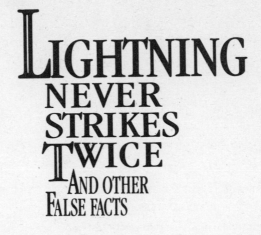

LIGHTNING
NEVER
STRIKES
TWICE
AND OTHER
FALSE FACTS

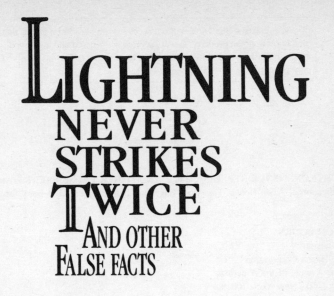

LIGHTNING NEVER STRIKES TWICE
AND OTHER FALSE FACTS

LAURENCE MOORE

AVON BOOKS  NEW YORK

LIGHTNING NEVER STRIKES TWICE AND OTHER FALSE FACTS is an original publication of Avon Books. This work has never before appeared in book form.

AVON BOOKS
A division of
The Hearst Corporation
1350 Avenue of the Americas
New York, New York 10019

Copyright © 1994 by Laurence A. Moore
Cover art by William Bramhall
Interior design by Suzanne H. Holt
Published by arrangement with the author
Library of Congress Catalog Card Number: 93-40648
ISBN: 0-380-77477-1

Library of Congress Cataloging-in-Publication Data:

Moore, Laurence A.
  Lightning never strikes twice and other false facts / Laurence Moore.
    p. cm.
  1. Curiosities and wonders. 2. Handbooks, vade-mecums, etc. I. Title.
AG243.M657   1994   93-40648
031.02—dc20   CIP

First Avon Books Trade Printing: June 1994

AVON TRADEMARK REG. U.S. PAT. OFF. AND IN OTHER COUNTRIES, MARCA REGISTRADA, HECHO EN U.S.A.

Printed in the U.S.A.

OPM 10 9 8 7 6 5 4 3 2 1

Contents

Introduction

We believe an astounding number of things.

One of the most astounding things we believe is that everything we believe is true.

When something is accepted as common knowledge, we rarely think of checking it.

"Of course the world's largest pyramid is in Egypt. Everybody knows that."

The world's largest pyramid isn't in Egypt, though.

We all take pride in what we know, and in increasing our stock of knowledge.

We also like to be surprised, and take a certain perverse pleasure in learning that a commonly believed "fact" is false.

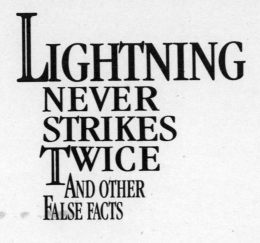

LIGHTNING NEVER STRIKES TWICE

AND OTHER FALSE FACTS

Animals

FALLACY: Saint Bernard dogs carry casks of brandy for people stranded in the snow in the Swiss Alps.

FACT: Saint Bernard dogs do not—and never did—carry casks of brandy or of anything else. The belief that they do comes from fiction and advertising, which is probably redundant.

//

FALLACY: A "razorback" is a hog native to Arkansas.

FACT: A sharp-crested ridge or hill is called a razorback. A rorqual whale is called a razorback. A feral hog of the southeastern United States is called a razorback. Feral hogs are descendants of domestic hogs that hied their hocks into the hills before they became breakfast. They are called by different names in different parts of the country. A "razorback" is no more native to Arkansas than it is to other parts of the Southeast—unless the word is capitalized: "The Razorbacks today won their fourth straight game."

//

FALLACY: Vampire bats suck blood through their hollow teeth.

FACT: There are only two things wrong with that: vampire bats do not suck blood, and they do not have hollow teeth. Vampire bats make small incisions with their razor-sharp incisor teeth, then lap up the blood that comes out. The process is so painless that most hosts, including humans, don't even wake up.

FALLACY: In spite of some nineteenth-century suggestions in this country, horses have never been required to wear diapers.

FACT: Nothing significant came of the nineteenth-century suggestions. As we approach the twenty-first century, however, wonders are beginning to appear. The city commission of the nation's oldest city, Saint Augustine, Florida, passed a law in 1992 requiring diapers on horses that pull tourist carriages through the town. Don't know which laundromat they use, but I'd avoid it.

//

FALLACY: If you're being chased by a bear, climb a tree; bears are too big to climb trees.

FACT: A common belief, but a dangerous one if you're being chased by a bear. Not only can most bears climb trees, they can climb quite well. Polar bears, on the other paw, are not noted for their tree-climbing ability.

//

FALLACY: Ladybugs are the females of the species; there are no male ladybugs.

FACT: A ladybug is any of several beetles of the family Coccinellidae. Most are small, hemispherical, and brightly colored, often red with black spots. They feed on other insects, such as aphids and scale insects. Both the male and the female are called ladybugs, proving that entomologists were ahead of the game when it came to names. They'd have a lot of explaining to do if they'd named them gentlemanbugs.

//

FALLACY: Bombay ducks are a species of duck found only in India.

FACT: Ducks are members of the family Anatidae. Bombay ducks aren't even distantly related to ducks, Indian or otherwise. They're small, thin, nearly transparent lizardfish, *Harpodon nehereus,* native to Asia. Restaurants probably sell a lot more Bombay Duck than they would Bombay Lizardfish.

FALLACY: Baboons are apes; chimpanzees are monkeys.
FACT: Apes are tailless, anthropoid members of the family Pongidae, closely related to humans. The gibbon, a small ape, and the orangutan, the smallest of the great apes, live in the forests of Southeast Asia. The chimpanzee and the gorilla, both great apes, live in the forests of Africa. Monkeys include baboons, capuchins, guenons, macaques, marmosets, and tamarins. Monkeys, unlike apes, have long tails and cannot swing arm over arm through the trees. *Homo sapiens sapiens'* closest relative is the chimpanzee, although most chimpanzees won't admit that.

/ /

FALLACY: You can tell a red fox by its red fur.
FACT: The two best-known red foxes are *Vulpes fulva* of North America and *Vulpes vulpes* of Europe. The North American species is common from Mexico to the Arctic Ocean, except along the west coast. You can't tell a red fox by its red fur: although many have red fur, many others sport black fur, or brown, or silver. A Redd Foxx is a different matter entirely.

/ /

FALLACY: A hummingbird sucks nectar out of a flower with its long bill.
FACT: Those hypodermic-looking hummingbird bills are merely bills. They're not airtight, and hummingbirds cannot suck anything up through them. The secret is the hummingbird's extremely long tongue, which goes all the way to the end of its bill. Hummingbirds don't suck the nectar out of a flower, they use their tongue to lap it up. Among the shortest-lived of birds, the oldest known hummingbird lived in a zoo until the ripe old age of ten.

/ /

FALLACY: There are about a million different species of living things.
FACT: There are approximately 1.5 million species of living things known today. Scientists who specialize in such matters estimate that this represents somewhere between 2 percent and 15 percent of the number of existing species. Humans make up one—just one—of those 10 million to 75 million species.

FALLACY: A woolly bear is a bear.

FACT: A woolly bear is reddish brown in the middle and black at both ends. Would make for a mighty small bear, though. A woolly bear is a North American caterpillar.

//

FALLACY: Mountain lions are lions.

FACT: Mountain lions, *Felis concolor,* are common in mountainous regions of the Western Hemisphere. People living near them definitely know they're nearby because of their piercing screams at night, and have given them many local names. People call them catamounts, cougars, mountain cats, painters, panthers, and pumas, but the most common name is mountain lion; this is strange, because lions don't live in the Western Hemisphere, and *Felis concolor* is not even in the same genus as the lion, *Panthera leo.* In spite of its formal name, the lion is not a panther, which is actually just another name for a black leopard. Cats are hard to categorize.

//

FALLACY: Only male members of the deer family have antlers.

FACT: Caribou, part of the deer family, are unisex when it comes to growing antlers. They are native to the Arctic and sub-Arctic, roaming free in Canada and Siberia. Reindeer, Rudolph included, are a domesticated subspecies of caribou.

//

FALLACY: Dolphins live in the ocean.

FACT: Many dolphins live in the ocean, but at least five species don't. There are species of river dolphins in China, India, Pakistan, South America, and Southeast Asia. Rather than rounded, blunt, or bottle-nosed faces, they have long beaks with sharp teeth for catching fish. Unlike the more common dolphins, the Amazon River dolphin has pink skin, and is often called the pink dolphin. Flipper was a bottle-nosed ocean dolphin, and wouldn't have been caught dead in pink skin.

FALLACY: The horse was introduced to North America by the Spaniards.

FACT: The horse and North America had been introduced long before Spaniards—or Spain—existed. The horse is a plant-eating hoofed mammal of the family Equidae. The only surviving genus, which includes the domestic horse, the wild Przewalski's horse, the ass, and the zebra, is *Equus*. The modern horse evolved in North America, spread across the continents, and then became extinct in North America about 11,000 years ago at the end of the most recent Ice Age. It was hunted as food by primitive humans, and finally domesticated in Asia. Spaniards did not introduce the horse to North America—they reintroduced it.

//

FALLACY: Only a few species of snakes have snake oil.

FACT: The only species of snake that has snake oil is the very slippery human snake-oil salesman. "Snake oil" is any worthless medical potion foisted on the public as a cure. The term came into common usage during the time of the traveling medicine show.

//

FALLACY: The elephant is the largest living animal.

FACT: No beating around the bush: the African bush elephant is the largest living land animal, averaging 10.5 feet at the shoulder and weighing more than 6 tons. The largest living animal, however, is the blue or sulfur-bottom whale. One female blue whale killed in 1909 was 110.2 feet long; another female, killed in 1947, was 90.5 feet long and weighed 209 tons.

//

FALLACY: For obvious reasons, all fish lay their eggs in water.

FACT: Not the grunion (*Leuresthes tenuis*) of the coastal waters of California and Mexico. Thousands of people—mostly young couples—go out to the coast on spring high-tide nights to watch the running of the grunion. Huge masses of the small silvery fish ride the high-tide waves far up onto sandy beaches. The males and females writhe together, mixing eggs and sperm and burying the fertilized eggs, then catch the next outgoing wave. By the time of the following month's high tide the eggs are ready to hatch, and the new grunion bodysurf to the ocean on returning waves. If there are grunion naturalists, they are probably equally interested in the mating behavior of the human couples on the beach.

//

FALLACY: Turkeys can't fly.
FACT: That one on your platter is certainly in no shape for take-off. Long before women (and, more recently, men) enlarged their chests with implants, turkey breeders were enlarging the chest of the domestic turkey with selective breeding. Thanksgiving turkeys may be aromatic, but they're a long way from aerodynamic. The table turkey is no work of art; nature did a much better job with the original. Members of the Meleagrididae family, and related to grouse and pheasants, wild turkeys are excellent fliers.

//

FALLACY: When you see a sheep with an udder, you're looking at a ewe.
FACT: When you see a sheep with an "udder," you're looking at a ram. Female sheep don't have udders. Male sheep, however, have very large scrotums.

//

FALLACY: Porcupines shoot their quills at an attacker.
FACT: Porcupines can't shoot their quills at an attacker because they have no "launch mechanisms" at the quill roots. The quills are very loosely attached to the porcupine, and when once stuck into an attacker, they stay stuck.

//

FALLACY: Even the smallest living things are made up of many cells.
FACT: Strange as it may seem, there are living things that consist of only one cell. Bacteria, for example, are unicellular, and so are protozoans such as amoebas, ciliates, flagellates, and sporozoans. Size doesn't count when it comes to being alive, either.

FALLACY: Morning doves are called that because they are seen only in the morning.

FACT: The word is *mourning,* not *morning.* They were named mourning doves because of their plaintive call. Mourning doves are about a foot in length, have long, tapered tails, pink and violet neck markings, and a white-bordered tail. They can be seen at any time of the day, but like some humans, they do migrate south for the winter.

//

FALLACY: The Great Apes are native to Africa.

FACT: "Great Apes" is a term for any of the anthropoid apes of the family Pongidae, the best known of which are the chimpanzee, the gorilla, and the orangutan. The chimpanzee (*Pan troglodytes*) and the gorilla (*Gorilla gorilla*) are native to Africa, but the orangutan (*Pongo pygmaeus*) is not. Arboreal swinger that it is, the orangutan is from the islands of Borneo and Sumatra.

//

FALLACY: Pigs and hogs can't interbreed because they belong to different families.

FACT: They not only belong to the same family, Suidae, but they're the same animal. When a pig grows to more than 120 pounds, it's called a hog. That most popular of hog calls, *Suuuuu-eee!,* may come from the family name rather than from the legal terms suer/suee.

//

FALLACY: The dodo was a mythical animal.

FACT: The dodo was a very real bird, native to the island of Mauritius in the Indian Ocean. *Raphus cucullatus* was as large as a turkey. It couldn't fly, but didn't need to because it had no natural predators. European sailors and then colonists used the easily caught birds as food, and their domestic animals destroyed the dodo's eggs. The first report of a dodo was in 1598; by 1681, the dodo was extinct.

FALLACY: The koala bear is a bear.

FACT: The koala bear is not even related to bears. Bears, such as the grizzly, *Ursus horribilis,* belong to the order Carnivora and are ground dwellers. Bears in the wild live as long as thirty-five years. Koalas, *Phascolarctos cinereus,* belong to the order Marsupialia, are not carnivorous, and live in trees. The name comes from the aboriginal Dharuk language of southeast Australia. Koalas live as long as twenty years, except the one that works for Quantas, which seems to live forever.

//

FALLACY: Moby Dick aside, there is no such thing as a white whale.

FACT: The beluga whale, *Delphinapterus leucas,* lives in northern waters. A newborn beluga is dark and about five feet long, but a full-grown adult is up to eighteen feet in length—and white. The beluga sturgeon, whose row is called beluga caviar, lives in the Black and Caspian seas. The only relation between the two is the Russian word *byelii* (white), which is the root of both *byeluga* (sturgeon) and *byelukha* (white whale). It would give a whole new perspective to that classic if Moby Dick were a beluga whale rather than a sperm whale.

//

FALLACY: Vultures are not city birds.

FACT: Humans who flock to Miami during the winter are called snowbirds. Vultures who flock to Miami during the winter are called vultures. About ten thousand vultures fly in each winter from eastern states and as far north as Canada. The Dade County Courthouse, with a roof like a stepped pyramid, or ziggurat, makes a perfect day roost for them. At night they roost in mangroves and other trees around the area. They arrive by Halloween and, appropriately, leave by tax day.

//

FALLACY: Flying fish flap their fins like wings.

FACT: Flying fish do not flap their fins, nor do they fly in either water or air. What they do is build up speed, leap out of the water, and glide. The common puffin, a bird, does flap its wings underwater, making it one of the few creatures to fly in both water and air.

FALLACY: A tarantula is not a spider.
FACT: Tarantulas are large and hairy, and look like spiders. They can inflict a painful though not very poisonous bite. There is a reason for their looking like spiders; they are members of the family Theraphosidae: hairy spiders.

/ /

FALLACY: Because they're slow and directionless, butterflies seldom get more than a few miles from where they're born.
FACT: They may appear to be slow and directionless, but they do get around. Monarch butterflies migrate as far as three thousand miles each year, from Canada to the Sierra Madre mountains in Mexico's Michoacan state. Monarchs produce several generations each year; the first starts the migration, and the last completes it.

/ /

FALLACY: Penguins live only in the Arctic and the Antarctic.
FACT: Not a single penguin lives in the Arctic. All seventeen species of the order Sphenisciformes are native to the Southern Hemisphere. Most are around Antarctica, but many others live near islands well above the Antarctic Circle, such as Australia's Macquarie Island. An estimated two million penguins live near Punta Tombo, Argentina; the southern Chilean coast and archipelago are home to many more.

/ /

FALLACY: The main use for pigskin is making footballs.
FACT: The main use for pigskin is holding pigs together.

/ /

FALLACY: Elephants drink through their trunk, and are afraid of mice.
FACT: An elephant's trunk is its nose. Elephants draw water up into their trunk, then squirt the water into their mouth, onto their back, or elsewhere. If they tried to drink through their trunk, the water would go

into their lungs, not their stomach. They are not in the least afraid of mice, and probably notice a single mouse about as much as we notice a single ant when we're walking outdoors. The average elephant lives about sixty years, unless it tries to drink water through its nose.

/ /

FALLACY: An ox and a steer are the same thing.
FACT: An ox is an adult castrated male bovine, used as a draft animal. A steer is a young male bovine, castrated before sexual maturity and raised as a food animal. No bull.

/ /

FALLACY: Passenger pigeons are used to carry messages.
FACT: Homing pigeons, sometimes called carrier pigeons, are used to carry messages. Passenger pigeons are a whole different story. Until the nineteenth-century, there were huge flocks of passenger pigeons (*Ectopistes migratorious*) throughout most of North America. It has been estimated that in colonial times there were as many as six billion of them. John James Audubon described a flock in Kentucky in 1813 which took three days to pass. Shot, trapped, and netted by professional hunters, and poisoned by farmers, the passenger pigeon became extinct in the wild in 1900. The last member of the species died in captivity at the Cincinnati Zoo in 1914.

/ /

FALLACY: All mammals have their nostrils somewhere on their face.
FACT: Cyrano de Bergerac's nose was all over his face, but whales and dolphins, both mammals, have their nostrils on top of their head.

/ /

FALLACY: Marsupials live only in Australia.
FACT: Australia is identified with a marsupial, the kangaroo, and is the only remaining home of most of the world's other marsupials, including wombats. Bandicoots do live in Australia, but they also live in New Guinea. There is one species of marsupial, however, that lives quite

happily in the Americas: *Didelphis marsupialis,* better known as opossums, and a major ingredient in possum pie.

// /

FALLACY: Geoduck is short for that bird known as the "Earth duck."
FACT: Geoducks live on the Pacific coast from Washington state to Alaska, and are flightless, featherless—clams. They can weigh more than five pounds. Geoduck, by the way, is pronounced "gooey duck."

// /

FALLACY: A sea wasp is a wasp.
FACT: A sea wasp has venom, and can give a potentially fatal sting, but it has no wings and is no more a wasp than a sea horse is a horse. A sea wasp is any of several difficult-to-pronounce scyphozoan jellyfishes.

// /

FALLACY: Some whales have teeth and some don't, but none have tusks.
FACT: The Arctic narwhal grows to about eighteen feet. It has only two teeth, both in its upper jaw. In males of the species, the left tooth grows into a tusk as long as eight feet—almost half as long as its body. This "unicorn of the sea" has traditionally been hunted more for its tusk than for its oil or its flesh; dishonest humans sold the tusk as unicorn horn, and foolish humans bought it.

// /

FALLACY: Flying squirrels and one type of fox, the flying fox, are the only mammals that can fly.
FACT: Flying squirrels don't fly; they jump out of trees and glide. Flying foxes aren't foxes; that's a common name for the fruit bat. Bats—which are mammals, not rodents—are the only mammals that can fly. Humans ride.

// /

FALLACY: The same animal goes by three different names: burro, donkey, and mule.

FACT: A burro, not to be confused with a burrito or a taco, is a small donkey. A donkey is a domesticated ass, *Equus asinus*. A mule is a sterile hybrid offspring of a female horse and a male donkey. Just to keep things gender-balanced here, the hybrid offspring of a male horse and a female donkey is a hinny. An ass? We all have our own candidates for that word, but in the equine world it refers to an animal that resembles and is related to the horse, but is smaller and has larger ears.

//

FALLACY: Any small fish is a minnow.

FACT: Any small fish is a small fish; a minnow is a member of the family Cyprinidae, and lives only in fresh water. One minnow, the squawfish of western North America, weighs up to 100 pounds. What would you catch if you used *that* minnow as bait?

//

FALLACY: No bird can fly backward.

FACT: They're not songbirds, and they couldn't hum a tune if their lives depended on it, but there is one type of bird that can fly backward. Hummingbirds get their name from the sound their wings make while moving so fast that they're blurred. Small species have wingbeats up to seventy per second. Hummingbirds can, indeed, fly backward—or any other direction. In that regard they're more like helicopters than airplanes. They're the only birds capable of flying backward.

//

FALLACY: Cats are afraid of water.

FACT: Cats are not afraid of water. In fact, most cats can swim. The reason cats don't like to get wet is the elaborate cleaning ritual they put themselves through afterward.

//

FALLACY: A "snipe hunt" ends with a naive person being deserted in the woods; there is no such thing as a snipe.

FACT: In this case a little knowledge could be dangerous, so you may not want to read any further. Although desertion is the intent of most snipe hunts, there actually is such a thing as a snipe. It's a long-billed bird, common to marshes but not to forests.

//

FALLACY: Mosquitoes live on the blood of animals.
FACT: Both male and female mosquitoes can live on the juice of plants; male mosquitoes have no choice, because they don't have the apparatus to bite through animal skin. Although it is not necessary for females to feed on the blood of animals, doing so greatly increases the number of their offspring. The fact that male mosquitoes live on the juice of plants is doubtless a welcome bit of news to animals because it greatly reduces their odds of being bitten; the news is probably less welcome to plants.

//

FALLACY: Fish can catch insects on or near the surface of the water, but an insect flying a yard above the surface is safe.
FACT: Depends on who is below that surface. There is a member of the Toxotidae family called the archerfish that can accurately hit an insect flying six feet above the water. The archerfish puts its lips just above the surface, then slams its gills closed, firing a jet of water that can knock an insect off a rock or overhanging vegetation, or right out of the air. This is a fish that can spit in your eye.

//

FALLACY: Worms crawl toward buildings when it rains because they want to get in out of the rain.
FACT: The fact that worms crawl toward buildings when it rains has nothing to do with the buildings. Worms live in tunnels. When it rains, the tunnels flood and the worms are in danger of drowning. First they come to the surface, then they head uphill. Most building sites are higher than the surrounding land. Worms from all directions will climb uphill toward that higher ground, whether or not there is a building on it. "Half an inch, half an inch, half an inch onward!"

FALLACY: Dinosaurs were the largest animals that have ever lived.

FACT: The largest known dinosaurs weighed somewhere between 50 tons and 100 tons. A more exact estimate would require more complete skeletons. Major entries in the 50-ton-plus category include *Antarctosaurus gigantus, Brachiosaurus altithorax, Seismorsaurus halli,* and *Supersaurus vivianae.* (The desktop *Thesaurus,* although numerous, is not large.) The largest animal ever to live, however, is still alive: the blue whale. A newborn can be more than 20 feet long and weigh over 3 tons. Adults grow to more than 110 feet in length, and can weigh more than 200 tons. The blue whale was once common in all the world's oceans, with an estimated population of 220,000 at the beginning of the twentieth century. The current estimate is about 11,000, because of slaughter by humans. They are now an endangered species.

/ /

FALLACY: Mohair is the hair of an animal locally called a "mo."

FACT: There's no mo. Mohair is the hair of an Angora goat. The word is a corruption of the Arabic word *muhayyar.*

/ /

FALLACY: A beheaded chicken stays alive and runs around; a beheaded snake stays alive and can crawl until sundown.

FACT: Many a city slicker has been amazed to see a headless chicken run or a headless snake crawl. In neither case is the animal alive, and there's nothing supernatural about it. It's simply that nerve and muscle bundles in the body continue to fire for a while after the animal dies. Sundown has no effect on animal muscles, but it may have an effect on human superstitions.

/ /

FALLACY: Electric eels can electrocute a human.

FACT: "Electrocute" is a combination of "electro" and "(exe)cute"; not even the most ill-intentioned eel can do that to a human. There is a South American electric eel (*Electrophorus electricus*) that can deliver 650 volts, stunning a human like a blow to the head. The amperage is low, however, so not even this most electric of eels can electrocute a human.

FALLACY: Pterodactyls were the first birds.

FACT: The first of the two known types of pterosaurs was the rhamphourhynchoid. The pterodactyl came later. The pterosaurs were flying reptiles unrelated to birds. Pteranodon, a descendant of the pterodactyl, was the largest of all flying reptiles, with a wingspan of more than fifty feet. Pterosaurs, which belonged to a different order from the dinosaurs, lived from 200 million years ago until the great extinction 65 million years ago. Birds evolved from the dinosaur group of reptiles. The oldest known fossils of a bird are those of Archaeopteryx, which lived about 150 million years ago.

//

FALLACY: Although the females of some species mature early, none mature so early that they can get pregnant right after birth.

FACT: Aphids can see "right after birth" and raise it one. Some aphids are *born* pregnant.

//

FALLACY: A hippopotamus can't go any deeper under the water than nostril-level.

FACT: Hippos routinely walk on the bottom of a river, with their nostrils many feet below the surface. They can hold their breath for quite a while. Although they open their eyes underwater, they keep their nostrils tightly closed. The name hippopotamus means "river horse." Hippos live about forty years, unless they try to breathe underwater.

//

FALLACY: A polecat is a large wildcat.

FACT: A polecat is not a cat. It is a nocturnal European weasel, *Mustela putorius*. "Polecat" is sometimes used as a general name for the entire Mustelidae family, including minks, otters, and other weasels. In some parts of the United States, skunks are commonly called polecats— the term being applied equally to human and four-footed varieties.

FALLACY: No bird can fly faster than a speeding car.

FACT: In 1990, Lamborghini claimed a road-car speed record of 202 miles per hour for its Diablo. In 1992, Jaguar claimed a road-car speed record of 217 miles per hour for its XJ220. Spine-tail swifts have been clocked at 220 miles per hour: "Faster than a speeding pullet!"

//

FALLACY: Some whales are known as sperm whales because that was the commercially most valuable product derived from them.

FACT: Two species of whale are known as sperm whales because the whalers weren't very good at either anatomy or physiology. The front of a sperm whale's head contains a large reservoir of oil, probably used as a liquid lens to focus the sounds they make. This fluid was named spermaceti oil, from the Latin *sperma ceti,* whale sperm. When removed from the warm-blooded mammal and allowed to cool, it forms a waxy substance formerly used in candles and cosmetics. Spermaceti has absolutely nothing to do with the whale's reproductive system. Neither does ambergris, which is formed in the intestines of sperm whales and used as a fixative in some perfumes.

//

FALLACY: Antlers are horns.

FACT: Horns are bony projections from the skull, which grow throughout an animal's life. They are covered with keratin, which is harder than bone. In most horned species, such as antelope, bovines, and goats, both sexes have horns. Antlers, unlike horns, are not covered with keratin, and last for one season only; a completely new set of antlers is grown every year. In most antlered species, including elk and moose but not all species of deer, only the males have antlers. The expression "horny as a goat" means something else entirely.

//

FALLACY: A female peacock is called a female peacock.

FACT: There is no such thing as a female peacock. Male peafowl are peacocks; female peafowl are peahens. Peafowl go to great lengths to display their physical attributes so that members of the opposite sex will view them as sex objects, unlike humans who are more interested in personality than in pulchritude. At least that's what humans say.

FALLACY: Porcupines are the world's largest rodents.

FACT: With more than 1,500 species, rodents make up the largest order of mammals. Fortunately for us, they're predominately vegetarian. The world's largest rodent is the Latin American capybara (*Hydrochoerus hydrochaeris*). It weighs as much as 125 pounds in the wild, and up to twice that in captivity. Porcupines weigh about sixty pounds. Capybaras are also known as carpinchos or water hogs.

// /

FALLACY: Sea cows are the largest marine mammals after whales.

FACT: Steller's Sea Cow (*Hydrodamalis gigas*) was the largest marine mammal after whales. Recorded by German naturalist Georg Wilhelm Steller in the Bering Sea in 1741, they weighed up to fourteen thousand pounds. Because of wholesale slaughter by seal and whale hunters, Steller's Sea Cow was extinct by about 1767. Dugongs and manatees are also called sea cows, and are the surviving members of the order Sirenia. They rarely exceed six hundred pounds. Bull walruses, on the other hand, weigh up to three thousand pounds, and that's a lot of bull.

/ /

FALLACY: Moles eat the roots of vegetables in a garden.

FACT: Moles would no sooner eat vegetable roots, or vegetables for that matter, than you would eat a book. Moles are meat-eaters; more specifically, they are insect-eaters.

/ /

FALLACY: Great auks are an endangered species.

FACT: Great auks (*Pinguinus impennis*), flightless birds hunted for their flesh, feathers, and oil, were an endangered species until 1844, when they became an extinct species.

/ /

FALLACY: Snails, like other sexually reproducing animals, are divided into male and female.

FACT: Snails do reproduce sexually, but each of them has both male and female sex organs. The same is true of earthworms, sea cucumbers, sea hares, and many other species. When two snails mate, they both become fertilized and they both lay eggs. What we have here is true equality of the sexes.

//

FALLACY: Fire ants, which arrived in the United States in the 1960s, have been eradicated.

FACT: Fire ants arrived in Texas from South America in the 1940s. They have a fierce sting, and have by no means been eradicated. Interestingly, they are attracted to electrical fields; unfortunately, they often cause short circuits in electrical equipment. That's rough on the fried circuit, but it's a lot rougher on the fried ant.

//

FALLACY: Silkworms are among the fattest of all worms.

FACT: Silkworms are not worms. They are the caterpillars (larvae) of various species of moths, and feed on mulberry leaves. As is true of other caterpillars, they attach themselves to a twig and spin a cocoon around themselves. The cocoon is made of a single strand of silk, commonly half a mile long.

//

FALLACY: Whooping cranes are extinct.

FACT: Whooping cranes (*Grus americana*), the tallest birds in North America at five feet, are not extinct. They're not far from it, though. The main flock of wild birds numbers less than two hundred. It spends its winters in Canada's Northwest Territories, and its summers along the Texas Gulf Coast. An attempt was begun in 1975 to establish a second flock in New Mexico, but it was unsuccessful and finally abandoned in 1992. A new attempt was begun in 1993 at Three Lakes Wildlife Management Area near Kenansville, Florida.

//

FALLACY: Of all animals, the African elephant has the longest tail.

FACT: Not counting snakes, which are tail from head to foot, the animal with the longest tail, about eight feet, is the male giraffe. Moving from backside to frontside, he also has the longest neck. It's not true, by the way, that elephants are banned from beaches because they won't keep their trunks up.

///

FALLACY: Wild boar are descendants of escaped domestic hogs.
FACT: Some hunters refer to feral descendants of domestic hogs as wild boar, but they aren't. Wild boar are undomesticated pigs native to Eurasia and northern Africa that have dense, dark bristles. Those hunters who go into boring detail about hunting the "wild boar" descendants of domestic hogs have it exactly backward: wild boar are the ancestors of domestic hogs.

///

FALLACY: When horses in a field stand side by side, nose to tail, they're doing the same thing that dogs do when they sniff each other.
FACT: That's a canine behavior trait, not equine. What the horses are doing is taking advantage of each other's whisking tail to keep flies away from their faces.

///

FALLACY: The Great White is the largest of the sharks.
FACT: The great white shark, *Carcharodon carcharias,* averages 15 feet in length and weighs about 1,500 pounds. The largest ever caught was 21 feet long and weighed 7,302 pounds. It is definitely the largest of the meat-eating sharks. The great white is a mere minnow, though, compared to the whale shark, *Rhincodon typus,* which feeds on plankton. One captured whale shark measured 41.5 feet in length; its weight was estimated at 33,000 pounds. Although that's one whale of a shark, there are undoubtedly much larger whale sharks in the ocean.

///

FALLACY: A jackrabbit is a rabbit.
FACT: You'd think so from the name, but jackrabbits are hares, not rabbits. Hares are born with fur, and with their eyes open. Rabbits,

among the best known of which are the cottontails, are born without fur and with their eyelids sealed.

/ /

FALLACY: The African elephant has the world's longest penis.
FACT: Only if African elephants have a Natural History Museum. Proving yet again that size doesn't matter, in this case because the species reproduces so slowly, the world's longest penis is sported by the blue whale. Although they undoubtedly go to greater lengths, the longest blue whale penis measured by humans was approximately ten feet long.

/ /

FALLACY: Ostriches bury their heads to hide.
FACT: This is strictly a human trait—no ostrich has ever been known to do it. Their huge legs are great for kicking anything that attacks them, and if that doesn't work those legs can move them like the wind. They don't often have to do either, though; the ostrich is the world's largest bird, and some males stand eight feet tall and weigh more than two hundred pounds. An ostrich lives about twenty-five years, unless it buries its head and suffocates.

/ /

FALLACY: Whalebone is exactly that.
FACT: Whales are divided into two types: toothed and baleen. In place of teeth, baleen whales have two rows of fringed plates attached to their upper jaw. These plates strain their food, mainly plankton, out of huge volumes of water. The horny substance of which these plates are made is called whalebone, but it is not bone. Whalebone and whale bone are different things.

/ /

FALLACY: A homing pigeon will take a message anywhere it has been before, and return to its home base with an answer.
FACT: Homing pigeons are strictly one-way. The only place they can find is home. You take one with you, then send a message back to

its base by releasing it. They're firm believers in what Dorothy said in the last line of *The Wizard of Oz*: "There's no place like home."

//

FALLACY: Horseshoe crabs are crabs.
FACT: Horseshoe crabs are not crabs. True crabs are crustaceans. Horseshoe crabs are related to arachnids (spiders, scorpions, mites, ticks). Spiky tail-like section included, they can be as long as two feet. Before you feel superior to a creature with such relatives, though, keep in mind that the current model of human has been around about 35,000 years. The horseshoe crab has existed in virtually the same form for at least 175 million years. They must be doing something right.

//

FALLACY: Camels store water in their humps.
FACT: There is a one-humped Dromedary camel from Africa and the Middle East, and a two-humped Bactrian camel from Asia. None of the humps is hollow, and none is used to store water. One of the first things to look at when you're buying a camel is the hump. If the animal has been well fed, the hump will be large and firm. If the camel has not been well cared for, the hump will be small and shrunken, and may flop over to one side. Camels store fat, not water, in their humps. The reason they can go so long between drinks is that they have amazingly efficient recycling systems, allowing them to exhale and excrete very little moisture.

//

FALLACY: Snakes are cold and slimy.
FACT: As with other reptiles, snakes have no internal thermostat to maintain a constant temperature. When they get cold, they move to a warmer place; when they get hot, they move to a cooler place. You'll often see snakes basking on a blacktop road early in the year, because that's the warmest place around. Since humans maintain a relatively high body temperature, a snake will usually feel slightly cool, but not cold. As for snakes feeling slimy to a human, that's exactly backward. A snake's skin, made up of overlapping scales, is dry. A human's skin, on the other hand, is moist, which might feel slimy to a snake.

FALLACY: A centipede has 100 legs; a millipede has 1,000 legs.
FACT: That's what the names say, but it's not true. The *Himantarum gabrielis* centipede, for example, has about 350 legs. Putting the shoe on the other foot, no millipede has been found to have more than the 750 legs of the *Illacme plenipes*.

//

FALLACY: Hummingbirds never land.
FACT: Hummingbirds, and all other birds, do land. Because of the speed at which they flap their wings, often just a blur to human eyes, it takes a huge amount of energy to keep them in flight. Even though they land when they aren't going anywhere, they still have to eat half their weight in food every day. And they never put on a pound.

//

FALLACY: There is no such thing as a fish that *really* flies.
FACT: Well, so-called flying fish certainly don't—they merely glide. There are fish, however, that do fly. Some of the rays (there are more than four hundred species) propel themselves through the water by flapping their winglike pectoral fins. They literally fly through the water. The best known are the manta rays, sometimes called devilfish. They are the largest of the rays, growing to more than twenty feet from tip to tip of their wings, and weighing up to three thousand pounds.

//

FALLACY: The farthest that any birds migrate is from North America to South America.
FACT: Arctic terns (*Sterna paradisea*) migrate a lot farther than that. They breed and spend the Northern Hemisphere's summer as far north as the northernmost Arctic islands. Then they begin a migration that lasts almost three months—all the way to Antarctica. After spending the Southern Hemisphere's summer in Antarctica, they fly back north, for a total distance of as much as twenty-two thousand miles. Sooty terns (*Sterna fuscata*) seem to enjoy flying more than almost anything else. As soon as they're old enough they take off, and they don't land again for three to ten years. What finally brings them back to Earth is the only thing they seem to enjoy more than flying: they land to mate.

FALLACY: Boa constrictors are the world's largest snakes.

FACT: Boa constrictors (*Constrictor constrictor*), anacondas (*Eunectes murinus*), and reticulated pythons (*Python reticulatus*) are closely related. Tropical American boa constrictors are indeed impressive snakes, growing as long as 10 feet. The largest Asian reticulated python measured, however, was 32 feet 9.5 inches. The largest measured South American anaconda, although only 27 feet 9 inches long, had a circumference of 44 inches and weighed about 500 pounds—twice as much as a reticulated python of the same length. Anacondas are the world's largest snakes.

//

FALLACY: Fireflies are flies that fly.

FACT: Fireflies are not flies. The name "firefly" applies to any of about 1,500 species of nocturnal beetles that flash their luminous abdomens. The common American firefly is *Photinus pyralis*. Only mature male fireflies both glow and fly. Larvae glow, but do not fly. Females glow, but have nonfunctional wings or no wings at all. Lightning bugs don't bug, either.

//

FALLACY: There is no such thing as a vampire.

FACT: There are indeed two-legged mammals that are vampires. Commonly known as vampire bats, they belong to the genera *Desmodus* and *Diphylla* of the family Desmodontidae, and live only in Latin America. They're named after the legendary vampires of Transylvania because they do live on the blood of a wide variety of warm-blooded animals, including birds and mammals.

//

FALLACY: The titmouse got its name because that species of mouse has relatively large breasts.

FACT: The titmouse doesn't have any breasts at all. Found mainly in the Northern Hemisphere, titmice are small gray-and-brown birds of the family Paridae. Chickadees and tits belong to the same family as the titmouse.

FALLACY: Angora wool comes from Angora sheep.

FACT: It would be very difficult to shear an Angora sheep, because there is no such thing. There are Angora cats, and goats, and rabbits, but no sheep. The "wool" comes from the Angora goat or the red-eyed Angora rabbit.

FALLACY: Giant clams that can kill a human are pure fiction.

FACT: This might put you off your clam chowder, but there are such giant clams in the Indian and Pacific oceans. If they close on a hand or foot, the human will drown. They grow up to four feet in width and weigh as much as five hundred pounds, which makes quite an anchor.

FALLACY: Once a skunk fires, it can't fire again for at least an hour.

FACT: Dangerous belief, that. A skunk fires only a portion of its potion in the first shot. It can shoot that strong-smelling liquid up to ten feet with amazing accuracy, and it can fire again almost immediately. Skunks come in many varieties, but "single shot" is not one of them.

FALLACY: You can tell the size of a bird by the size of its egg.

FACT: The world's largest bird is the ostrich, weighing up to 300 pounds. It lays an egg weighing up to three pounds—1/100th of its weight. The kiwi (bird, not fruit) weighs about four pounds. It lays an egg weighing about one pound—1/4th of its weight. Ouch!

FALLACY: Horses are always mounted from the left side because approaching them from the right makes them nervous.

FACT: Horses are a lot more sensible than humans, and don't care which side they're approached from. The reason for mounting them from the left is nothing more than tradition. Most people are right-handed. They therefore wore their sword on their left hip. Mounting a horse from its left kept the sword out of the way.

//

FALLACY: The largest member of the cat family is the lion.
FACT: The average adult lion is about nine feet long, three feet at the shoulder, and weighs about 400 pounds. The largest ever recorded weighed 690 pounds. The largest member of the cat family, though, is the Siberian tiger. Adult male Siberian tigers average ten feet in length, well over three feet at the shoulder, and weigh about 600 pounds. The largest ever recorded weighed 847 pounds. The Siberian tiger is not a lap cat.

//

FALLACY: Mammals give live birth to their young; they don't lay eggs.
FACT: Some mammals do lay eggs: members of the Monotremata order. Echidnas (spiny anteaters) do, and so do duck-billed platypuses. Which makes them, by the way, the only mammals that don't have navels. I'm not going to say a word about duck-billed platitudes.

//

FALLACY: The swallows always return to Capistrano on St. Joseph's Day, 19 March.
FACT: That's an enjoyable religious legend, but in fact they don't. Although they return every year to San Juan Capistrano, between Laguna Beach and San Clemente, they start to arrive on any day in February or March. The other half of the legend is that they always leave on 23 October, the date of St. John of Capistrano's death. In fact, they leave for their six thousand-mile flight to Argentina as they arrived—over a long period, starting whenever they're ready. What made these swallows more famous than any others in the world was Leon Rene's 1939 song, "When the Swallows Come Back to Capistrano."

FALLACY: Whales spout water.

FACT: Whales no more spout water when they surface than does a human swimmer. The whale's blowhole is its nostril. The air at the surface of the ocean is cool and damp. Just as you can see your breath on a cool, damp day, you can see the whale's breath when it exhales. Any water in the blast of warm, moist air from the spout comes from outside the whale, not inside. Preadolescent whales may occasionally spout cola to impress their friends or distress their elders, but that's another matter entirely.

//

FALLACY: Hens cannot lay eggs without the help of a rooster.

FACT: Hens can lay eggs without a rooster even laying eyes on them. Not fertile eggs, but eggs. Nearly all the eggs you buy in a store are from "virgin" hens.

//

FALLACY: There is no "chamois" animal for a chamois cloth, any more than there is a "nauga" animal for a nauga hide.

FACT: The chamois is a hoofed animal, *Rupricapra rupricapra,* about the size of a large goat and found in the mountains of Europe and the eastern Mediterranean. The original "chamois cloth" was the treated skin of the chamois, but most today are the treated skin of deer or sheep. Naugahyde is a trademark for fabrics coated with vinyl; the vinyl is not an endangered species.

//

FALLACY: Bats are "blind as a bat."

FACT: Bats are not blind, but their echolocation system of high-frequency sounds is more acute than their eyesight. Their sonar is so accurate that they can locate and catch a single insect flying at night. A bat probably catches more insects at night than any other creature except a motorcycle rider.

//

FALLACY: Sea snakes are the ancestors of land snakes.

FACT: Just the opposite. As with the ancestors of several other marine animals—including dolphins, porpoises, and whales—sea snakes' ancestors evolved on land. Sea snakes belong to the family Hydrophidae, one of sixteen families and 2,700 species of snakes.

//

FALLACY: Dogs circle several times before lying down because they can't decide exactly where to settle.
FACT: If you watch them go through the process outdoors, it makes more sense. What they're doing is flattening the grass into a bed and checking for obstacles such as rocks and sticks. Indoors, the lying-down ritual sometimes arranges their bed, but is usually just a habit.

//

FALLACY: Rabbits are rodents.
FACT: Beavers, mice, porcupines, rats, squirrels, and about 1,500 other species are rodents, and belong to the order Rodentia. Rabbits, hares, and pikas are not rodents; they belong to the order Lagomorpha. Rodents have only one pair of upper incisors, and nearly naked feet; lagomorphs have two pairs of upper incisors, and fully furry feet. Hobbits have furry feet, too, but that's a different story.

//

FALLACY: Goats eat tin cans.
FACT: Goats do not eat tin cans. The belief that they do may come from the fact that goats will, if they're hungry enough, eat the paper labels and the glue. Goats eat what's on the outside of a tin can, and we eat what's inside, but neither of us can digest the can itself.

//

FALLACY: Bees collect pollen and honey from flowers.
FACT: Pollen is a powdery substance produced by flowering plants that acts as the male element in fertilization, and bees do collect it. Bees would probably be happy to collect honey from flowers, but they can't because flowers don't produce honey. Flowers do produce nectar,

however, which bees collect and take back to the hive. Sucrose in the nectar is transformed into fructose and glucose by enzyme action in the worker bee's honey sac; the honey is then stored in the honeycomb to age and thicken. And that's the whole ball of wax.

//

FALLACY: Most people buy female canaries because they sing better.
FACT: Canaries are small finches, *Serinus canaria,* native to the Canary Islands off the northwest coast of Africa. Among canaries, only the males sing. That is probably unrelated to the fact that among humans, males do most of the singing in the shower.

//

FALLACY: The color red makes bulls mad.
FACT: There's one small problem with that theory. Bulls can't see the color red. They're color-blind. What attracts their attention is movement, not the color of what's moving. You'd be just as safe wearing red clothes as you would going naked. Depending on what's flapping in the breeze, maybe safer.

//

FALLACY: Grasshoppers and locusts are only distantly related.
FACT: The deadliest known grasshopper is the one made of crème de menthe, crème de cacao, and cream. In the insect world, grasshoppers are orthopterous members of the families Acrididae and Tettigoniidae. Locusts belong to the Acrididae family: they are not only related to grasshoppers, they *are* grasshoppers.

//

FALLACY: The birds popularly known as puffins belong to the genus *Puffinus.*
FACT: The birds popularly known as puffins do not belong to the genus *Puffinus.* They belong to *Fratercula* or *Lunda*—not even the same family. The birds that belong to the genus *Puffinus* are popularly known as shearwaters. How's that for confusing?

FALLACY: A daddy longlegs is a spider.
FACT: Several different insects are called daddy longlegs, but none of them is a spider. The most common is the harvestman, which looks like a spider and bounces up and down when agitated. It doesn't bite. Crane flies, sometimes called mosquito hawks, have daddy-longlegs–long legs, and fly, and look like giant mosquitoes. They don't bite, either.

/ /

FALLACY: Flounder are born with both eyes on one side of their head.
FACT: Flounder, as with the other five hundred or so species of flatfish, do end up with both eyes on one side of the head. They aren't born that way, though. They start with the normal arrangement of one eye on each side. Gradually one eye migrates to the other side. Which is fortunate, because flatfish lie flat on the bottom, and their bottom eye would be getting an eyeful of nothing but mud. This is completely unrelated, of course, to the old adage: "Absinthe makes the heart grow flounder."

/ /

FALLACY: Catgut is exactly that.
FACT: Catgut is used for many things, including musical instruments, surgical sutures, and tennis rackets. It is made from the gut of several different animals, usually sheep, but not from cat gut. A cathouse isn't exactly that, either.

2

Arts, Entertainment, Language, Literature, Religion

FALLACY: Nietzsche was a glum, serious philosopher with no sense of humor.

FACT: Friedrich Nietzsche wrote some decidedly heavy philosophy, but he had his light moments. This, for example, from *Thus Spoke Zarathustra*: "To get to the bottom of this mystery I went over the sea, and I have seen truth naked—verily, barefoot up to the throat."

//

FALLACY: Only about 10 percent of the Americans chosen for Rhodes scholarships are women.

FACT: From 1902 when the scholarships were established, until 1976, zero percent of the people chosen for Rhodes scholarships were women. Cecil Rhodes didn't allow women. Things have improved steadily since 1976. In 1992, for the first time, half of the Americans chosen for the scholarships to Oxford University in England were women. Cecil would have a fit.

//

FALLACY: The *New York Times* is the largest-circulation newspaper in the country.

FACT: Whether referring to daily circulation or Sunday circulation, the *New York Times* doesn't make it. The leader in daily circulation is the *Wall Street Journal*. It's followed, in order, by *USA Today*, the *Los Angeles Times*, and only then the *New York Times*. Advertising takes up far more room than news in most newspapers, but they do fill up the blanks around the advertising with news: "All the news that fits, we print."

//

FALLACY: There is one letter of the alphabet that isn't on telephones.
FACT: Both *Q* and *Z* are still missing from our telephones. Be glad you don't have a phone with all but two of the seventy-four letters in the Cambodian alphabet. If you let your fingers do the walking they'd get tired feet.

//

FALLACY: The largest concentration of Moonies in the United States is in Los Angeles County.
FACT: It's not enough that Southern California is expecting a huge earthquake? According to officials of Reverend Sun Myung Moon's Unification Church, the largest concentration of "Unificationists" is in Westchester County, New York. May have something to do with the fact that Reverend Moon lives there, in Tarrytown.

//

FALLACY: A mugwump is someone who won't make a decision; who sits on the fence, mug on one side and wump on the other.
FACT: Not at all. "Mugwump" comes from the Native American Natick word *mugwomp*, which means "captain." In American politics, it first referred to Republicans who left the party in 1884 rather than support presidential candidate James G. Blaine. More generally, it means an independent in politics, although that meaning seems to be dying out along with the species.

//

FALLACY: Madonna University, in the entertainer's hometown, is named for her.
FACT: There is no Madonna University in her hometown of Bay

City, Michigan. There is a Madonna University in Livonia, Michigan, west of Detroit and considerably south of Bay City. Originally all-female, it is now coed. Although there's no denying that Madonna has been an education, this is a religious school, named for another Madonna.

//

FALLACY: The first video game was created in the 1970s.
FACT: Video games are now a billion-dollar industry, but the first one was created as a mere diversion; its creator didn't even take out a patent. The first video game, tennis, was created by Willy Higinbotham in 1958. Each player had a button to hit the ball, and a knob to determine its height. Willy was not a teenage genius working in a garage. He was a physicist at Brookhaven National Laboratory, had worked on the Manhattan Project, and watched the detonation of the world's first atomic bomb. In today's video games, you can watch the detonation of the world.

//

FALLACY: When she asks, "O Romeo, Romeo! wherefore art thou Romeo?" Juliet is asking where he is.
FACT: Romeo is hiding in the bushes beneath Juliet's balcony, but she's not asking where he is. In Shakespeare's time "wherefore" meant "why." She's lamenting that his name is Romeo Montague, because the Montagues are locked in a deadly feud with her family, the Capulets.

//

FALLACY: The mamba is a South American dance.
FACT: The mamba didn't originate in South America. It's native to southern Africa. Members of the genus *Dendraspis,* mambas are extremely poisonous snakes. They're closely related to cobras, but have no hoods. The mambo, a dance in ¼ time with a lot of hip movement, didn't originate in South America, either. It's native to Cuba. The similarity of the two words gives new meaning to the expression "snake hips."

//

FALLACY: The expression "separation of church and state" comes from the Constitution.

FACT: Separation of church and state is required by the First Amendment to the Constitution, but that expression is not from the Constitution. In 1802, Thomas Jefferson said: "I contemplate with sovereign reverence that act of the whole American people which declared that their legislature should make no law respecting an establishment of religion, or prohibit the free exercise thereof, thus building a wall of separation between church and state." Ever since, there has been a holy war over whether or not that wall should be holey.

//

FALLACY: When you hear the word *vittles*, you know that the speaker doesn't know English very well.
FACT: Only someone who doesn't know English very well would think that. *Victuals,* pronounced "vittles," are food supplies. *Victual,* singular, means food fit for human consumption. Ma and Pa Kettle knew that.

//

FALLACY: "Sator arepo tenet opera rotas" is a medieval magic spell.
FACT: It is definitely old, but it's not a medieval magic spell. Written out like that it loses its original form, which was:

```
S  A  T  O  R
A  R  E  P  O
T  E  N  E  T
O  P  E  R  A
R  O  T  A  S
```

and showed that it was a word game. Such "word squares" were popular thousands of years ago, and this particular one was found at Pompeii. To be a word square it has to be readable in two directions. This is among the more famous because it can be read in four directions.

//

FALLACY: Paul McCartney recordings are distributed by the Beatles' original Apple Records.
FACT: Apple Records went the way of the Beatles. Thorn-EMI Plc. owns Capitol Records, which distributes Paul McCartney's recordings in the United States, and EMI Records, which distributes them internationally. McCartney signed a deal with EMI to start with his 1993 record,

Off The Ground and continue, according to a Capitol spokesman, "basically for the rest of his recording career."

//

FALLACY: Although most national anthems have way too many stanzas, all of them have at least two.
FACT: At least three national anthems—those of Japan, Jordan, and San Marino—manage to get by with only one four-line stanza each. The Spanish national anthem, along with those of ten other countries, has no words at all. The national anthem of the United States has many stanzas, but that's okay because nobody remembers them.

//

FALLACY: Bram Stoker, author of *Dracula,* was German.
FACT: Abraham "Bram" Stoker, author of the 1897 classic novel, was born on 8 November 1847 in Dublin. He was a contemporary of Oscar Wilde, another famous Irish writer. Transylvania I can believe as Dracula's hangout; I'd have a harder time believing Tipperary.

//

FALLACY: Lynching means hanging.
FACT: Although lynch victims are sometimes hanged, that is not the meaning of the word. "Lynch" means to kill by mob action without legal sanction—regardless of how the murder is accomplished. Among the first things lynched when a mob forms are logic, reason, and common sense.

//

FALLACY: A polymath is someone who is expert in several different fields of mathematics.
FACT: The odds are against a polymath being expert in several different fields of mathematics; it's entirely possible for someone to be a polymath without being an expert in any field of mathematics. The "math" part comes from the Greek word *mathaneim,* to learn. A polymath is someone of wide and deep learning, regardless of the fields of learning. Sounds odd, but it does add up.

//

FALLACY: Orson Welles's career began with his "War of the Worlds" broadcast, and ended with his motion picture *Citizen Kane.*

FACT: Known most recently for "We shall sell no wine before its time" ads, Orson Welles broadcast his adaptation of H. G. Wells's *War of the Worlds* in October 1938, on his "Mercury Theater of the Air." That was not the beginning of his career; at the age of twenty-three, he was already a major figure in the New York theatrical world. Welles co-wrote, directed, and played the title role in the motion picture *Citizen Kane,* which appeared only three years later. That was not the end of his career; among his later films were *Macbeth* in 1948, *Touch of Evil* in 1958, and *The Trial* in 1962. Somewhat of a perfectionist, he refused to release any film before its time.

//

FALLACY: The Shroud of Turin is the burial shroud of Jesus.

FACT: A French nobleman, Geoffrey I de Charny, claimed in 1356 that he had discovered the burial shroud of Jesus. The Bishop of Troyes said at the time that it was a fraud, which had been painted by a local artist. Scientific carbon-14 dating has shown that the flax in the cloth was grown sometime between 1260 and 1390. On 13 October 1988, Roman Catholic Cardinal Anastasio Ballestrero, the shroud's official custodian, announced that the Shroud of Turin could not be the burial shroud of Jesus because it was made in the Middle Ages.

//

FALLACY: Pluto is Mickey Mouse's dog; Goofy is not a dog.

FACT: Pluto is definitely a dog. He first appeared as Rover, several years before Goofy arrived on the scene. As for Goofy, when he first appeared his name was Dippy Dawg—a definite clue.

//

FALLACY: Lizzie Borden was convicted of killing her parents with an ax.

FACT: In the words of the famous ballad, "Lizzie Borden took an ax and gave her mother forty whacks. When she saw what she had done, she gave her father forty-one." Andrew J. and Abby Gray Borden were killed in Fall River, Massachusetts, on August 4th of 1892. Although many experts believe that Lizzie Borden did commit the murders, on June

30th of 1893 she was acquitted of the crimes, not convicted. Her occupation in 1892? She was a Sunday school teacher.

/ /

FALLACY: Most of the poets who have read their work at presidential inaugurations have been women.

FACT: Until 1993, not a single female poet had been invited to read a poem at a presidential inauguration. The first woman invited to do so was author and poet Maya Angelou, who read ''On the Pulse of Morning'' at President Clinton's inauguration. She was the first ''official poet'' at an inauguration since Robert Frost read ''The Gift Outright'' at John F. Kennedy's.

/ /

FALLACY: The most commonly used words in the English language are *it, the,* and *and.*

FACT: Depends on whether you mean written English, or spoken English. The most commonly used words in written English are, in order, *the, of, and, to,* and *a.* The most commonly used word in spoken English is *I.* Proves that we should write more and talk less.

/ /

FALLACY: Frank Zappa named his first child Dweezil.

FACT: What a silly notion—of course that's not true. Frank and Gail Zappa named their *second* child Dweezil. They named their first child Moon Unit. Ahmet Rodin is their third child, and Diva their fourth.

/ /

FALLACY: Shakespeare's plays are not only based on history, they are historically accurate.

FACT: Many of Shakespeare's plays are based on history, but he was a better wordsmith than historian. Also a pragmatist, he was acutely aware of current royalty as he shaped stories about past royalty. Obviously not a science-fiction writer, he penned some amazing anachronisms. In *Antony and Cleopatra,* for example, he referred to the game of billiards, which hadn't been invented. In *King John* he employed cannon, which hadn't been invented. His greatest feat of time travel, though, was in *Julius Caesar,* where he had a clock striking the hour more than a thousand years before such a clock existed. *A Comedy of Errors,* or *Much Ado About Nothing?*

//

FALLACY: Horace Greeley originated the expression "Go West, young man, go West."
FACT: He may have said it, but he didn't originate it. When that first appeared in his *New York Tribune,* it was a reprint. It was originally written in 1851 by John Lane Soule in the Terre Haute, Indiana, *Express.* Horace Greeley never claimed authorship, and repeatedly gave the original source.

//

FALLACY: San Franciscans hate the word *Frisco.*
FACT: Some traditionalists do, but most San Franciscans don't; many of them use the nickname. Even Herb Caen, Mr. San Francisco himself, who has had a column in the *San Francisco Chronicle* for more than fifty years, has changed his mind on the formerly forbidden word. Not that he'd ever use the word himself, but he no longer considers its use a capital crime.

//

FALLACY: Buddhism was founded by a man named Buddha.
FACT: Buddha is a title, not a name. It comes from Sanskrit and means "enlightened." His name was Siddhartha Gautama. It's not true that Dolly Parton tried to become a Buddhist, but couldn't contemplate her navel.

//

FALLACY: The world's largest painting on canvas was hundreds of feet long.
FACT: The world's largest painting on canvas was twelve feet

high and three miles long. First displayed by artist John Banvard in 1846, it was titled *Panorama of the Mississippi.* The painting was kept in huge rolls; a complete showing took two hours, with or without popcorn.

/ /

FALLACY: Most of our common proverbs, such as Haste makes waste, are from unknown authors of the last century.
FACT: Most of our common proverbs are much older than that, and most of the authors are known. Many come from such well-known sources as Alexander Pope and William Shakespeare, but some relatively unknown people contributed generously. These, for example, are all from *The Proverbs of John Heywood,* published in 1546:

> *Haste makes waste.*
> *When the sun shineth, make hay.*
> *Look ere you leap.*
> *Two heads are better than one.*
> *Love me, love my dog.*
> *Beggars should be no choosers.*
> *All is well that ends well.*
> *The fat is in the fire.*
> *I know on which side my bread is buttered.*
> *One good turn asketh another.*
> *A penny for your thought.*
> *Rome was not built in one day.*
> *Better late than never.*
> *The more the merrier.*
> *You cannot see the wood for the trees.*
> *This hitteth the nail on the head.*

/ /

FALLACY: When Tonto called the Lone Ranger *Kemo Sabe,* he was calling him "faithful friend."
FACT: That's what the radio and television shows contended, but what Tonto meant may have depended on how he felt about the Lone Ranger at the moment. In Apache, the words mean "white shirt." In Navajo, they mean "soggy shrub."

FALLACY: Harvard University and Boston College are in Boston.
FACT: Harvard and Radcliffe colleges, the core of Harvard University, are in Cambridge, not Boston. Boston College isn't in Boston, either; it's in Chestnut Hill.

//

FALLACY: In most of the western world, whistling at a public event is like clapping, and indicates approval.
FACT: In most of the western world, whistling at a public event is like booing, and indicates disapproval. After Luciano Pavarotti made two very minor errors while singing at the La Scala opera house in Milan, Italy, there were whistles among the applause. The applause was from fans who ignored or didn't know about the errors; the whistles were from opera fan(atic)s who were letting him know that they knew. Pavarotti later said, "If I make mistakes, I'm ready to accept whistling." For that he should be given a hand.

//

FALLACY: Joyce Kilmer, who wrote "Trees," is one of America's most famous female poets.

> *I think that I shall never see*
> *A poem lovely as a tree.*

FACT: Joyce Kilmer wrote that in 1914. Those are definitely the two most famous lines to come from the pen of that poet. Joyce was not a woman, though. His full name was Alfred Joyce Kilmer.

//

FALLACY: John Wayne was in the Marine Corps during World War II.
FACT: John Wayne was not in the Marine Corps during World War II. Marion Morrison, whose stage name was John Wayne, was never in any of the armed forces.

//

FALLACY: It's impossible to read tomorrow's newspaper today.
FACT: It's very possible. Morning newspapers are printed the

evening of the previous day. Most of tomorrow's newspaper is written by the close of the normal working day at 5:00 or 6:00 P.M. At a large regional newspaper, editions sent to outlying areas are printed first. Many newspapers use the number of stars on the front-page masthead to mark the different editions. Considering that what you read in the morning was published the previous day, it's surprising how much of it you will hear on the evening "news." No matter when you get it, though, there's no gnus like good gnus.

//

FALLACY: Worldwide, more people speak English than any other language.

FACT: Worldwide, more people speak Chinese than any other language. English, including American English and New York English, is second.

//

FALLACY: More Jews live in Israel than in any other country.

FACT: First off, a clarification. Jew refers to a member of the Jewish faith, just as Catholic refers to a member of the Catholic faith. Hebrew refers to a member of an ethnic group, just as Arab refers to a member of an ethnic group; both Arabs and Hebrews belong to the larger group Semite. According to the 1990 *American Jewish Yearbook,* the Jewish population of Israel was 3,659,000. That was the second listing. The first listing was the United States, home to 5,700,000 Jews.

//

FALLACY: Actors in Shakespeare's plays included men, women, boys, and girls.

FACT: All the roles in Shakespeare's plays were acted by men and boys. In England at that time, it was not considered proper for women, much less girls, to appear on stage. It wasn't until half a century after Shakespeare's death that a woman acted in an English play. *Romeo and Juliet* were both males, as were *Antony and Cleopatra,* and all the cast members of *The Merry Wives of Windsor.*

FALLACY: The letters *L.S.* at the bottom of a contract stand for Legal Signature.

FACT: The letters *L.S.* stand for the Latin words *Locus Sigilli,* which mean Place of the Seal. Contracts used to require an official seal, but a signature is now legally binding without a seal. The only reason that some contract forms still have *L.S.* at the bottom, where the signature is now located, is tradition. Unless you read the contract very carefully, *L.S.* near your signature may stand for Lost Soul.

//

FALLACY: Guy Lombardo first played "Auld Lang Syne" for New Year's Eve during World War II.

FACT: Gaetano Albert Lombardo first broadcast "Auld Lang Syne" from the Roosevelt Grill in New York City at the stroke of midnight on New Year's Eve/Day, 1929/1930. When the Roosevelt Grill closed in the 1960s, he moved his band to the grand ballroom of the Waldorf Astoria Hotel, where he welcomed every New Year in with "Auld Lang Syne" up to and including 1977.

//

FALLACY: In spite of the movie *Amadeus,* no emperor ever told Mozart that one of his works had "too many notes."

FACT: That one we can't blame on Hollywood. One of Mozart's most popular works, *The Marriage of Figaro,* had its first performance on 1 May 1786. Ferdinand of Austria, emperor and critic, said to the composer afterward: "Far too noisy, my dear Mozart. Far too many notes."

//

FALLACY: "The road to Hell is paved with good intentions," is from the Bible.

FACT: "The road to Hell is paved with good intentions" is from *Das Kapital,* by Karl Marx.

//

FALLACY: The 1969 Woodstock festival was held in Woodstock, New York.

FACT: The 1969 Woodstock festival was originally planned for Woodstock, but that didn't work out. The farm where the Happening happened was in Bethel, New York, about forty miles from Woodstock.

//

FALLACY: Beethoven was deaf when he wrote his greatest works.
FACT: Beethoven was born in 1770. When he mentioned in an 1801 letter that he was getting hard of hearing, he had already written the *Moonlight* sonata and the First Symphony. Between then and 1814, he wrote the *Emperor* concerto, the *Appassionata* sonata, the Second through Eighth symphonies, his only opera, *Fidelio,* and many other works. He didn't become completely deaf until about 1818.

//

FALLACY: There is no bone in bone china.
FACT: Bone ash, or calcium phosphate, is added to the mixture for bone china to make it whiter and more translucent.

//

FALLACY: Humphrey Bogart's most famous line in the film *Casablanca* is "Play it again, Sam."
FACT: Humphrey Bogart never says that in *Casablanca.* Nobody does. Ingrid Bergman comes closest with: "Play it, Sam. Play 'As Time Goes By.' " What Bogart says is: "If she can stand it, I can. Play it!" Whereupon Dooley Wilson not only plays it, he sings it, too. It's hard to say what Bogart's most famous line is. Might be: "Here's looking at *you,* kid." Might be the last words in the film: "Louie, I think this is the beginning of a beautiful friendship." Reportedly, the last thing that Humphrey Bogart ever said was: "I should never have switched from Scotch to martinis."

//

FALLACY: Being caught *flagrante delicto* means being caught in the midst of a sex act.
FACT: Being caught *flagrante delicto* has nothing to do with sex,

in spite of how it sounds in English. It means being caught in the act of committing a crime. Literally, "while the crime is blazing."

/ /

FALLACY: A ten-gallon hat holds ten gallons.
FACT: Ten-gallon hats, which have a tall crown and a very wide brim, come in the same head sizes as any other hat. The overall size is much larger than that of other hats because of the crown and the brim, so they may have been called "ten-gallon" hats as a joke. Then again, the name may be a derivation of Spanish *galloon,* for the braid wrapped in rows above the brim. Ten-gallon hats, though, definitely do not hold ten gallons. Take a look at a gallon jug of water or milk, then imagine the size a true "ten-gallon" hat would have to be; everything in Texas is larger than the same thing anywhere else, but not even Texans have heads big enough for that hat.

/ /

FALLACY: Malcolm X wrote *The Autobiography of Malcolm X.*
FACT: *The Autobiography of Malcolm X,* published in 1965, was ghostwritten by Alex Haley, the author of *Roots.* Malcolm X was, however, the coauthor of six daughters, including twins who were born to his wife, Betty Shabazz, after Malcolm's death in 1965.

/ /

FALLACY: The English horn is an English horn.
FACT: The English horn, which is not a horn but a double-reed woodwind resembling a large oboe, was created in France, not in England. The French horn, on the other hand, is a French horn.

/ /

FALLACY: The liquor gin and the cotton gin got their name from engine.
FACT: The cotton gin, yes; the liquor gin, no. Gin was created in the Netherlands, and is made by distilling rye or other grains with juniper berries. Our word "gin" is a shortened form of *geneva,* from the Dutch *genever,* meaning "juniper." Wicked little berries, those.

FALLACY: Nathan Hale's last words were: "I regret that I have but one life to give for my country."

FACT: That actually goes, "I only regret that I have but one life to lose for my country," but that's not the point. The point is that according to a document written by an eyewitness, Nathan Hale's last words in 1776 were, "It is the duty of every good officer to obey any orders given him by his commander-in-chief." Interestingly, the following two lines reminiscent of famous Revolutionary War quotes are found in *Cato* by Joseph Addison (1672–1719). "Liberty or death." "What pity is it that we can die but once to serve our country!"

//

FALLACY: An XXX-rated movie has more sex than an X-rated movie.

FACT: There is no such thing as an XXX-rated movie. As established by the Motion Picture Association of America, the X rating was for any movie that should be seen only by adults because of its subject matter. Over time, the two major reasons for an X rating became violence and sex. Then sex became the predominant reason, as violence moved into mainstream films. Advertisers apparently decided that XXX looked sexier than X, so they invented the XXX "rating." The world's least-read words are probably the subtitles on X-rated films.

//

FALLACY: *Peter Rabbit,* the popular American children's book, is protected by copyright.

FACT: *The Tale of Peter Rabbit* was written by British author and illustrator Beatrix Potter, who was born in 1866 and died in 1943. Under the old copyright law, it would long ago have been in the public domain. Under the new copyright law, *The Tale of Peter Rabbit* was protected by copyright until fifty years after her death: 1993. *The Tale of Peter Rabbit* is now in the public domain. That is not true, however, of the twenty-two other books she wrote about Flopsy, Mopsy, Cottontail, and Peter. The publisher and copyright holder of Beatrix Potter's works is Frederick Warne & Co. Although by no means a killer rabbit, Peter did manage to get into more trouble than the average bunny. One of his mother's classic cautions was: "Don't go into Mr. McGregor's garden: your father had an accident there; he was put in a pie by Mrs. McGregor."

FALLACY: Entertainers with easy-to-remember real names, such as George Burns or John Wayne, don't make up stage names.

FACT: Nothing is quite what it seems in the entertainment world. Donald Wayne wasn't satisfied with his name, and Caryn Johnson changed hers, too. Here are a few well-known names, and the names those people were born with:

George Burns	Nathan Birnbaum
Cher	Cherilyn Sarkisian
Tom Cruise	Thomas Mapother
Werner Erhard	John Paul Rosenberg
W. C. Fields	William Claude Dukenfield
Judy Garland	Frances Gumm
James Garner	James Bumgarner
Whoopi Goldberg	Caryn Johnson
Cary Grant	Archibald Alexander Leach
Elton John	Reginald Dwight
Don Johnson	Donald Wayne
Michael Keaton	Michael Douglas
Boris Karloff	William Henry Pratt
Jerry Lewis	Joseph Levich
Madonna	Madonna Louise Ciccone
George Michael	Georgios Kyriakou Panayiotou
Demi Moore	Demi Guynes
Prince	Prince Rogers Nelson
Joan Rivers	Joan Sandra Molinsky
Roy Rogers	Leonard Slye
Soupy Sales	Milton Hines
Sting	Gordon Sumner
Tina Turner	Annie Mae Bullock
John Wayne	Marion Michael Morrison

//

FALLACY: Toulouse Lautrec was a French painter who had no legs.

FACT: Toulouse was not his first name, and he did have legs. His name was Henri de Toulouse-Lautrec. Because of an accident when he was fifteen, his physical growth was permanently stunted. Capturing what he saw around him in cabarets, circuses, bordellos, and music halls, he went on to become one of France's most famous painters and lithographers.

／／

FALLACY: "The pen is mightier than the sword" is from the Bible.
FACT: The original quote is: "Beneath the rule of men entirely great, The pen is mightier than the sword." It's from Edward George Bulwer-Lytton's *Richelieu,* published in 1838. Another famous quote from him is the opening sentence of his 1830 work *Paul Clifford:* "It was a dark and stormy night; the rain fell in torrents—except at occasional intervals, when it was checked by a violent gust of wind which swept up the streets (for it is in London that our scene lies), rattling along the housetops, and fiercely agitating the scanty flame of the lamps that struggled against the darkness." He certainly did have a way with words. And words. And words.

／／

FALLACY: Bluebeard was a pirate.
FACT: Bluebird was a fictional wife murderer in Charles Perrault's novel *Conte du Temps,* published in 1679. He was not a pirate. His name is often confused with Blackbeard, a pirate who died in 1718. Blackbeard was a privateer who operated in the West Indies and along the Atlantic Coast. I have that on the authority of a graybeard.

／／

FALLACY: Only the company that holds the copyright on the title can put out a *Webster's* dictionary.
FACT: Anyone can put out a *Webster's* dictionary, and many companies do. A title cannot be copyrighted. Interestingly, Noah Webster didn't use the word in the title of his dictionary, *An American Dictionary of the English Language.*

／／

FALLACY: "Tit for tat" is an anatomical reference.
FACT: Nope. That's not where it comes from. Comes from the Netherlands, where *Dit vor dat* means "This for that." Sorry about dat.

FALLACY: That famous quote, "Now is the winter of our discontent," means that the speaker is discontented.

FACT: That famous quote is only half the quote. The full quote, spoken by Richard III in Shakespeare's play of that name, means exactly the opposite:

> *Now is the winter of our discontent*
> *Made glorious summer by this sun of York.*

//

FALLACY: "Happy Birthday" is a folk song that long ago passed into the public domain.

FACT: "Happy Birthday to You" was originally written by sisters Mildred and Patty Hill as "Good Morning to You." It didn't make a big splash. After the word changes it was published again in 1935, and the rest is history. "Happy Birthday to You" is still covered by copyright—it is not in the public domain.

//

FALLACY: The Bible says that Adam and Eve were thrown out of the Garden of Eden for eating an apple from the tree of knowledge of good and evil.

FACT: According to the Bible they both did eat fruit from that tree, but it was probably not an apple because the climate was too hot; there is no mention of Eve being thrown out of the garden; and neither of them was thrown out for eating fruit from *that* tree.

And out of the ground made the Lord God to grow every tree that is pleasant to the sight, and good for food; the tree of life also in the midst of the garden, and the tree of knowledge of good and evil. . . .

And the Lord God said, Behold, the man is become as one of us, to know good and evil: and now, lest he put forth his hand, and take also of the tree of life, and eat, and live forever:

Therefore the Lord God sent him forth from the garden of Eden, to till the ground from whence he was taken.

FALLACY: India ink is from India.

FACT: India ink is a solid black pigment, made from lampblack mixed with a binding agent. The bottle of "India ink" you buy in an art store is a fine suspension of India ink in a liquid. India ink can easily be made anywhere—even India.

//

FALLACY: W. C. Fields said: "Anybody who hates dogs and children can't be all bad."

FACT: That famous tongue-in-cheeker was not said by W. C. Fields; it was said *about* him, by Leo C. Rosten, during a speech at a Masquers' Club dinner on February 16, 1939. Rosten's original was: "The only thing I can say about Mr. W. C. Fields, whom I have admired since the day he advanced upon Baby LeRoy with an ice pick, is this: Any man who hates babies and dogs can't be all bad."

//

FALLACY: The story of the Dutch boy who put his finger in the dike is an ancient legend from Holland.

FACT: The story of that Dutch boy is a recent legend. It comes from the book *Hans Brinker, or the Silver Skates,* published in 1865. And that book did not come from the Netherlands. It was written by American author Mary Mapes Dodge.

//

FALLACY: Since the beginning of Hollywood, if a star is arrested, convicted, and serves jail time, his or her career is over.

FACT: Often true, but not always the case. Robert Mitchum's was a case for which it wasn't true. He was arrested in 1948 for "conspiracy to possess marijuana," convicted, and served the full two-month sentence.

//

FALLACY: The expression "survival of the fittest" is from Darwin's book on evolution.

FACT: The expression "survival of the fittest" is from Herbert Spencer's *Principles of Biology,* describing Darwin's theory of natural selection. Charles Darwin, in *The Descent of Man,* said, "I have called this principle, by which each slight variation, if useful, is preserved, by the term of Natural Selection." He went on to say, "The expression often used by Mr. Herbert Spencer of the Survival of the Fittest is more accurate, and is sometimes equally convenient."

//

FALLACY: Most ships tie up at wharves.
FACT: A wharf runs parallel to the shoreline. Boats frequently tie up at wharves, but ships rarely do because the water is usually far too shallow. What ships tie up to are docks, which run perpendicular to the shoreline out into deeper water. And what's the difference between a boat and a ship? Traditionally, a boat can be carried on a ship but a ship can't be carried on a boat.

//

FALLACY: Assault and battery means physically attacking someone.
FACT: "Assault" and "battery" have very different meanings. Attempting, or even threatening, to batter someone is assault. Carrying out the threat is battery.

//

FALLACY: "Tell the truth and shame the devil," is from the Bible.
FACT: "Tell truth, and shame the devil," (only one "the") is from *Mary the Cookmaid's Letter,* by the same man who wrote *Gulliver's Travels*: Jonathan Swift. Even more satirical than that classic was *A Modest Proposal for Preventing the Children of Ireland from being a Burden to their Parents or Country,* commonly shortened to *A Modest Proposal.* This sentence will give you some idea:

> I have been assured by a very knowing American of my acquaintance in London, that a young healthy child well nursed is at a year old a most delicious, nourishing, and wholesome food, whether stewed, roasted, baked, or boiled, and I make no doubt that it will equally serve in a fricassee, or a ragout.

FALLACY: A chauvinist is a male who thinks that females are inferior.

FACT: Chauvinism originally had nothing to do with sex. The word comes from Nicholas Chauvin, a French soldier who constantly and endlessly praised Napoleon. His name became part of the language when he was used as a character in a number of works, including Theodore and Hippolyte Cogniard's play *La cocarde tricolore* and Emmuska Orczy's *Scarlet Pimpernel.* The word meant someone who was blindly devoted to a nation or group. Only recently has it been applied to sexual groups, as in "male chauvinist" or "female chauvinist."

//

FALLACY: There is no such thing as a language without an alphabet.

FACT: The vast majority of spoken languages have no alphabet. Cherokee was one until Sequoyah (1766–1843) created an eighty-five-character alphabet which represented all the spoken sounds; redwoods, the world's largest trees, were named *sequoias* in his honor. Another notable example is the world's most widely spoken language, Chinese, which uses pictographs rather than the letters of an alphabet.

//

FALLACY: The word *infantry* means "warriors."

FACT: The word *infantry* comes from "infant-ry," and originally meant children who were foot soldiers.

//

FALLACY: Genghis Khan was the name of a conqueror; Kublai Khan was the name of a poem.

FACT: "Genghis Khan" was a Mongol title meaning "Supreme Conqueror," not a name. The name of the man was Temüjin, and he was the grandfather of Kublai Khan. While Marco Polo was in Asia, he spent most of his time at the court of Kublai Khan in what is now Beijing. Using a slightly different spelling, Samuel Taylor Coleridge wrote in his famous poem, *Kubla Khan*:

In Xanadu did Kubla Khan,
A stately pleasure-dome decree:
Where Alph, the sacred river, ran
Through caverns measureless to man
Down to a sunless sea.

//

FALLACY: The word *butterfly* started out as "flutterby."
FACT: In Modern English it has always been "butterfly," which came from Middle English *butterflye,* which came from Old English *butorfleoge.* That, in turn, may well have come from the Dutch *boterschijte,* which referred not to the color of the insect's wings as it flew away, but to the color of what it left behind.

//

FALLACY: The original 3-D film was MGM's 1953 *Bwana Devil.*
FACT: Everybody who has seen *Bwana Devil* in 3-D remembers the glasses they had to wear, and many people remember the spear that seems to come out of the screen, but almost nobody remembers the story. It was that good. The original 3-D film, though, was *The Power of Love,* made in 1922.

//

FALLACY: *Whistler's Mother* was painted by James MacNeill Whistler.
FACT: The painting that brings that title to mind was painted by Whistler, but that's not what he named it. The name of that painting is *Arrangement in Grey and Black #1.* In case you're wondering, *Arrangement in Grey and Black #2* is a painting of Thomas Carlyle.

//

FALLACY: When you go in the front door of a church, you walk down the aisle to the back of the church.

FACT: When you go in the front door of a church, you walk down the nave. Aisles are on the sides of the room, between the pews and the walls. And if you went in the front door of a church and walked the full length of the nave, you'd be at the front of the church—the front door is in the back wall.

//

FALLACY: James Garner was the only actor who played "Maverick" on that TV show.

FACT: James Garner was the first of three actors to portray the character "Maverick" on TV. The other two were Jack Kelly and Roger Moore.

//

FALLACY: Because it is sung every year, the most-sung song in the United States is "Auld Lang Syne."

FACT: Because it is sung every day, the most-sung song in the United States is "Happy Birthday to You."

//

FALLACY: Sherlock Holmes says "Elementary, my dear Watson," at least once in each of the Arthur Conan Doyle stories.

FACT: He never says it, in any of the stories. That's one more we can chalk up to Hollywood.

//

FALLACY: George Bernard Shaw was English.

FACT: George Bernard Shaw was born in Dublin, Ireland, in 1856. He didn't move to England until after his twentieth birthday. Other famous "English" writers who were actually Irish include John Synge, Oscar Wilde, and William Butler Yeats.

//

FALLACY: Delilah cut Samson's hair, the source of his strength.

FACT: According to the biblical story, Samson's long hair was the source of his strength. It was not Delilah who cut Samson's hair, however. "But she made him sleep upon her knees, and lay his head in her bosom. And she called a barber, and shaved his seven locks, and began to drive him away, and thrust him from her: for immediately his strength departed from him." It was the barber, called in by Samson's bosom buddy, who cut Samson's hair.

//

FALLACY: The first color comic strips appeared in the twentieth century.

FACT: The first color comic strip, a series of panels of an already existing single-panel color comic, was "The Yellow Kid" by Frank Outcault. It appeared in the 24 October 1897 Sunday Supplement to the *New York Journal*. We still need our Sunday Funnies.

//

FALLACY: A dirigible has a rigid frame; a blimp does not.

FACT: A blimp is a nonrigid, lighter-than-air craft; a dirigible is a steerable, lighter-than-air craft. "Dirigible" comes from the Latin *dirigere* (capable of being steered). Therefore any lighter-than-air craft that can be steered, whether or not it has a rigid frame, is a dirigible.

//

FALLACY: There were really four, not three, Marx Brothers.

FACT: Chico (Leonard), Harpo (Arthur), and Groucho (Julius) were three of the five Marx Brothers, and the ones seen and heard most often. The other two were Gummo (Milton) and Zeppo (Herbert). It was Groucho who first came up with: "Military intelligence is a contradiction in terms."

//

FALLACY: "Three sheets to the wind" refers to someone who has had a lot to drink and is staggering around like a ship with three sails hoisted in a storm.

FACT: "Sheets" aren't sails. They're ropes used to control sails. When three sheets are untied and blowing in the wind, the sails are out of control and cause the ship to stagger around like someone who has had a lot to drink.

//

FALLACY: Umbrellas were invented to keep the rain off.
FACT: Umbrellas were invented to keep the sun off. The word comes from the Latin *umbella,* meaning "little shaded area."

//

FALLACY: A bookworm is a person; there is no real "bookworm."
FACT: Figuratively, a bookworm is a person who spends a lot of time reading or researching. Literally, a bookworm is any of various insect larvae that feed on the paste in book bindings. If you come across many books that have been attacked by bookworms, you'll come to believe that there is such a thing as justifiable insecticide.

//

FALLACY: It was illegal to show pubic hair in photographs until *Playboy* did it and won in court.
FACT: It was never specifically illegal. It was just that censors, people who stick their NOs in other people's business, wouldn't allow it. Publishers knew that their publication would be banned, and they'd lose money. The first major magazine to show pubic hair without being censored was not *Playboy,* but the April 1970 issue of *Penthouse.*

//

FALLACY: After Ayatollah Khomeini's death, the reward for killing Salman Rushdie, author of *The Satanic Verses,* was dropped.
FACT: In 1989 Iran's Fifteenth Khordad Foundation, a government agency, offered $1 million to any non-Iranian who murdered Salman Rushdie; an Iranian would receive much more. In 1991 the offer was increased to $2 million. In 1992 the offer was increased again. I've heard of rough critics, but this is ridiculous.

FALLACY: *Corpus delicti* is Latin for a corpse.

FACT: *Corpus delicti* is Latin for "body of the crime." The term refers to the material substance upon which a crime has been committed, or to the material evidence proving that a crime has been committed. Although a corpse would certainly be part of the *corpus delicti* in a murder case, that is not what the phrase means.

///

FALLACY: The *Encyclopaedia Britannica* is from Britain.

FACT: The *Encyclopaedia Britannica* is from the United States. It originated in Scotland in 1771. From 1928 to 1943 it was owned by Sears Roebuck. Since then, it has been owned by the University of Chicago. You can look it up.

///

FALLACY: Michael Angelo was one of the most famous Renaissance painters.

FACT: That's Michelangelo, not Michael Angelo. Michelangelo Buonarroti was not only one of the most famous painters of the Renaissance, he was also one of its most famous architects, poets, and sculptors. He thought of himself primarily as a sculptor. His best-known painting is on the ceiling of the Sistine Chapel; his best-known sculpture is *David.*

///

FALLACY: "Call me Ishmael" is from the Bible.

FACT: The opening words in Chapter One of Herman Melville's *Moby Dick* are: "Call me Ishmael." That phrase is not in the Bible.

///

FALLACY: The first motion picture to take all major Academy Awards was *One Flew Over the Cuckoo's Nest.*

FACT: Close, but no Oscar. *One Flew Over the Cuckoo's Nest* was the second motion picture to take all major Academy Awards, in 1975. The first film to do that was *It Happened One Night,* starring Clark Gable and Claudette Colbert, in 1934—in spite of the fact that it didn't happen that night.

/ /

FALLACY: Camel's-hair brushes are made of camel's hair.
FACT: Although camel's-hair cloth is made of either camel's hair or camel's hair mixed with wool, camel's-hair brushes are not. That camel's-hair brush you pull through your hair is usually made of squirrel's hair.

/ /

FALLACY: The story of Robinson Crusoe was fiction.
FACT: The main character's name was changed by Daniel Defoe, author of *Robinson Crusoe,* for reasons known only to Daniel Defoe. The story itself was based on the definitely nonfictional adventures of a Scotsman named Alexander Selkirk, who was a castaway on Juan Fernandez Island in the Pacific for more than four years. He was rescued by an English sea captain named Woodes Rogers. Rogers was a "privateer" to the English, but a "pirate" to the Spanish: he plundered Spanish treasure ships that were carrying home what they had plundered from Native Americans.

/ /

FALLACY: *Bustard* is a polite form of an impolite word.
FACT: While it is true that the parents of bustards are not married, it would be more than surprising if they were. A bustard is a large bird of Europe and Australia that can fly, but prefers to run. The largest species is about the size of a turkey.

/ /

FALLACY: Belgian is spoken not only in Belgium, but in Belgium's former colonies such as the Congo.
FACT: "Belgian" is spoken nowhere. There is no such language. The two official languages of Belgium are Dutch and French. Dutch is

spoken in Flanders, the northern part of Belgium, which shares a border with the Netherlands; French is spoken in Wallonia, the southern part, which shares a border with France.

// //

FALLACY: The Korean War lasted a lot longer than the television series based on it, M*A*S*H.

FACT: Happy to say, the Korean War lasted less than a third as long as the original series of M*A*S*H episodes. The reruns will probably last longer than the Hundred Years War.

// //

FALLACY: Frankenstein was a monster.

FACT: Possibly, but that sounds like an ex-mate's opinion. In Mary Shelley's 1818 novel *Frankenstein, or The Modern Prometheus,* Frankenstein was the man who built the monster. Frankenstein, by the way, was not a doctor. He was a student of physiology.

// //

FALLACY: "The Battle Hymn of the Republic" was written by a Union soldier during the Civil War.

FACT: "The Battle Hymn of the Republic" was written by Julia Ward Howe, an author and a leader in the women's suffrage movement.

// //

FALLACY: Grouchy was one of The Seven Dwarfs.

FACT: The dwarfs in Disney's 1937 *Snow White and the Seven Dwarfs* were: Bashful, Doc, Dopey, Grumpy, Happy, Sleepy, and Sneezy.

// //

FALLACY: The Catholic doctrine of Immaculate Conception says that Jesus was conceived free of Original Sin.

FACT: That doctrine, which became dogma in 1854, does not refer to the conception of Jesus. What it says is that his mother, unlike other humans, was conceived free of Original Sin.

//

FALLACY: When someone tells you that your fly is open, they mean that your pants buttons are unbuttoned or your zipper is down.

FACT: That may be what they mean, but that's not what they said. The fly is not the buttons or the zipper, but the flap of cloth that covers them.

//

FALLACY: Catch-22 is a general term for rules that make themselves impossible; it never referred to anything specific.

FACT: In Joseph Heller's novel of that name, Catch-22 referred specifically to the U.S. Air Force regulations about a combat pilot asking to be grounded because of insanity. The pilot "would be crazy to fly more missions and sane if he didn't, but if he was sane, he had to fly them. If he flew them he was crazy and didn't have to; but if he didn't, he was sane and had to."

//

FALLACY: There is no such word as *ain't*.

FACT: Sure there is, and has been for hundreds of years. *Ain't* is the contraction for *am not*. In spite of that fact, *ain't* is considered "non-standard" at best. Seems silly to outlaw a useful word, but I amn't going to argue with lexicographers.

3

Astronomy

FALLACY: The closest planet to Earth is Mars.
FACT: Because each of the planets has its own orbit, the distances among them vary constantly. The closest that Mars can come to Earth is thirty-five million miles. That's closer than any other planet—except Venus. At closest approach, Venus is only twenty-six million miles from Earth. Getting from here to there would involve a *much* longer curved path, but in straight-line travel time at one thousand miles per hour it would take a mere twenty-six thousand hours, or about three years, to drop in on our nearest neighbor.

//

FALLACY: From the bottom of a dark well, you can see stars during the day.
FACT: The depth and darkness of a well would make no difference. The reason we can't see stars during the day is that the Sun makes our atmosphere so bright that we can't see through it. If you fell to the bottom of a dark well and landed on your head, then you might see stars.

//

FALLACY: Earth is the only Solar System body with volcanoes.
FACT: Io, the ninth moon out from Jupiter and one of the four brightest, is the most volcanically active body in the Solar System. Its volcanoes erupt sulfur and sodium. Earth is second. Venus also has volcanoes, and the volcanoes on Neptune's largest moon, Triton, eject carbon-

rich material as high as five miles. The largest volcanic mountain ever discovered, however, is not on any of those. Discovered on Mars by the *Mariner 9* spacecraft, the extinct volcano Olympus Mons has a crater more than 50 miles from rim to rim. Its base is about 350 miles wide, and it rises nearly 90,000 feet into the thin Martian atmosphere. Put Mount Everest on top of Mount Everest. Then put another Mount Everest on top of those. That's how high Olympus Mons is. The base of Olympus Mons is so large that it could cover the total land areas of Connecticut, Delaware, Hawaii, Indiana, Maryland, Massachusetts, New Hampshire, New Jersey, Rhode Island, and Vermont—with 2,000 square miles left over. Them's a lot of leftovers.

//

FALLACY: None of our space probes has headed for the star nearest to the Sun.
FACT: None of our space probes has headed *directly* for the Sun's nearest neighbor, but there is one on its way there. Launched from Cape Canaveral on 2 March 1972, *Pioneer 10* headed for Jupiter. It reached there in 1973, studied the planet, and kept on going. On 13 June 1983, it left the Solar System. On 13 June 1993, it was 5.5 billion miles from Earth and traveling at a speed of 50,000 kilometers per hour. The nearest star group is Alpha Centauri; of those three stars the closest is Proxima Centauri. That's the direction *Pioneer 10* is heading. You'll have to be patient, though. It won't arrive there for another 32,600 years, because Proxima Centauri is twenty-five trillion miles from Earth.

//

FALLACY: By paying a fee, you can officially name an unnamed star or other heavenly body.
FACT: No matter how much you paid, you couldn't name a moon, an asteroid, or a star. Official names for heavenly bodies are conferred by the International Astronomical Union. In 1988, for example, the General Assembly of the IAU named the ten moons of Uranus discovered by *Voyager 2*. More recently, the IAU gave names to four asteroids: Lennon, McCartney, Harrison, and Starr.

FALLACY: Venus and Mars have about the same gravity.
FACT: The only planet with a gravity close to that of Venus's
8.85 meters/second^2 is Earth, with 9.81 m/s^2. Mars, with 3.72 m/s^2, is a
close match with Mercury, at 3.70. Saturn, Uranus, and Neptune are similar to each other, at 11.67, 11.48, and 11.97. The closest to Pluto's 1.96
is not another planet's, but our Moon's 1.62. The Solar System Planetary
Gravity Record is held by Jupiter, with its 26.39 m/s^2.

// /

FALLACY: The tides in the ocean are caused by the Moon.
FACT: If the Moon were the only cause of the tides in the ocean,
those tides would be far simpler and more regular than they are. The Moon
raises two high tides: one on the part of Earth closest to it, and another
on the opposite side. In the first case the Moon is pulling the water away
from Earth, and in the second it is pulling Earth away from the water.
The Moon causes only about two-thirds of the total tidal effects, however;
the other third is contributed by the Sun. The cycle of the tides is determined by the Moon, but their height is determined by the position of the
Sun. The tide with the highest rise and fall, called a spring tide, occurs
when the Sun lines up with the Moon, as it does around the time of a
new moon or a full moon. The tide with the lowest rise and fall, called a
neap tide, occurs when the Sun and the Moon pull at right angles, as they
do around the time of a first-quarter or third-quarter moon. Tides occur
not only in the ocean, where they average about one meter, but also in
the land, where they average about twenty centimeters. It's true: sometimes you're taller.

// /

FALLACY: A light-year is a very long time.
FACT: A light-year is no time at all. It's the very long *distance*
that light travels in a year: 5,878,500,000,000 miles.

// /

FALLACY: The area of the Milky Way around our Sun is fairly typical.
FACT: The area of the Milky Way around our Sun is fairly
empty. The low-density bubble we're embedded in extends about three
hundred light-years from the Solar System, and may have been caused by

a supernova explosion that blew away the gas and dust that would have made this area fairly typical. For as far as light travels in three hundred years, there's a whole lot of not very much out there.

/ /

FALLACY: Saturn has rings, but no moons.
FACT: In addition to its magnificent ring system, Saturn has at least eighteen moons. The smallest is Pan, about twelve miles in diameter, discovered in 1990. The largest is Titan, which could potentially harbor life. For comparison, Earth's Moon has a diameter of 2,160 miles; the planet Mercury has a diameter of 3,029 miles; Titan has a diameter of 3,200 miles. Titan has the densest atmosphere of any moon in the solar system; atmospheric pressure at Titan's surface is 1.6 times that at Earth's surface.

/ /

FALLACY: The Sun is a huge ball of fire.
FACT: Surprising as it sounds, there is no fire at all on the Sun. Fire requires three things: temperature, fuel, and oxygen. The Sun has an abundance of the first two, but not oxygen. It is indeed huge, though, with a diameter of about 865,000 miles, and a mass 332,000 times that of Earth. The main energy source is the fusion of hydrogen atoms into helium atoms, which goes on in the 15,000,000°C core. This releases energy in many forms, much of which ends up as heat and light. What looks like fire is the visible surface of the Sun, called the photosphere, and occasional solar flares and prominences in the chromosphere above it. In spite of all that heat and light, though, there's no fire. Have you ever nestled in front of an electric heater on a cold, dark day? It, too, gives off heat and light without fire.

/ /

FALLACY: A compass points toward the North Star.
FACT: A compass points generally toward Earth's magnetic north pole, not Earth's geographic north pole. It is the geographic pole, determined by Earth's axis of rotation, that points toward Polaris, the North Star. A compass, therefore, does not point toward the North Star. Polaris is a second-magnitude supergiant star five hundred to eight hundred light-years from Earth, at the end of the handle of the Little Dipper, in the

constellation Ursa Minor or Little Bear. One reason it's so useful to navigators is that its height above the northern horizon tells your latitude: if Polaris is 35° above the horizon, you're at 35° North latitude; if Polaris is 90° above the horizon it's directly overhead, and you're standing on the geographic north pole. Because of its importance, many people think that Polaris is the brightest star in our sky; it's only forty-ninth. Seriously speaking, Sirius is the brightest.

//

FALLACY: The bigger a planet is, the slower it rotates.

FACT: Earth, with an equatorial diameter of 7,926 miles, rotates at about 1,000 miles per hour; it takes 23.9 hours to make one full rotation. Jupiter, with an equatorial diameter of 88,700 miles, rotates at about 22,000 miles per hour; it takes 9.8 hours to make one full rotation. Jupiter, the largest of all the planets, has the shortest period of rotation. Mercury, with an equatorial diameter of 3,030 miles, takes fifty-nine days to make one full rotation. The Sun, with an equatorial diameter of 864,930 miles, takes an average of twenty-seven days to complete a rotation, at an estimated 630,000 miles per hour.

//

FALLACY: Shooting stars, meteors, and meteorites are all the same thing.

FACT: A ''shooting star'' is a meteor heated to incandescence by friction with the atmosphere. As long as it's in the air, it's a meteor; once it lands, it's a meteorite. With love or alcohol or whatever, we've all had that experience.

//

FALLACY: Except for *Sputnik,* the United States has had all the ''firsts'' in the exploration of space.

FACT: The United States got off to a slow start, but has had some of the most impressive ''firsts.'' The Soviet Union, however, racked up most of the first ''firsts.'' *Sputnik 1* went into orbit on October 4, 1957, weighed 184.3 pounds, and had a diameter of 22.8 inches. On November 3, 1957, *Sputnik 2* carried Laika, a female dog, into orbit. On January 2, 1959, *Lunik 1* broke away from Earth's gravity, passed within 4,000 miles of the Moon, and went on to become the first manmade object in solar orbit. On September 12, 1959, *Lunik 2* crashed on the Moon. On October 4, 1959, *Lunik 3* was launched to become the first manmade object in orbit around the Moon, and sent photos back to Earth. On April 12, 1961, *Vostok 1* lifted off with Yuri Gagarin, the world's first human in orbit. On June 16, 1963, *Vostok 6* lifted off with Valentina Tereshkova, the world's first female human in orbit.

//

FALLACY: You can balance an egg on its small end at the summer solstice, but at no other time.

FACT: Sometimes "summer solstice" is replaced in this statement with "winter solstice" or with either of the equinoxes. Whether or not you can balance an egg on its end and have it stay there depends on several factors, including the shape of the egg, the texture of the surface you're trying to stand it on, and the steadiness of your hand. It has nothing to do with the position of the Sun in the sky, which is what the solstices and the equinoxes are all about. As massive as the Sun is, it's ninety-three million miles away, so its gravitational effect on the egg is insignificant compared to Earth's. It's also insignificant, as a matter of fact, compared to that of the very close human who is trying to stand it on end.

//

FALLACY: The Moon is always the same distance from Earth because its orbit is circular.

FACT: The Moon's distance from Earth varies constantly because its orbit is slightly elliptical. The mean distance between the centers of Earth and the Moon is 238,857 miles, but sometimes the Moon is as far away as 252,710 miles, and sometimes it's as close as 221,463 miles— that's when the Moon hits your eye like a big pizza pie.

//

FALLACY: Because the ocean covers so much of our planet, there's more land area on Mars than there is on Earth.

FACT: Earth's diameter is 12,756 kilometers (7,922 miles), whereas Mars has a diameter of 6,786 kilometers (4,214 miles). That gives Earth a planetary surface area of 197,160,169 square miles, compared to

55,787,714 for Mars. Approximately 71 percent of Earth's surface is covered by the ocean, however, leaving 57,168,886 square miles of land (some under icecap). Earth has 1,381,172 square miles more land area than does Mars. And before you consider moving to Mars, keep in mind that gravity there is only 38 percent of Earth's, its atmosphere is 95 percent carbon dioxide, and temperatures range from a high of 27° Centigrade down to −124° (81° to −191° Fahrenheit).

//

FALLACY: A long time ago, the Sun actually stopped in the sky.
FACT: As we know, the apparent motion of the Sun across the sky is caused by Earth's rotation on its axis. For the Sun to appear to stop, Earth would have to suddenly stop rotating. Considering that Earth is rotating at approximately one thousand miles per hour, the forces caused by its coming to a sudden halt would destroy it.

//

FALLACY: Every light in the Northern Hemisphere's night sky that can be seen with the naked eye is part of our Milky Way galaxy.
FACT: All except one. You can also see another galaxy, larger than the Milky Way. The Andromeda galaxy (M31) is the most distant light visible to the naked eye from the Northern Hemisphere. It is 2.5 million light-years away, about 120,000 light-years in diameter, and contains more than 200 billion stars. When you get a chance, take a look—it's an eyeful, whether or not you're naked.

//

FALLACY: The Great Wall of China is the only manmade object that can be seen from the Moon.
FACT: *No* manmade object can be seen from the Moon. Not China's Great Wall, not America's freeway system, not even the world's largest cities until they are illuminated at night.

//

FALLACY: The Sun creates a huge amount of energy from hydrogen fusion, but since it has been doing that for so long, it obviously doesn't use much hydrogen to do it.

FACT: The Sun is much larger than most people think. It has two thousand trillion trillion tons (2×10^{30} kilograms) of matter, and most of that is hydrogen. In its core, the Sun fuses 600 million tons of hydrogen into helium every second. The Sun has been fusing its hydrogen into helium for about 4.6 billion years, but has used up less than half of its original supply; it will keep on keeping on as it is for at least another 4.6 billion years. There will be big changes when it runs out of hydrogen, but that's a different story, involving a Red Giant.

//

FALLACY: The dark side of the Moon has been photographed.
FACT: That wouldn't be easy, because there is no "dark side of the Moon." Like Earth, the Moon rotates on its axis, exposing its entire surface to the Sun. Over time, the Moon's rotation has slowed to the point where one rotation takes just as long as one orbit around Earth: 27.322 days. Therefore, the same side of the Moon is always facing Earth. We call the one facing us the "near side," and even Gary Larson calls the other one the "far side." The Soviet *Lunik 3* satellite, launched in 1959, was the first to photograph the far side, which had never before been seen by humans; since then, *Mariner 10* and *Galileo* have also studied parts of the far side. Compared to the side facing us it has a much thicker crust, far fewer maria ("seas" created when volcanic lava filled basins gouged out by meteorites), and a more regular pattern of craters.

//

FALLACY: Some of the brightest stars in the constellation Orion are in his sword.
FACT: The constellation Orion has seven stars of second magnitude or brighter, the most of any constellation. None of them, however, is in his sword. His right (eastern) shoulder is marked by the only one that is red, Betelgeuse. His left shoulder is Bellatrix; his belt stars are Alnitak, Alnilam, and Mintaka; and his knees are Saiph and Rigel. Rigel is the brightest of the seven. The most interesting thing about the Hunter's sword, three stars hanging down between his legs, is the fuzzy patch around Theta Orionis, the middle star. That's the Orion Nebula, also known as M42. It is a star nursery, where new stars are condensing out of an immense cloud of hydrogen gas. The Orion Nebula is so bright (fourth magnitude) that it can be seen from Earth with nothing more than binoculars, because it's shining with the light of hot, brilliant, newborn

stars. Just to the southeast of Orion is Sirius, the faithful Dog Star following Orion the Hunter. Sirius is the brightest star in Earth's night sky, even though few of us go out to look anymore.

//

FALLACY: Sputnik was the first satellite to orbit Earth.

FACT: On October 4, 1957, *Iskustvenyi Sputnik Zewli* (Artificial Companion of the Earth) became the first *manmade* satellite to orbit Earth. The first of ten Sputniks, it reentered Earth's atmosphere on January 4, 1958. A much earlier satellite, although probably not the first, is still up there: the Moon.

//

FALLACY: Jupiter is as large as ten Earths.

FACT: Jupiter has more than twice the mass of all the other planets combined. It has 318 times the mass of Earth, and 1,323 times the volume of Earth. That makes it not only larger than Orson Welles, but larger even than President William Howard Taft.

//

FALLACY: Galileo was brought before the Inquisition because he was the first one to say that Earth went around the Sun.

FACT: Galileo Galilei was brought before the Inquisition in 1633 because in 1632 he had published *Dialogue Concerning the Two Chief World Systems*, which supported the theory that Earth went around the Sun. He didn't claim to have originated that theory, however. He was supporting the Copernican system, proposed by Copernicus in 1530. Unfortunately, the rulers of the Church favored the older Ptolomaic system, which said that the entire universe revolved around Earth. Galileo was forced to renounce all of his beliefs and writings which contradicted the Ptolomaic system. But even Copernicus was not the first to come up with the heliocentric theory. Eighteen centuries earlier a Greek astronomer named Aristarchus of Samos had proposed it. You just can't keep a good idea down.

FALLACY: It takes a full year for us to see all of the Sun's surface.
FACT: For us to see all of the Sun's surface takes about twenty-seven days. The Sun is a chubby little devil, but like the planets it rotates on its axis.

//

FALLACY: The surface of the Moon is very cold.
FACT: Depends on what time you go out for your stroll on the Moon's surface. Even at the equator, in the depths of the lunar night the temperature gets down to $-261°$ Fahrenheit. When the Sun is directly overhead, though, the temperature gets up to a toasty 243° Fahrenheit.

//

FALLACY: Pluto is the most distant planet from the Sun.
FACT: Pluto is usually the most distant of the nine known planets from the Sun. Because its orbit is more of an ellipse than a circle, however, it is occasionally closer to the Sun than Neptune is. It takes Pluto 247.7 Earth years, traveling at 10,440 miles per hour, to make one orbit around the Sun. For twenty of those years, Pluto is inside Neptune's orbit. Neptune's main claim to fame at the moment is that between January 1979 and March 1999, it is the most distant planet from the Sun.

//

FALLACY: The nearest object to our Milky Way galaxy is the Andromeda galaxy.
FACT: From the Northern Hemisphere it would appear that way. The Andromeda galaxy is the only thing that can be seen from there with the naked eye that isn't part of the Milky Way. Taking that same naked eye down to the Southern Hemisphere, however, gives a whole new perspective. The Magellanic Clouds, two satellite galaxies of the Milky Way, are visible from there. The Large Magellanic Cloud, about 15,000 light-years in diameter, is 170,000 light-years from Earth; the Small Magellanic Cloud, about 10,000 light-years in diameter, is 200,000 light-years away. Andromeda, by comparison, is 2,500,000 light-years from us.

//

FALLACY: All comets come from the Oort cloud.
FACT: In 1950, Jan Oort proposed that comets come from a

spherical cloud of comets orbiting near the edge of the Solar System. The Oort cloud is still the most famous cometary source and is responsible for long-period comets, but the Kuiper comet belt, much closer to Neptune's orbit, is the source of many short-period (two hundred years or less) comets. The most famous of all comets, Halley's, is a short-period comet; the first recorded sighting was by Chinese observers in 240 B.C., and it has returned every seventy-six years since. Although NASA didn't have the money, the European Space Agency, Japan, and the Soviet Union sent a total of five probes out to study Halley during its 1986 visit.

//

FALLACY: Moons have to be close to their planets, or they'd fly away.
FACT: Depends on both the moon and the planet. Mars's inner moon, Phobos, for example, is only 5,827 miles from the center of its planet. At the other extreme, Jupiter's outermost moon, Sinope, is 14,700,000 miles from the center of its planet. First you decide how closely you want to be mooned, then you pick your planet.

//

FALLACY: Alpha Centauri is the star closest to Earth.
FACT: The star closest to Earth is the Sun, at about 93 million miles, or 8.32 light-minutes. Next nearest is the three-star group Alpha Centauri. Alpha Centauri A and B are a binary system 4.35 light-years from us. Alpha Centauri C is also known as Proxima Centauri, because it is currently the nearest to us of the three, at 4.22 light-years, or 25 trillion miles. Moving on from the Alpha Centauri group, Barnard's star is the next nearest to us, at 6 light-years. Those are the *closest* stars.

//

FALLACY: Saturn and Jupiter are the only planets that have rings.
FACT: None of the inner planets (Mercury, Venus, Earth, Mars) has a ring. Until 1977, Saturn was the only one of the outer planets (Jupiter, Saturn, Uranus, Neptune, Pluto) known to have rings. Since then, rings have been discovered around Jupiter, Uranus, and Neptune. Neptune, for example, has at least four rings in addition to its eight known satellites. Only Pluto, of the five outer planets, has no ring; an organization has been formed to buy it one.

FALLACY: When Neil Armstrong stepped onto the Moon, he said: "That's one small step for a man, one giant leap for mankind."

FACT: That's how the script read, but what he actually said was: "That's one small step for man, one giant leap for mankind." The poor guy was bound to get into grammatical, logical, or sexual trouble no matter how he worded that.

/ /

FALLACY: Hundreds of asteroids orbit Earth.

FACT: Asteroids, like planets, orbit the Sun. No asteroids orbit Earth. Most of them are in the asteroid belt, between Mars and Jupiter. Ceres was the first discovered, in 1801; not by coincidence it is also the largest, with a diameter of 470 miles. The Apollo asteroids have very elliptical orbits, and come close to Earth. There are also two groups of Trojan asteroids in Jupiter's orbit, one 60° ahead of the gas giant and the other 60° behind.

/ /

FALLACY: The Sun, being a ball of gas, is the same color from surface to center.

FACT: The Sun is a ball of gas about 865,000 miles in diameter. It produces light in its photosphere, a gaseous layer which is the visible surface seen from Earth. The photosphere separates the Sun's opaque interior from its transparent exterior. There is no light, and therefore no color, at the center of the Sun.

/ /

FALLACY: On a moonless night in the desert you can see all the stars.

FACT: On a moonless night in the desert you can see a few thousand stars. In our Milky Way galaxy alone, there are more than 100 billion stars. There are probably as many galaxies in the universe as there are stars in ours.

FALLACY: Every fourth year is a leap year.

FACT: Every fourth year that can be divided by four is a leap year—except years ending in 00 that cannot be divided by four hundred. The years 1800 and 1900 can be divided by four, but end in 00 and cannot be divided by 400, so they were not leap years. The year 2000 will be a leap year. The rate of Earth's rotation occasionally increases or decreases, with the overall trend being toward a slower speed and a longer day. Adding leap-year days doesn't bring our calendar into exact synchronization with atomic clocks, so leap seconds are added to some years. At midnight on 30 June 1992, the International Earth Rotation Service added a leap second. Because 1992 was also a leap year, it was the longest year since leap seconds were first added in 1972. The record is still held by 1972, though, because not only was that a leap year, but *two* leap seconds were added to it. Bisextile, by the way, is not a term from the Sexual Revolution; it means ''of or pertaining to leap year or leap-year day.''

//

FALLACY: Jupiter is the largest and densest planet.

FACT: Jupiter is definitely the largest planet, but size and density are not necessarily related. Depends on what the planet is made of. Jupiter is a gas planet, and has a density of only 1.267 (the density of water is 1.000). The Solar System Density Record is 5.515, held by a rocky planet with an iron core: Earth.

//

FALLACY: The Sun rises in the morning.

FACT: We still say that, and teach our children that, but we know it's not true. When Earth turns on its axis to bring our part of the planet around to where we first see the Sun in the morning, we say that the Sun is ''rising''—even though we're the ones who are moving. The Sun doesn't mind.

//

FALLACY: The sky is blue.

FACT: Beyond our atmosphere, the sky is black. And no, the atmosphere itself isn't blue, either; it's colorless. Because we evolved on this planet, it's no coincidence that our Sun emits the full range of frequencies (colors) that we call the "visible" spectrum. The blue end of the visible spectrum is the short-wavelength end. Light arriving from our local star is scattered by particles in the atmosphere. Because of the composition of our atmosphere, short-wavelength light scatters more than any other, so our sky looks blue. Several other planets, including Mars, Neptune, and Uranus, have an atmosphere, but the color depends on the composition.

//

FALLACY: The planets have always been known because they're visible in the night sky.
FACT: Until late in the eighteenth century, humans knew of only six planets. The outer three planets known today are so far away that they're not visible to the naked eye. The three most recently discovered were Uranus in 1781, Neptune in 1846, and Pluto in 1930. Astrologers had a lot of explaining to do.

//

FALLACY: Earth is near the center of the Milky Way galaxy.
FACT: Our spiral Milky Way galaxy is about 100,000 light-years across. A light-year is roughly 6 trillion miles. From Earth, the center of the Galaxy is in the direction of the constellation Sagittarius. It's a long walk, though, because Earth is about 25,000 light-years from the center. While Earth is orbiting around the Sun, the Sun is orbiting around the center of the Milky Way. Takes it about 200 million Earth years to complete one of its years (one orbit). That's a *long* time between birthdays.

//

FALLACY: Galileo invented the telescope.
FACT: Galileo Galilei is justly honored for many scientific feats, but inventing the telescope is not one of them. Johann Lippershey of the Netherlands invented the telescope. After learning of Lippershey's invention, Galileo constructed the first *astronomical* telescope. He used it to make many significant discoveries, including the four largest satellites of Jupiter and the fact that the Milky Way is composed of stars.

//

FALLACY: Earth is closest to the Sun in the summer.
FACT: Earth is closest to the Sun during the Northern Hemis-

phere's winter, in January, and farthest from it in July. It isn't our distance from the Sun that causes the temperature difference between summer and winter—one and a half million miles either way counts little when the average distance is ninety-three million miles. At the time of summer solstice the Northern Hemisphere is tilted 23.5° toward the Sun, giving us our longest day and shortest night. It is because of the more direct rays of the Sun and the extra hours of sunlight that summer is hotter than winter. The theory that winter days are shorter and summer days are longer because things shrink when they're cold and expand when they're hot has not been proven.

//

FALLACY: The difference between planets and moons is that planets are bigger.
FACT: There are moons in our solar system larger than planets. Jupiter's moon Ganymede is larger than the planet Mercury, for example, and Earth's Moon is larger than the planet Pluto. The difference between planets and moons is that planets orbit the Sun, and moons orbit planets. Of the nine known planets, all but Mercury and Venus have at least one moon; Jupiter has at least seventeen. There's going to be some wild writing when poets get to Jupiter.

//

FALLACY: Because the universe is expanding, all the galaxies are moving away from each other.
FACT: Although most galaxies are moving away from each other due to the universe's expansion, the Andromeda galaxy and the Milky Way are moving closer to each other at 120 kilometers per second because of gravitational attraction: 10 million kilometers closer every day. As a romantic would put it, the Andromeda galaxy and the Milky Way are falling into each other's spiral arms.

//

FALLACY: A moon has to orbit its planet in the same direction that the planet rotates.
FACT: Earth's Moon orbits in the same direction that Earth rotates: west to east. Almost all other moons also orbit their planets in the

same direction the planets rotate, but that's merely a fact, not a necessity. Neptune's moon Triton, for example, orbits in the opposite direction from which Neptune rotates. Earth's Moon is spiraling outward from Earth; Triton is spiraling inward toward Neptune.

/ /

FALLACY: Earth orbits the Sun at about 1,000 miles per hour.
FACT: Earth rotates on its own axis at about 1,000 miles per hour. In its orbit around the Sun, Earth zips along at about 67,000 miles per hour. The Moon's orbital velocity around Earth, by the way, is about 2,300 miles per hour.

/ /

FALLACY: When we look at the night sky, we see the stars as they are.
FACT: The night sky is like a time machine. We see the stars as they were when the light left them. Since no two stars are exactly the same distance from Earth, we see each star as it was at a different time in the past. Alpha Centauri is the nearest star system to the Sun. It's approximately four and a quarter light-years from Earth, so we see Alpha Centauri as it was four and a quarter years ago. Light from a supernova in Galaxy M-99 first reached us in 1986. M-99 is seventy million light-years away, so we were watching an explosion that happened seventy million years ago. When that star exploded into a supernova, dinosaurs were still the dominant form of life on Earth. We do not even see our Sun, the star nearest to us, as it is because the Sun is more than eight light-minutes from Earth. If every star in the universe went out right now, we wouldn't know anything about it. More than eight minutes from now both sides of Earth would have a permanent night sky. Four and a quarter years from now, Alpha Centauri would disappear. A decade from now, only eleven stars would be missing from our sky. We would still see light from all the others, even though there were no stars burning anywhere in the universe.

4

Earth

FALLACY: There's a difference of several hundred miles between the lowest point on Earth and the highest.

FACT: The lowest point on Earth is the bottom of the Mariana Trench southwest of Guam, at 35,810 feet below sea level. The highest point on Earth is the top of Mount Everest, at 29,022 feet (and 3.9 inches) above sea level. The difference is only 12.28 miles. With an equatorial diameter of 7,926.38 miles, Earth is smoother than a baby's bottom.

//

FALLACY: Air is mostly oxygen.

FACT: Air is mostly nitrogen: 78 percent nitrogen and only 21 percent oxygen. The remaining 1 percent is mainly argon, with trace amounts of carbon dioxide, helium, hydrogen, krypton, neon, xenon, and other gases. This is true of clean air. Polluted air can contain anything, and often does.

//

FALLACY: Canada used to be the second largest country in the world; now that the Soviet Union has disbanded, Canada is the largest.

FACT: Now that the Soviet Union has disbanded, Canada is still the second largest country in the world, with an area of 3,849,000 square miles. The United States is the fifth largest, after China and Brazil. The world's largest country now, with an area of 6,592,800 square miles, or 11.5 percent of Earth's land surface, is Russia.

FALLACY: South America is due south of the United States.
FACT: Disregarding everything in between, if the United States moved directly south only a small part of it would bump into South America. A line due south from Pittsburgh would run offshore from Florida's easternmost point, and would be roughly 80° longitude. With the exception of a tiny coastal sliver, all of South America is east of 80° longitude. South America's easternmost point is much closer to Africa than it is to the United States.

// //

FALLACY: Like the ocean, Great Salt Lake in Utah is teeming with fish and other saltwater life.
FACT: Great Salt Lake is hotter and saltier than the ocean; much too hot and salty for most forms of life. There are no fish in the lake. Brine shrimp live in its waters, and algae, but that's about all. The opposite of a fish out of water, Great Salt Lake is a water out of fish.

// //

FALLACY: The magnetic South Pole is on the continent of Antarctica.
FACT: The magnetic South Pole is not on the continent of Antarctica; it is not even geographically south of the Antarctic Circle. The magnetic South Pole is in the ocean, offshore from Antarctica, at about latitude 66° South and longitude 139° East.

// //

FALLACY: Nevada City is in Nevada.
FACT: Nevada City is in California, near Grass Valley and Auburn. To keep things fair, though, the Virginia City made famous by TV's *Bonanza* isn't in Virginia. It's in Nevada.

// //

FALLACY: Grand Canyon is the deepest gorge in North America.
FACT: Grand Canyon is not only the largest gorge in North America, but the largest land gorge on Earth. It is 277 miles in length,

from Marble Gorge to Grand Wash Cliffs, and varies from 4 to 13 miles in width—but is only about 1 mile deep. Great Gorge, below Mount Dickey on the flank of Alaska's Mount McKinley, is the deepest gorge in North America. Total distance from the top of Mount Dickey's peak to the bottom of Great Gorge's glacier is 9,000 feet. The deepest land gorge on Earth is El Cañon de Colca in Peru, at 10,574 feet.

//

FALLACY: Counties are larger than cities.
FACT: A county usually contains several cities. In the case of New York City, however, the opposite is true. Each of New York City's five boroughs is a county unto itself: New York County (Manhattan), Bronx County, Queens County, King's County (Brooklyn), and Richmond County (Staten Island).

//

FALLACY: Lake Victoria, one of the main sources of the Nile River, is the highest major lake on Earth.
FACT: Lake Victoria is the largest freshwater lake in Africa. At 3,720 feet it is one of the highest, but is surpassed by 4,180-foot Lake Urmia and 5,279-foot Lake Issyk Kul, both in Asia, and by the world's highest, 12,506-foot Lake Titicaca on the border between Bolivia and Peru.

//

FALLACY: There is no such place as 0° latitude and 0° longitude.
FACT: There's no land there, but there is such a place. That's where the prime meridian crosses the equator. It's in the Gulf of Guinea off Africa's west coast, south of Accra, Ghana, and west of Libreville, Gabon.

//

FALLACY: At noon on summer solstice, the Sun is directly overhead.
FACT: Not on most of the planet, and not exactly at noon even if you leave out Daylight Saving Time. At noon on a summer solstice,

the Sun is, however, as close to overhead as it's ever going to get. In the Northern Hemisphere, that solstice occurs about June 21st; in the Southern Hemisphere, it occurs about December 22nd. The Tropic of Cancer, 23° 27' north of the equator, is the farthest north where the Sun can be directly overhead on one of the solstices. The Tropic of Capricorn, 23° 27' south of the equator, is the farthest south where the Sun can be directly overhead on the other solstice. At the equator, the Sun is directly overhead on both equinoxes; standing up, you wouldn't get much of a tan.

//

FALLACY: Old Faithful erupts faithfully every sixty minutes.
FACT: Old Faithful Geyser in Yellowstone National Park in northwestern Wyoming isn't quite that faithful. It erupts on average every sixty-five minutes, but the eruptions can be as close together as thirty-three minutes or as far apart as an hour and a half. Each eruption lasts about four minutes, shooting steam and water from 115 to 175 feet into the air.

//

FALLACY: Sometimes it's too cold to snow.
FACT: What leads to the belief that it sometimes gets too cold to snow is that the lower the temperature, the less moisture there is in the air. The less moisture there is, the less snow will fall, and the smaller the flakes will be, but it's never too cold to snow. Those polar ice caps were built up from snow.

//

FALLACY: Mt. Everest is the world's tallest mountain.
FACT: Actually, there are three ''world's tallest'' mountains. According to October 1987 satellite measurements, Mount Everest (Qomolangma) rises 29,022 feet and 3.9 inches above sea level, making it the world's tallest from sea level to its peak. Because the Earth bulges slightly at the equator, however, the peak of 20,561-foot Mount Chimborazo in Ecuador is more than 7,000 feet farther from the center of Earth than the peak of Mount Everest. That makes Mount Chimborazo the world's tallest

from the center of Earth to its peak. Mauna Kea in Hawaii rises only 13,796 feet above sea level—but its base is on the ocean floor 19,680 feet *below* sea level, so the total height of Mauna Kea is 33,476 feet. That makes Mauna Kea the world's tallest mountain from its base to its peak.

//

FALLACY: The Suez Canal is the longest canal in the world.
FACT: The Panama Canal is about 50 miles long. The Suez Canal is about 100 miles long. Started in the sixth century B.C. and extended several times, the Grand Canal in China is about 1,000 miles long, making it the world's longest canal. It runs from Beijing's port city of Tientsin (Tianjin) in the north to the Yangtze River in the south.

//

FALLACY: Earth has only one North Pole.
FACT: Earth has two North Poles. The one most commonly thought of is the geographic North Pole, at 90° North latitude, where all the lines of longitude meet. The other is the magnetic North Pole, the northern end of Earth's magnetic-field lines, which attract compass needles. A line through the geographic North and South Poles is the axis around which Earth rotates once a day. The geographic North Pole does not coincide with the magnetic North Pole, which is near latitude 76° North, longitude 101° West. Quite a distance apart, but if you're determined to travel "from Pole to Pole" you'll save a lot of time by making them both North Poles.

//

FALLACY: Lake Superior is the world's largest lake.
FACT: Lake Superior, in Michigan, Minnesota, Ontario, and Wisconsin, has a surface area of 31,700 square miles, a depth of 1,330 feet, and a volume of 2,900 cubic miles. Although Lake Superior has the largest surface area of any freshwater lake, it is not the world's largest lake. At 143,244 square miles, the lake with the largest surface area is the Caspian Sea. Lake Baikal, at 5,315 feet, is the world's deepest lake. The Caspian Sea, in Azerbaijan, Iran, Kazakhstan, Russia, and Turkmenistan, has a volume of 21,500 cubic miles, and is the world's largest lake.

FALLACY: Antarctica is the only continent with no volcanoes.
FACT: Antarctica does have volcanoes. Big Ben erupted in 1960.
Deception Island Volcano erupted in 1970. Antarctica's largest volcano,
12,450-foot Mount Erebus on Ross Island, erupted in 1991. Mount Erebus
is one of the few volcanoes on Earth to have a lava lake in its crater. The
only continent with no volcanoes is Australia.

//

FALLACY: The Grand Canyon of the Colorado is in Colorado.
FACT: The Grand Canyon of the Colorado, usually shortened to
just the Grand Canyon, is in northwestern Arizona. It gets its name from
the river that carved it, not from the state it's in.

//

FALLACY: Tidal waves are caused by the pull of the Moon.
FACT: Not only does the Moon have nothing to do with tidal
waves, there is no such thing as a "tidal" wave. What used to be called
tidal waves, and are now called tsunamis, are caused by earthquakes, land-
slides, and eruptions beneath the ocean or along its edge. Don't even
consider it: not even in Florida can you get away with saying "Tsunami
Vice."

//

FALLACY: Earth's core is so hot that the rock there is molten.
FACT: Earth's core is definitely hot, with temperatures as high as
6,130°C, or 11,060°F. It doesn't consist of rock, however, in whatever
form. The inner core is made of iron. Although temperatures are well
above the melting point of iron, pressures are so great that the inner core
remains solid. Around the solid inner core is the outer core, and this is
where you first find molten matter—liquid iron mixed with other elements.
Above the inner core is the mantle, and above the mantle is Earth's crust.
It's that extremely thin crust that we call "solid earth."

//

FALLACY: If it's raining, the humidity is 100 percent.
FACT: Not necessarily. Humidity is measured at ground level;

rain falls from clouds. When it rains in the desert, for example, the humidity at ground level is usually well below 100 percent. Conversely, when there's fog at ground level the humidity is 100 percent, even though there's not a raincloud in sight.

//

FALLACY: More snow falls at the South Pole in Antarctica than any where else in the world.

FACT: The world record for amount of snow in a single year is held by Paradise, on Mount Rainier, in Washington state: 1,224.5 inches. The world record for amount of snow from a single storm is held by Ski Bowl, on Mount Shasta, in (believe it or not) California: 189 inches. Actually, very little snow falls at the South Pole, or anywhere else in Antarctica. The snow that does fall, however, stays; it's too cold for it to melt. The ice sheet that covers much of the continent has been collecting for a long, long time. There's a sign down there that reads:

> GEOGRAPHIC
> SOUTH POLE
> 9,301' ELEVATION AVE. TEMP. −56°F
> ICE THICKNESS IN EXCESS OF 9000'

//

FALLACY: Pittsburg is in Pennsylvania.

FACT: There's a town named Pittsburg in California. There are also towns named Pittsburg in Kansas, Kentucky, New Hampshire, Oklahoma, and Texas. The one in Pennsylvania is Pittsburgh—with an *h*.

//

FALLACY: The farther west you go, the earlier it gets.

FACT: It comes as a surprise to many that by taking a single step westward, you can make the opposite happen—it gets an entire day later. A Monday sunrise on the east side of the International Date Line is a Tuesday sunrise on the west side. If the International Date Line ran through the United States, there would be a mass migration from west to east on Tax Day.

FALLACY: Utah's Great Salt Lake is the saltiest lake in the world.

FACT: Although saltier than the ocean, Great Salt Lake is not as salty as the Dead Sea, which is the saltiest lake in the world. The Dead Sea is also the lowest nonoceanic point on Earth, its surface being about 1,300 feet below sea level.

/ /

FALLACY: The only place on Earth where the Midnight Sun can be seen is at the North Pole.

FACT: Although the Midnight Sun (meaning the Sun is visible twenty-four hours a day) can be seen at the North Pole for approximately six months between the vernal and autumnal equinoxes, it can also be seen for an increasingly shorter number of days as far south as the Arctic Circle. The same is true for the area between the South Pole and the Antarctic Circle, during the other half of the year. When the Sun finally sets at the North Pole, it doesn't rise again for 176 days. When it sets at the South Pole, it doesn't rise again for 182 days. This gives a whole new meaning to the phrase "Movies till Dawn."

/ /

FALLACY: Grand Teton National Park does not mean Big Breast National Park.

FACT: That, or a shorter colloquial word, is exactly what it means. At 13,766 feet, Grand Teton is the highest mountain of the Teton Range in northwestern Wyoming. The name was bestowed by lonely and imaginative French explorers.

/ /

FALLACY: Mount McKinley was discovered by President William McKinley.

FACT: That mountain, the tallest in North America, was discovered by Native Americans thousands of years before McKinley was born. In the Athabascan language they called it, and still call it, *Denali* (High One or Great One). The name was changed to Mount McKinley in 1896 to boost the presidential candidacy of William McKinley. He won.

FALLACY: The Amazon is the world's longest river.

FACT: The Amazon begins in Laguna McIntyre, high in the Peruvian Andes near the Pacific Ocean, and flows across the continent to empty into the Atlantic Ocean from northern Brazil. Ships entering from the Atlantic can travel 2,300 miles upriver, completely across Brazil, to Iquitos, Peru. At 3,900 miles, the Amazon is the world's second longest river—about 250 miles shorter than the Nile. It carries more water than the Nile, though, draining 40 percent of the entire continent of South America.

//

FALLACY: Hawaii is the state farthest west, Alaska farthest north, Florida farthest south, and Maine farthest east.

FACT: Hawaii is the state farthest *south*; Alaska holds all the other records. It is farthest north; farthest west because the Aleutian Islands extend all the way to the 180th meridian, which divides west from east; and farthest east because the Aleutians cross the 180th meridian.

//

FALLACY: "Cyclone" and "tornado" are regional names for the same thing.

FACT: Only in *The Wizard of Oz*. A cyclone is a huge atmospheric disturbance, as large as a thousand miles in diameter, with winds rotating around a low-pressure center; counterclockwise in the Northern Hemisphere and clockwise in the Southern Hemisphere. A cyclonic weather pattern usually brings with it storms and rain. A tornado is a column of air up to several hundred yards in diameter, with a downward-reaching funnel, rotating as fast as three hundred miles per hour.

//

FALLACY: Water falls down waterfalls, never up.

FACT: The Bay of Fundy, between New Brunswick and Nova Scotia, is 170 miles long and up to 50 miles wide. It is most famous for its tidal bore, which is caused by forty- to fifty-foot tides. Its other main claim to fame is the "reversing waterfall" of the Saint John River, which occurs when those huge tides raise the level of the river above the top of the waterfall.

//

FALLACY: The west side of the Mississippi River is its left bank.
FACT: Although the west side of the Mississippi River is on the left side as you look at a map, that is its right bank. The right/left distinction is made by looking downstream.

//

FALLACY: If you dug a hole in the United States deep enough, you'd come out in China.
FACT: Leaving aside the problem of Earth's molten interior and metallic core, it would depend on where you started the hole. Starting at latitude 40° North, longitude 100° West, near the middle of the conterminous United States on the Nebraska-Kansas border, you'd come out in the Indian Ocean about even with the southern tip of the Australian mainland. Nearest land would be Saint Paul and Amsterdam islands, more than 1,500 miles from the nearest point in China. To come out in central China, you'd have to start digging at about 35°S 100°W—in the eastern South Pacific Ocean, about 2,000 miles from Santiago, Chile. Would be a bit damp.

//

FALLACY: Wisconsin calls itself "The Land of Ten Thousand Lakes," but it doesn't have anywhere near that number.
FACT: Wisconsin is being modest. Although some of them are small, Wisconsin actually has closer to fifteen thousand lakes. They were going-away presents from a glacier that used to live there.

//

FALLACY: Gravity decreases as you go up from Earth's surface and increases as you go down from Earth's surface.
FACT: Gravity definitely decreases as you go up from Earth's surface. If you go up high enough, it decreases to the point that you can stay in orbit; if you go even higher, you can escape Earth's gravity com-

pletely. Going down from Earth's surface doesn't work the other way, though. Gravity is related to mass. The more mass, and the closer you are to it, the greater the force of gravity. When you go up from Earth you're increasing your distance from it, thereby decreasing the gravity. When you're standing on the surface the entire mass of the planet is beneath you, and you're as close to it as you can get. That's when the force of gravity is strongest. If you go below the surface, you're below some of the mass. Not only is there less mass beneath you pulling in that direction, but there's some mass above you pulling in the opposite direction. If you went all the way to the gravitational center of Earth you'd have equal amounts of mass pulling in all directions, and the gravitational forces would cancel each other out. Other forces, including pressure, would cancel you out.

//

FALLACY: About 60 percent of Earth is covered by the oceans.
FACT: About 139,500,000 square miles, or 71 percent of Earth's surface, is covered by the ocean. Although there is only one ocean on Earth, for convenience it is often divided into four areas: Arctic, Atlantic, Indian, and Pacific. When we think of Earth's surface we think of land, but Earth is actually a water-covered planet, with land rising above the ocean's surface only here and there.

//

FALLACY: A compass in the Northern Hemisphere points to the north pole, and a compass in the Southern Hemisphere points to the south pole.
FACT: A compass points north in either hemisphere—but not directly toward the magnetic North Pole. Except for a few anomalies, the magnetic field at Earth's surface is made up of lines that start at the magnetic South Pole and end up at the magnetic North Pole. These are not straight lines, however. They wander widely along the way. A compass needle is not attracted by the magnetic North Pole, but aligns itself with these magnetic lines. Since the lines do not point directly toward the magnetic North Pole, neither does the compass. You have to get up pretty early in the morning to fool a compass.

//

FALLACY: Boulder Dam is near Boulder, Colorado.
FACT: Started in 1931, Boulder Dam existed from 1933 to 1947

on the Colorado River between Arizona and Nevada, nowhere near Boulder, Colorado. The lake it formed in Nevada is still called Lake Mead, but in 1947 the name of the dam was changed to Hoover. To build the dam, concrete had to be poured continuously—*for two years*. It is 45 feet thick and 1,244 feet long at the top, 600 feet thick at the base, and 726 feet high. Lake Mead is still the largest manmade reservoir in the United States, but Boulder Dam is no more.

/ /

FALLACY: Because Ecuador's capital is near the equator, it is always hot.
FACT: Quito, the oldest capital in South America, is just south of the equator at the foot of Pichincha volcano in the Andes. Even though it's so near the equator and at the bottom of the volcano, it sits at an altitude of 9,350 feet. Because it's near the equator its climate is much the same year-round; because of its altitude that climate is temperate, not tropical.

/ /

FALLACY: The Great Lakes are the source of the Mississippi River.
FACT: The source of the Mississippi River is Lake Itaska in northwestern Minnesota, well north of all the Great Lakes except Superior, and north of much of that. From Lake Itaska the Mississippi flows about 2,350 miles to the Gulf of Mexico. Including its major tributary, the Missouri River, it is the third largest river system in the world after the Nile and the Amazon. In an average year the Mississippi empties 1.64 million cubic feet of water per second into the Gulf. To put that in perspective, 1.64 million cubic feet of water is 12,268,052 gallons. Per second.

/ /

FALLACY: Brooklyn was created as one of the five boroughs of New York City.
FACT: Brooklyn was created as the town of Brooklyn Ferry in 1816. In 1834 it became just plain Brooklyn. Absorbing neighboring areas such as Flatbush and Gravesend, by 1855 it had become the third largest city in the United States. It wasn't until 1898 that Brooklyn became part of New York City; Brooklyn still claims that it's the other way around.

At the southwestern end of Long Island, seventy-one-square-mile Brooklyn is all of Kings County.

///

FALLACY: Heat lightning is caused by hot weather.
FACT: Heat lightning has nothing to do with temperature. It's merely regular lightning so far away that you don't see the stroke itself, but only a reflection of it in the atmosphere. Because of the great distance, you don't hear thunder, either. Despite the similarity, heat lightning is not the same thing as a hot flash.

///

FALLACY: Because of earthquake danger, tall buildings are forbidden in both San Francisco and Los Angeles.
FACT: San Francisco's Transamerica Pyramid is 853 feet tall, and First Interstate World Center in Los Angeles is 1,017 feet—taller than any building in Boston, Cleveland, Dallas, Detroit, Houston, New Orleans, Philadelphia, or Pittsburgh. The 1,454-foot Sears Tower in Chicago, which is only 437 feet taller than Los Angeles's First Interstate World Center, is the tallest building in the United States.

///

FALLACY: Of all the major canals in the world, the Panama Canal is best known in this country only because it's the closest.
FACT: There's also the fact that the United States completed it (France started it in 1881) on 15 August 1914, and controls it until 31 December 1999.

///

FALLACY: One number up on the Richter scale means the earthquake releases ten times as much energy.
FACT: Although there's often confusion about it, the Richter (M_L) scale is easy to understand. One whole number up means that the earthquake causes ten times as much ground motion, and releases thirty-two times as much energy. A Richter 6 earthquake, for example, causes ten

times as much ground motion as a Richter 5, and releases thirty-two times as much built-up strain. The Richter scale was originally developed by Charles Richter to measure the magnitude of local earthquakes in southern California, hence the designation M_L (Magnitude, Local).

/ /

FALLACY: The Himalayas are the world's largest mountain system.
FACT: The Himalaya Mountains, still being pushed up as India crashes into Asia, comprise the world's highest mountain system, but not the largest. By far the largest is the Mid-Ocean Ridge. It runs down the Atlantic Ocean from the Arctic, south of Africa and Australia, and back up the Pacific Ocean toward North America. The Himalaya Mountains extend for about 1,500 miles; the Mid-Ocean Ridge is more than 40,000 miles long.

/ /

FALLACY: Reno, Nevada, is east of Los Angeles.
FACT: You can safely bet your ass or mule against that one. Below a line drawn from Cape Mendocino to Lake Tahoe, the California borders run northwest-southeast, not north-south. Almost all of Nevada is west of California's easternmost point. Reno is about a hundred miles west of Los Angeles.

/ /

FALLACY: The East Indies are just east of the West Indies.
FACT: "East Indies" was a name for parts of southeast Asia, including India, Indonesia, and Malaya. "West Indies" comes from the same mistake that caused Native Americans to be called Indians: Columbus didn't know where he was. The West Indies are an archipelago stretching from Florida to Venezuela, setting the boundary between the Atlantic Ocean to the east, and the Caribbean Sea and the Gulf of Mexico to the west. Among the better-known islands, from north to south, are the Bahamas, Cuba, Jamaica, Hispaniola, Puerto Rico, Barbados, Trinidad, and Aruba.

/ /

FALLACY: Canada's Northwest Territories are the northwestern part of Canada.

FACT: The northwestern part of Canada is the province of Yukon. Canada's Northwest Territories are above the tier of provinces that border the United States. They span the width of Canada from the eastern border of Yukon to the eastern edge of Ellesmere Island, which is further east than parts of Greenland. The only part of upper Canada that is *not* part of the Northwest Territories is the northwestern part.

/ /

FALLACY: The largest earthquake in the United States was the 1906 Great Earthquake, which destroyed San Francisco.

FACT: Although the 8 April 1906 quake on the San Andreas Fault led to widespread destruction in San Francisco, most of the damage was caused by fire. And San Francisco wasn't destroyed. Rebuilding began almost immediately, and in 1915 San Francisco hosted the Panama-Pacific International Exhibition. The 1906 quake, estimated at 8.3 on the Richter (M_L) scale, was smaller than the 8.4 M_L quake which struck Prince William Sound, Alaska, on 27 March 1964. Even that, however, was dwarfed by the largest known earthquakes in the United States so far: a series in 1811–1812 on the New Madrid Fault in Missouri, estimated at up to Richter 8.7. Changes caused by the New Madrid Fault are visible on the surface; if you're interested, go look—Missouri loves company.

/ /

FALLACY: Carbon dioxide hasn't increased in Earth's atmosphere nearly as much as we thought it had.

FACT: The increase in carbon dioxide in Earth's atmosphere is much greater than we believed only a short while ago. There was an increase of roughly 20 percent just between 1957 and 1992. Since the beginning of the Industrial Revolution, the concentration has increased from 280 parts per million to 350 parts. That is the highest carbon dioxide level found in ice-core samples stretching back 160,000 years.

/ /

FALLACY: There may not be any land exactly at the geographic North Pole, but there's land nearby.

FACT: There's no land within a hundred miles of the geographic North Pole. Or within two-hundred miles, or three-hundred miles, or four-hundred miles. The nearest land is Oodaq Ø, which is only one hundred feet across. It's located at 83°40'32.5"N, 30°40'10.1"W, 439 miles south of the geographic North Pole. Santa's house is not well grounded.

//

FALLACY: Full-moon nights are no noisier than any other night.
FACT: Except in brightly lighted cities, full-moon nights are much noisier than darker nights. There's nothing strange or supernatural about it, though. Most diurnal creatures react to light. Full-moon nights are bright, and more creatures, including humans, are more active on bright nights than on dark ones. This is especially true in the countryside, where there's a noticeable difference between the quiet of a dark night and the scurry and scuttle of a full-moon night. None of this applies to Roseanne's Full Moon, which is definitely something else.

//

FALLACY: Deserts are hot, sandy, and dry.
FACT: There is a sandless desert in Antarctica where temperatures at the height of summer rarely go above 0° Fahrenheit. What makes an area a desert is dryness, to the degree that it can support little or no vegetation. Although 95 percent of Antarctica is under an icecap, there is no liquid water. The world's largest traditional desert, the 3,500,000-square-mile Sahara in northern Africa, has sand and is definitely hot, but the only thing that makes it a desert is that it is dry.

//

FALLACY: Earth's crust, taken as a whole, is a fairly even mix of all the chemical elements.
FACT: First problem with that is that the vast majority of Earth's iron is in its core, a long way down from the crust. The composition of Earth's crust, taken as a whole, is a very uneven mix of chemical elements: 47 percent oxygen, 28 percent silicon, 8 percent aluminum, 4.5 percent iron, 3.5 percent calcium, 2.5 percent potassium, 2.5 percent sodium, 2.2 percent magnesium, and less than 1 percent each carbon, hydrogen, phosphorus, and sulfur. Or you could call it dirt.

FALLACY: The United States is several times as large as Australia.
FACT: Without Alaska and Hawaii, the United States is 2 percent larger than Australia. Including Alaska and Hawaii, the land area of the United States is 3,618,770 square miles, only 18 percent larger than Australia's 2,966,200 square miles. One of Australia's claims to fame is that it is the only nation in the world that covers an entire continent. Perfect fit, too.

//

FALLACY: All cities use oil, gas, or coal for heat.
FACT: Iceland sits near the northern end of the Mid-Atlantic Ridge, a geologically active spreading zone. This tectonic activity provides the country with volcanoes that build new land, and with countless hot springs. Iceland's entire capital city, Reykjavik, is heated with hot water. Reykjavik, not Los Angeles, is the hot tub capital of the world.

//

FALLACY: The shortest distance between two points is a straight line.
FACT: True on a flat surface, but nowhere else. For example, the shortest distance between Washington and Tokyo, slightly south of Washington, is a "great circle" route that seems to curve far north toward the pole. Technically speaking, a straight line between Washington and Tokyo would tunnel through the planet.

//

FALLACY: Thanks to satellites, all of Earth's surface has been photographed in detail.
FACT: Satellites have photographed all of the surface that they can see. Approximately 71 percent of Earth's surface, however, is covered by its ocean, and most of the sub-sea surface is less well known than the face of the Moon.

//

FALLACY: The Pacific Ocean end of the Panama Canal is west of the Atlantic end.

FACT: The Pacific Ocean end of the Panama Canal is *east* of the Atlantic end. Panama, the lower end of a land bridge between North and South America, runs roughly east-west. The canal cuts through from northwest (Atlantic end) to southeast (Pacific end).

// /

FALLACY: The geographic center of the United States is near Kansas City.
FACT: The geographic center of the United States is west of Castle Rock, South Dakota, at 44°58'N, 103°46'W. That's because the northernmost point is Point Barrow, Alaska, at 71°23'N, 156°29'W, and the westernmost point is Pochnoi, Alaska, on Semisopochonoi Island, at 51°17'N, 172°09'E. Including only the forty-eight conterminous states, the geographic center is near Lebanon, Kansas, at 39°50'N, 98°35'W, which is close to the middle of Kansas' northern border but a very long walk from Kansas City. The geographic center of the United States would be even farther north if it weren't for the fact that the southernmost point is Ka Lae, Hawaii, at 18°55'N, 155°41'W.

// /

FALLACY: Water draining out of a sink circles one direction in the Northern Hemisphere, and the opposite direction in the Southern Hemisphere.
FACT: No matter where you are, the draining water will circle in either direction. That effect works only on large bodies of water. The North Pacific and the North Atlantic, for example, circle clockwise, while the South Pacific and the South Atlantic circle counterclockwise. People in either hemisphere, looking for a drain after drinking a lot of beer, have been known to circle in both directions.

// /

FALLACY: There are seven continents.
FACT: As a look at a world map will show, there are only six continents: Africa, Antarctica, Australia, Eurasia, North America, and South America. "Europe" is defined by political and cultural boundaries, not by the edge of a continent.

FALLACY: California is going to sink into the ocean during a great earthquake.

FACT: The San Andreas Fault, which runs on land through western California from the Gulf of California in Mexico to just north of the small coastal town of Manchester, is part of the fault zone between the Pacific Plate and the North American Plate. These two plates, huge pieces of Earth's crust, are indeed moving relative to each other—but not up and down. Things on the western side of the San Andreas Fault, such as Los Angeles, are moving northwest relative to those on the eastern side, such as San Francisco. A "great" earthquake is a Richter (M_L) 8 or above. In the great San Francisco earthquake of 1906, there was twenty-one feet of movement between the two sides of the fault at one point—but the western side moved northwest, not up or down. Millions of years from now the part of California west of the San Andreas Fault will become an island heading toward Alaska, but no matter how many great quakes there are, California is not going to sink into the ocean. Sorry, Nevada—no oceanfront property.

/ /

FALLACY: More than 10 percent of all the water on Earth is locked up in the Antarctic ice cap.

FACT: Including fresh water, salt water, ice, and water vapor in the atmosphere, 97.2 percent of all the water on Earth is in the ocean. The Antarctic ice cap contains 1.9 percent of the total. Approximately 98 percent of Antarctica is covered with about 90 percent of the world's ice, which contains 70 percent of the world's fresh water.

5

Food, Drugs, Plants

FALLACY: Black-eyed peas are peas.
FACT: Black-eyed peas, also called "cow peas" when pronounced carefully, are not peas. They are the seeds of a tropical vine called *Vigna sinensis,* related to beans. Pea vines, on the other hand, are *Pisum sativum.*

//

FALLACY: If you punch a hole in a barrel cactus, water will run out.
FACT: To get liquid from a barrel cactus (any of several members of the genera *Echinocactus* and *Ferocactus*) takes a lot more work than that. The liquid, which is cactus juice and not water, is in the cactus's pulpy interior. To get it involves cutting into the cactus and mashing the pulp. The small amount of liquid you'll get is not pleasant; it tastes as if it were made from cactus spines.

//

FALLACY: Although the media play up student parties, college students don't have time to drink a great deal of beer.
FACT: Depends on what you consider a great deal. According to figures from the U.S. Surgeon General's Office in 1992, college students polish off 64 billion cans of beer per year. Although that works out to about 174 cans per student, several students may not be drinking their share.

FALLACY: Stone fruit is decorative fruit made of ceramic.
FACT: Stone fruit is a general name for fruit that has a stone or pit. Among the stone fruits are apricots, nectarines, peaches, and plums.

//

FALLACY: After you mow a lawn, the grass blades grow new tops.
FACT: Newly planted grass blades have pointed tips. When you mow a lawn, the blades of grass do not grow pointed new tips; the tops of the blades remain cut-off flat. Grass, like hair, grows from the bottom.

//

FALLACY: The name *frankfurter* for a hot dog is derived from Frankfurt, Germany, but *weenie* is just a nonsense word.
FACT: The frankfurter, hot dog, or weenie is a long, reddish sausage made of odds and ends of beef or beef and pork, up to 30 percent fat, and additives. The name *frankfurter* does derive from Frankfurt, Germany. *Hot dog* is an American invention, probably from the sausage-shaped dachshund. *Weenie* has every bit as honorable an heritage as *frankfurter*. It's a diminutive of *wiener*, which is short for *wienerwurst*, which translates as "Vienna sausage." Although we spell the name of Austria's capital city *Vienna*, they spell it *Wien*.

//

FALLACY: Peanuts came to North America from South America.
FACT: Although they were first cultivated by the Incas of western South America, the peanut plant (*Arachis hypogaea*) came to North America from Europe. Europeans who invaded South America took peanuts back home, then spread them to both Africa and North America.

//

FALLACY: If you don't use drugs, you can't fail a drug test.
FACT: As one of many examples, professional bicycle racer Alexi Grewal was fined $500 and suspended for three months in 1992 when he failed a drug test after eating a poppy-seed muffin. The poppy seeds commonly used in baked goods are the seeds of the opium poppy, *Papaver*

somniferum, and may contain extremely small amounts of substances that can cause a positive reaction on a morphine test. Inca tea, sold in health food stores, can lead to a false positive test result for cocaine use, and cough suppressants containing dextromethorphan can result in a false positive for opiates. Over-the-counter cold remedies can cause a false positive for amphetamine use, as can diet aids that contain phenylpropanolamine. After filling up at a fast-food ptomaine parlor, there's no telling what you might test positive for.

//

FALLACY: Sugarplums are plums.
FACT: Sugarplums have been popular since Victorian times, especially during the year-end holidays, and were immortalized in "The Sugarplum Fairy" from Tchaikovsky's *Nutcracker Suite.* There's not a bit of plum in a sugarplum, though. A sugarplum is a small round piece of sugary candy.

//

FALLACY: The yams and sweet potatoes in the market are completely different vegetables.
FACT: Depends on where the market is. A yam is the starchy root of tropical vines that belong to the genus *Dioscorea,* native to Asia and commonly grown in Africa. A sweet potato is also the starchy root of a tropical vine, *Ipomoea batatas,* native to the Americas. Yams are not grown commercially in the United States. All the "yams" you see in U.S. markets are actually different varieties of sweet potato. Now that that's cleared up, consider this: a potato is a tuber, not a root. Sweet potatoes, therefore, are not potatoes.

//

FALLACY: Avocados are aphrodisiacs.
FACT: Interesting how that belief came to be. The Aztecs first named the fruit, and through a long line of linguistic legerdemain it ended up as "avocado." In the Aztec language, Nahuatl, the word was *ahuacatl,* "testicle." They named it that because of the way it looked hanging from the tree. Avocados are not aphrodisiacs. Unless, of course, you believe they are.

FALLACY: The correct name is "Welsh rarebit," not "Welsh rabbit."

FACT: The original and still correct name for this cheese-on-toast dish is Welsh rabbit. It's a humorous name, akin to calling a hot dog a tube steak. "Rarebit" is merely a corruption of "rabbit."

//

FALLACY: The older whiskey is, the better it is.

FACT: Even in the best wooden casks, this is not true of any type of whiskey past a certain point. Gin and vodka don't improve at all with age. Rum may or may not, depending on which rum drinker you talk with. Bourbon improves to its peak in about ten years. No connoisseurs are more contentious than Scotch drinkers. Although experts say that a blended Scotch reaches its maximum at twelve years, many people contend that it continues to improve with age. Among those who contend this are the people who sell scotch and charge increasingly more for it as it gets older.

//

FALLACY: Cinnamon comes from the fruit of the cinnamon plant.

FACT: Although many spices come from the fruit or the seed of a plant, cinnamon comes from a tree. And it's not from the fruit or from the seed. Cinnamon is the bark of cinnamon trees of the genus *Cinnamomum*, which are members of the laurel family.

//

FALLACY: Spanish fly is an aphrodisiac made from a Latin American fly.

FACT: Cantharides, sometimes called Spanish fly, is not an aphrodisiac. It is a toxic preparation made from crushed blister beetles, *Lytta vesicatoria* or *Cantharis vesicatoria*. This vividly green beetle is found only in central and southern Europe. Cantharides was once used as a counterirritant for skin blisters. If taken orally, it causes intense irritation of the urinary tract on the way out. For reasons known only to them, some people believed that such intense discomfort would put a person in the mood. Probably true, but more likely in the mood to murder than to mate.

FALLACY: Cuscus is a traditional pasta dish from Africa.
FACT: A cuscus is a wild marsupial of the genus *Phalanger,* found from Australia to New Guinea. It has a long, prehensile tail, and large eyes because it's nocturnal. Unlike the domesticated pasta couscous, it is not a traditional dish in Africa.

//

FALLACY: Irish moss is a moss native to Ireland.
FACT: Also called carrageen, Irish moss is not a moss. It's a seaweed high in gelatin, used as a thickener in ice cream, jelly, and cosmetics. Irish moss is found commonly in the ocean, and is harvested commercially in such widely separated places as Europe, Japan, and Massachusetts.

//

FALLACY: Supermarkets don't carry fresh sardines because they're too small to put in the display case.
FACT: Supermarkets don't carry fresh sardines because there is no such fish. "Sardine" is a generic name for more than a score of different fish, including small brisling, herring, pilchards, and sprats.

//

FALLACY: A cornflower is exactly that.
FACT: A cornflower is not the flower of a corn plant. It is an annual herb, *Centaurea cyanus,* and has large heads of blue (sometimes pink, purple, or white) flowers of its own. Cornflower's flowers are used both for medicinal purposes, and to make a dye. Regional names for the cornflower include bachelor's button, bluebonnet, bluebottle, and ragged robin.

//

FALLACY: Cocaine and cocoa, from which chocolate is made, both come from the coco tree.

FACT:　　　Cocaine comes from the leaves of the coca shrub, *Erythroxylum coca*. Cocoa comes from the seeds of the cacao tree, *Theobroma cacao*. Coconuts, by the way, come from a palm tree, *Cocos nucifera*. As for Coco, that's a river starting in northern Nicaragua and running about three hundred miles down to the Caribbean Sea.

//

FALLACY:　Vinegarroon is a condiment.
FACT:　　　There's no accounting for taste, but this is not a condiment you'd want to put on the table. A vinegarroon is a whip scorpion (*Mastigoproctus giganteus*) of northern Mexico and the southern United States. Its name comes from the fact that when you irritate it—trying to use it as a condiment, for example—it emits a strong vinegary smell.

//

FALLACY:　You have to use cold water in a coffeemaker, or it won't run its full cycle.
FACT:　　　A coffeemaker will run its full cycle no matter what temperature the water is when you put it in. All the coffeemaker cares about is getting the water to the boiling point so that steam will force the water up and out over the coffee grounds. If you start with hot water, it'll get there sooner. As any fish can tell you, though, the colder water is the more oxygen it can hold; water that has been hot for a while tends to taste "flat." That's why cold water is recommended for coffee, or for any other drink, including a glass of water.

//

FALLACY:　Banana oil comes from bananas.
FACT:　　　Makes perfect sense, but it's not true. Banana oil is a colorless liquid mixture of amyl acetate ($CH_3COOC_5H_{11}$) and nitrocellulose. It is used as a lacquer and paint solvent, and as a flavoring agent; it smells more like bananas than like anything else.

//

FALLACY:　Aspirin is the most widely used drug in the world.
FACT:　　　Also known as acetylsalicylic acid or $CH_3COOC_6H_4COOH$,

aspirin is sometimes used *after* the most widely used drug in the world. Top spot goes to $C_2 H_5 OH$, also known as ethanol, ethyl alcohol, grain alcohol, or just plain old alcohol. Not only is alcohol the most widely used drug in the world, it has been used longer than any other drug; after thousands of years of noble experiments, there's still no cure for a hangover.

//

FALLACY: More peanuts are sold in the United States than any other nut.

FACT: More almonds are sold in the United States than any other nut. Peanuts grow underground, and are legumes, not nuts. In a nutshell: nuts grow on trees.

//

FALLACY: Removing an orchid from its natural setting is called orchidectomy.

FACT: Orchidectomy has to do with an entirely different type of bulb. It comes from the Greek word *orkhis* and means the removal of one or both testicles.

//

FALLACY: The oldest living thing is a bristlecone pine tree.

FACT: That 4,900-year-old bristlecone pine, which until recently was thought to be the oldest living thing, grows at the top of the White Mountains in California. A creosote plant (*Larrea tridentata*) discovered in the desert about eighty miles northeast of Los Angeles is estimated to be 11,700 years old. That seventy-foot by twenty-five-foot plant, nicknamed "King Clone," is the oldest living thing found on Earth so far.

//

FALLACY: Head cheese is cheese.

FACT: Head cheese is a combination of chopped and boiled meat from pig heads and feet, and sometimes hearts and tongues, held together in loaf shape by gelatin. It's popular enough to be found in most delicatessens, proving again that there's no accounting for taste.

FALLACY: Except for a few with four leaves, clover has three leaves.
FACT: The scientific name for clover is *Trifolium,* which translates as "three leaves." Three-leaf clover is by far the most common, but many other leaf numbers are found regularly. Four-leaf clover can be found in almost any clover patch, and, with increasing rarity, higher numbers. The highest number of leaves authenticated so far is fourteen. "I'm looking over, a fourteen-leaf clover"?

//

FALLACY: A "yard of ale" measures one yard by one yard by one yard: one cubic yard.
FACT: Considering that people have often been known to drink a yard of ale in only a few minutes, it would be truly amazing if that term referred to a cubic yard. A yard of ale is a slender, horn-shaped glass about one yard tall. It holds 2.5 pints of ale.

//

FALLACY: Prickly pears are pears.
FACT: Picking a prickly pear without pricking your fingers is a decidedly delicate operation. A prickly pear is any of several plants of the genus *Opuntia,* or the fruit of these plants. You won't find them in an orchard, though. A prickly pear is a cactus.

//

FALLACY: Beef jerky is called that because it's made by jerking beef into thin strips.
FACT: Jerking beef does not mean pulling or tugging on it. It means cutting it into strips and drying or smoking it. In this case the noun came first. "Jerky" is derived from the Spanish *charqui* (dried meat).

//

FALLACY: White wine comes from white grapes; red wine comes from red grapes.

FACT: White wine can come from grapes of any color. Although the skin and meat of some grapes is dark colored, the liquid in almost all grapes is light. To make red wine, the red skins are fermented along with the white grape juice. A good wine is a joy when you're drinking it, but beware the wrath of grapes.

//

FALLACY: The May apple is a tree that produces apples in May.
FACT: The May apple (*Podophyllum peltatum*) of eastern North America does not produce apples, and is not a tree. It is a plant that produces yellow berries which can be used for making jelly. Another popular name for it is mandrake, although it is not related to the poisonous mandrake (*Mandragora officinarum*) of the Mediterranean and the Himalayas.

//

FALLACY: Baskin-Robbins is the hyphenated last name of the English owner of the ice-cream chain.
FACT: Baskin-Robbins came to be in 1948, when Burton Baskin and Irvine Robbins merged their Southern California ice-cream chains.

//

FALLACY: The most expensive ingredient in a bucket of buttered movie popcorn is the popcorn.
FACT: The most expensive ingredient in a bucket of buttered movie popcorn is the bucket, which costs about five times as much as the popcorn. As for the butter, there is none. It's an artificial butter substitute, which costs about half as much as the popcorn.

//

FALLACY: Wild rice is exactly that.
FACT: Wild rice is not rice, or even related to rice. Rice is *Oryza sativa;* wild rice is *Zizania aquatica*. Although some still grows wild, most of it is now farmed commercially. Irritating rice will not make it wild.

FALLACY: The Rose of Sharon is an Irish rose.
FACT: The Rose of Sharon has nothing to do with Ireland, and is not a rose. It's a shrubby Asian plant belonging to the genus *Hibiscus*.

//

FALLACY: The Volstead Act introduced Prohibition and made it illegal to buy, possess, or drink alcohol.
FACT: It was not the Volstead Act, but the Eighteenth Amendment to the Constitution, that introduced Prohibition in 1919. The Volstead Act, also 1919, was passed by Congress to enforce that amendment. The exact wording of the Eighteenth Amendment is: "After one year from the ratification of this article the manufacture, sale, or transportation of intoxicating liquors within, the importation thereof into, or the exportation thereof from the United States and all territory subject to the jurisdiction thereof for beverage purposes is hereby prohibited." The Eighteenth Amendment made it illegal to manufacture, sell, or transport alcohol, but it did not make it illegal to buy, possess, or drink it. Amazingly popular stuff, considering that it's basically yeast urine. On 16 January 1920, Colonel Daniel Porter, the revenue agent in charge of enforcing the Volstead Act, spoke these prophetic words: "There will not be any violations to speak of."

//

FALLACY: Mulligatawny stew is from Ireland.
FACT: Mulligan stew, as any Mulligan will be glad to tell you, is from Ireland; it's a hearty stew of meat and vegetables. Mulligatawny soup, from eastern India, is a meat broth highly flavored with curry. The word *mulligatawny* comes from Tamil root words meaning "pepper" and "cool water."

//

FALLACY: The U.S. government is trying to eliminate tobacco smoking.
FACT: The U.S. government is very selective about its tobacco programs. On the one hand it is spending millions on various plans to reduce tobacco smoking in this country. On the other hand, the Agriculture Department gave tobacco farmers $3.5 million in 1992 to encourage tobacco

smoking in other countries. According to the Tobacco Merchants Association of the U.S., Inc., the United States exported 188 billion cigarettes in fiscal 1992. The right hand does know what the left hand is doing, but they're obviously not connected through a brain.

/ /

FALLACY: Tapioca is made from the fruit of the tapioca tree.
FACT: There is no tapioca tree. Tapioca is made from the potatolike tuber of the cassava or manioc plant.

/ /

FALLACY: The Hershey Bar was created as a quick-energy source for U.S. troops in World War I, and was named for General Lewis Blaine Hershey.
FACT: The Hershey Bar was created in 1894, well before the First World War. It wasn't, therefore, named for General Lewis Blaine Hershey, who was born in 1893. It was created as a quick-income source for Milton S. Hershey, a Pennsylvania candy maker.

/ /

FALLACY: The saguaro cactus, with its raised arms, is often mistaken for a human in dim light because it's about the size of a human.
FACT: Would have to be a huge human. The saguaro cactus, which lives in the Sonoran Desert, is the largest cactus species. It lives for up to two hundred years, grows to a height of nearly fifty feet, and can weigh over ten tons. If one is mistaken for a human in dim light, it's probably because the lack of light confuses perspective: a distant saguaro might look like a closer human.

/ /

FALLACY: All trees have green leaves or needles because of the chlorophyll in them.
FACT: All trees do have chlorophyll in their leaves or needles; it's essential for photosynthesis. The green of chlorophyll doesn't have to be the dominant color in the leaves or needles, though; the Japanese maple,

as one example, has dark red leaves. Trees with green leaves reduce their production of chlorophyll in the autumn. As the green of chlorophyll fades, it allows the yellow of the carotenoids to show. In some trees, such as maples and oaks, anthocyanins form when sugar is trapped in the leaves by a sudden freeze. Anthocyanins give the leaves their red colors.

//

FALLACY: Corn is the tallest of all grass plants.

FACT: Outside the United States, where 90 percent of it is used as cattle feed, corn is called maize and most of it is used to feed people. Corn is a common name for it only because more than 50 percent of the world total is grown in the United States. Although corn does grow tall, it doesn't compare with the world's tallest grass: bamboo. Some species of bamboo can grow three feet in twenty-four hours, and some species grow to a height of more than 100 feet. Most lawns are rye, fescue, or bluegrass; imagine trying to keep up with mowing a bamboo lawn.

//

FALLACY: The most common violet is the African violet.

FACT: Not only is the African violet not the most common violet, it is not even a violet. Violets belong to the genus *Viola*. African violets (there are several) belong to the genus *Saintpaulia*.

//

FALLACY: The Caesar salad was named after Julius Caesar.

FACT: The Caesar salad was named *a long time* after Julius Caesar. It was created about 1950 by Caesar Gardini of Caesar's restaurant in Tijuana, Mexico. Caesar's salad contained romaine lettuce, garlic, anchovies, croutons, olive oil, coddled eggs, lemon juice, and grated cheese.

//

FALLACY: More than 25 percent of the beer sold in the United States is imported.

FACT: Using round figures, 1990 for example, the U.S. imported 9,000,000 barrels of beer. Miller produced 43,550,000 barrels that year, and Anheuser-Busch produced 86,400,000 barrels. The total domestic production was 189,896,000 barrels. "A billion bottles of beer on the wall, a billion bottles of beer . . . ''

FALLACY: A weed is any large, ugly plant that grows wild.
FACT: A weed is any plant that grows where you don't want it to. Orchids can be weeds; so can wheat, marijuana, or seaweed.

FALLACY: The pressure cooker was invented in the 1900s.
FACT: The pressure cooker, originally called the New Digester, was invented by Denis Papin in 1679. Although it worked well as a cooker, it had an unfortunate tendency to explode. It wasn't until the early 1800s that a reasonably reliable version was developed.

FALLACY: Mandarin oranges are smaller, sweeter, and more expensive than tangerines.
FACT: Mandarin oranges are the fruit of a Southeast Asian evergreen tree, *Citrus reticulata*. Tangerines are the fruit of a Southeast Asian evergreen tree, *Citrus reticulata*. It's amazing what advertising can do. Even though mandarin orange and tangerine are nothing more than different names for the same fruit, people routinely pay more for one than for the other.

FALLACY: The Irish potato was brought to the New World from Ireland.
FACT: The potato plant (*Solanum tuberosum*) started out in the New World, which was actually no newer than any other part of the world. A member of the nightshade family, it is native to the Andes Mountains area near Lake Titicaca, on the border between Bolivia and Peru. The potato, of which there are more than 10,000 varieties, was widely cultivated by the Incas in Bolivia, Peru, and Ecuador. It was from Ecuador

that Spanish invaders carried it back to their own country in the early 1500s; from Spain, potato cultivation spread throughout Europe. Europeans called two different food items a ''potato'': the white potato, and the unrelated sweet potato (*Ipomoea batatas*) of the morning glory family. The white potato became the staple food of poor people in Ireland, leading to the name ''Irish potato'' to differentiate it from the sweet potato.

/ /

FALLACY: Eating chocolate causes acne.
FACT: Repeated experiments have shown that eating chocolate has nothing to do with acne. The hormonal changes of adolescence can lead to inflammation of oil glands and hair follicles. That's acne.

/ /

FALLACY: Beer has a lot more calories than milk.
FACT: One cup (eight ounces) of regular beer has about 95 calories; one cup of whole milk has 150 calories. One cup of light beer has about 70 calories; one cup of nonfat milk has 90 calories. The main reason why there are so many more beer bellies than there are milk bellies is that very few people sit down and polish off a six-pack of milk.

/ /

FALLACY: Chow mein and chop suey came to this country from China.
FACT: Chow mein did come from China, where *ch'ao mien* (not mein) is a dish comprising diced or shredded meat, vegetables, and fried noodles. A literal translation of *ch'ao mien* is ''fried dough.'' Chop suey, as we know it, was invented in this country. It has a Chinese name only because it was concocted by a Chinese cook. He named it *shap sui,* which translates as ''miscellaneous bits.'' Many of us, let loose among the leftovers, have created unnamed masterpieces which qualify for that name.

/ /

FALLACY: Black pepper belongs to the same group as green peppers and red peppers.
FACT: Black pepper is not related to green peppers, yellow peppers,

or red peppers, which are members of the genus *Capsicum.* Black pepper is the dried, blackish fruit of a woody, climbing vine related to betel and kava, and like them is a member of the genus *Piper.* White pepper, by the way, is simply black pepper with the dark outer layer removed.

/ /

FALLACY: *The Fannie Farmer Cookbook* was not written by someone named Fannie Farmer.
FACT: The original was named *The Boston Cooking School Cook Book,* published in 1896, and was written by Fannie Merritt Farmer. The 1979 and 1989 revisions were written by Marion Cunningham. Betty Crocker, on the other hand, never did exist. She was created in 1921 by the Washburn Crosby Company, which merged with General Mills in 1928.

/ /

FALLACY: Monkey bread is bread.
FACT: Monkey bread has nothing to do with a bakery, but a lot to do with the tropical African baobab tree (*Adansonia digitata*). Monkey bread is the long, hard-shelled, gourdlike fruit which hangs from that tree.

/ /

FALLACY: Coca-Cola, concocted in the early part of this century, hit the market years before its first competitor.
FACT: Coca-Cola, Dr Pepper (no period), and Hires Root Beer were all concocted in the last century, and hit the market in the same year—1886. In 1992, Coke, Diet Coke, and Caffeine Free Diet Coke had 31.4 percent of the U.S. soft drink market; Pepsi, Diet Pepsi, and Caffeine Free Diet Pepsi had 25.7 percent; Dr Pepper had 5.9 percent; and Hires Root Beer was not among the top ten. There were no reliable statistics on the percentage of the U.S. soft drink market held by water, which is a hard drink in only limited areas.

/ /

FALLACY: Banana trees produce a new crop of fruit every year.
FACT: There is no such thing as a banana tree. Bananas grow on

large perennial plants of the Musacae family, which produce fruit only once. When the plant has borne fruit, it is cut down. Although originally a natural plant, the banana has now been so modified by cultivation that its seeds, when there are any, are sterile. New banana plants are started each growing season from pieces of the root. Slippery sidenote: botanically, the banana is not a fruit; it's a berry.

//

FALLACY: Johnny Appleseed was a character in an American folktale; there was no such real person.

FACT: Although best known for his wanderings in the Ohio Valley, Johnny Appleseed was born in Massachusetts in 1774 as John Chapman. In the 1790s he was in Indiana and western Pennsylvania, where he gave apple seeds to families migrating west. In 1801 he appeared in Ohio, and between then and the time he died in 1845, he planted apple trees in an area of more than 100,000 square miles. Not only did he exist, but it's in large part because of him that we still say, "As American as apple pie," not to mention, "How 'bout *them* apples!"

//

FALLACY: Century plants take a century to bloom.

FACT: There are several species of century plant (*Agave*), but none of them takes a century to bloom. The Mexican *Agave americana* is typical, maturing and blooming in ten to twenty years. There is a Chinese bamboo, *Phyllostachus bambusoides,* that blooms only once every 120 years. In China, records of its blooming have been kept since the year 919.

//

FALLACY: A typical serving of ice cream is a small bowl, about a cup.

FACT: Most of us serve ourselves at least that much. Before we have seconds. On ice-cream packages, though, a "serving" was long given as four ounces, half a cup. That was to cut the listed fat and calories in half. A few companies pushed this even further, listing a serving as three ounces.

//

FALLACY: Burgundy is a red wine made from Burgundy grapes.

FACT: Originally, burgundy was an unblended wine, either red or white, made from grapes grown in the Burgundy region of France. In the United States, burgundy is a red wine made from a blend of grape juices. The French call American burgundy many things, but never burgundy.

/ /

FALLACY: Evaporated milk and condensed milk are the same thing.
FACT: Evaporated milk is thickened by evaporation alone. Condensed milk is thickened partially by evaporation, and partially by adding sugar.

/ /

FALLACY: The heels of a loaf of bread are more nutritious than the slices.
FACT: The ends of a loaf of bread are different from slices in only two ways. First, they are brown and crusty. Second, they are often cut thinner than the inside slices. It's all the same dough, though, and equal amounts have equal nutritional value.

/ /

FALLACY: Dandelion is a botanical name, and has nothing to do with a lion.
FACT: The botanical name of the dandelion, a member of the thistle family, is *Taraxacum officinale*. The popular name comes from the French *dent-de-lion,* "lion's tooth."

/ /

FALLACY: All liquors are distilled from grain.
FACT: All whiskeys are distilled from grain, but not all liquors. Vodka, for example, was traditionally made from potatoes; brandy is distilled from grapes, apples, or other fruit; and rum is distilled from sugar-cane molasses. American bourbon whiskey is distilled from 51 percent corn and 49 percent rye; reverse that ratio and you get rye whiskey. Irish whiskey is made from barley, wheat, oats, and rye. Mexican tequila, on the other hand, is distilled from pulque, a beverage made from the fermented juice of maguey plants.

FALLACY: Eggs with brown shells have more nutritional value than eggs with white shells.

FACT: There is no nutritional difference between brown-shelled eggs and white-shelled eggs. Some types of chickens lay one color, some lay the other. There's even a type, popularly called an Easter Egg Chicken and officially known as an Araucana, that delivers pastel blue or green eggs. Robins, too, lay blue eggs, but it takes an awful lot to make an omelette.

//

FALLACY: Popcorn was developed by Americans.

FACT: That's not what they called themselves, but Native Americans cultivated popcorn (*Zea mays everta*) for thousands of years before Europeans arrived. To be fair, though, the Europeans brought the butter.

//

FALLACY: Mexican jumping beans jump because they're drying and contracting.

FACT: Mexican jumping beans, like all other beans, lie perfectly still unless moved. Inside a Mexican jumping bean is the larva of a bean moth. When the larva has eaten the bean into a hollow shell, it emerges as a winged moth. Spasmodic movements of the larva cause the bean to "jump."

//

FALLACY: Dry-roasted nuts have a lot less fat, sodium, and calories than regular nuts.

FACT: Regular peanuts have 14 grams of fat, 110 milligrams of sodium, and 170 calories, per ounce. Dry-roasted peanuts have 14 grams of fat, 220 milligrams of sodium, and 160 calories, per ounce. Dry-roasted unsalted peanuts have 15 grams of fat, 0 milligrams of sodium, and 170 calories. Sweetened peanuts have 8 grams of fat, 20 milligrams of sodium, and 140 calories. By comparison, regular almonds have 14 grams of fat, 170 milligrams of sodium, and 150 calories; cashews have 14 grams of fat, 140 milligrams of sodium, and 170 calories. If you really want to put on the pounds, choose macadamia nuts; they have the highest fat and calorie count per ounce: 21 grams of fat and 200 calories, with 95 percent of those calories coming from fat.

//

FALLACY: Five-Star Napoleon brandy is the highest grade.
FACT: One star is as good as twenty, because the stars have nothing to do with age, grade, quality, or anything else. Some sellers put stars on the label because some buyers believe that they mean something, but they don't. The word *Napoleon* is sometimes put on the label for the same reason, and has every bit as much meaning as the stars.

//

FALLACY: There are hundreds of different kinds of tea plant.
FACT: There is only one tea shrub, *Camellia sinensis,* of the family Theaceae. If the leaves, leaf buds, and internodes are not fermented, it is green tea; if they're lightly fermented it is oolong tea; and if fully fermented it is black tea. Leaf size determines whether the tea is congou, orange pekoe, pekoe, or souchong. Explain that the next time you order a cup of tea and you'll probably get a cup of coffee.

//

FALLACY: Spice is the major export of the Islands of Langerhans in the Indian Ocean.
FACT: The major export of the Islands of Langerhans, which are not in the Indian Ocean and are not part of the Spice Islands, is insulin. The Islands of Langerhans are masses of small cells in the interstitial tissue of the pancreas.

//

FALLACY: Supermarkets put meat and milk at the back of the store because it's cooler there, and out of direct sunlight from the front windows.
FACT: There's a definite reason why most supermarkets put meat and milk at the back of the store, but it's neither of those. The temperature

in a store is roughly the same throughout, because of heating and air conditioning. Direct sunlight would cause deterioration of almost any product, so stores keep all their wares out of it. The reason why meat and milk are at the back of the store is that they are among the most commonly bought foods. While you're walking the full length of the store, twice, you have to pass many other products. To maximize the number of products that you have to pass, the front doors rarely open onto the central aisle. So, you go down one of the other aisles to get to the meat or milk, and come back along the widest, easiest, central aisle. Sneaky, those supermarkets.

//

FALLACY: Coconut oil, palm oil, and palm kernel oil, products of Hawaiian palm trees, are all equally saturated.
FACT: Coconut oil, palm oil, and palm kernel oil all come from the oil palm tree, *Elaeis guineensis,* which is native to tropical Africa. Those three tropical oils, derived from different parts of the tree's nuts, are not all equally saturated, however. Palm oil is 51 percent saturated, palm kernel oil is 86 percent saturated, and coconut oil is 92 percent saturated.

//

FALLACY: Bells of Ireland is a plant native to Ireland.
FACT: Brian Boru never saw a Bells of Ireland. Bells of Ireland (*Moluccella laevis*), a member of the mint family, is an annual plant of western Asia.

//

FALLACY: Hershey Bars are the biggest-selling chocolate candy in the country.
FACT: Hershey Bars are one of the best-known forms of chocolate candy, but they're not the biggest sellers. And no, it's not ET's Reese's Pieces, either. Far and away the top moneymaker among chocolate candies is the mouth-melter: Mars Corporation's M&M's.

FALLACY: Popcorn is just regular corn, processed differently.

FACT: Corn is any of several varieties of *Zea mays*. Popcorn is *Zea mays everta,* a variety with a harder hull that passes heat more rapidly to the interior. When corn is heated, the moisture inside turns to steam and, in most varieties, escapes. Because of the faster heat transmission and popcorn's harder hull, the steam is trapped until it builds up sufficient pressure to cause the kernel to explode. The same process, well known by those of us who have forgotten to puncture the skin, results in pop-potato.

✓ ✓

FALLACY: Moss grows only on the north side of trees.

FACT: Moss grows anywhere there is enough moisture and not too much hot, drying sunlight. Because the Sun never gets into the northern half of the sky north of the Tropic of Cancer (23°27'N; just above Mazatlan, Mexico), the north side of trees above that latitude never get direct sunlight. In a dense forest, though, that makes no difference because all sides of a tree are shaded. The southern limit on the Sun is the Tropic of Capricorn, 23°27'S; just north of Alice Springs, Australia, so a similar folktale in the Southern Hemisphere would say that moss grows only on the south side of trees. In the United States, there is no truth to the rumor that moss grows *only* on the north side of people appointed to plush government jobs.

✓ ✓

FALLACY: Plum pudding is a pudding made with plums.

FACT: Plum pudding is a customary treat of the winter holiday season. There are many recipes, almost all including bread crumbs, raisins, and fat. Regardless of recipe, plum pudding is not a pudding; it is solid and heavy, similar in consistency to Boston Brown Bread. One of the best-selling plum puddings in North America is made in Canada. Its ingredients are, in order: Raisins, water, wheat flour, sugar, bread crumbs, corn syrup solids, beef suet, orange peel, orange marmalade, rum, brandy, skim milk powder, cottonseed oil, spices, dried whole egg, salt, and baking soda. As for what is commonly thought of as a plum, and turns into a prune when dried, there's not a one in a plum pudding. The name comes from the fact that raisins, when added to cakes or puddings, were traditionally called plums. Increasing the amount of rum and brandy no doubt makes all this perfectly clear.

FALLACY: Rice paper is made from the rice plant.
FACT: Rice paper is not made from the rice plant, or from any relative of the rice plant. It is made from the pith of a small Asian tree of the ginseng family.

////

FALLACY: The fat-free version of a food product is much lower in calories than the regular version.
FACT: That makes sense, because fat is so high in calories. It isn't true, however, for many products. There's very little difference in calories between regular ice cream and fat-free ice cream, and with some foods it actually goes the other way. One well-known company's regular fig bars have 120 calories per ounce; their fat-free version has 140 calories per ounce. When a company removes fat from a product, they commonly add sugar. The same is true in reverse for sugar-free products: the calorie count remains about the same because they add fat.

////

FALLACY: The green color on some potato skins is poisonous.
FACT: The green color on some potato skins is just chlorophyll. That happens when part of the potato isn't covered by soil, and sunlight reaches it. What is poisonous is solanine, a bitter alkaloid ($C_{45}H_{73}NO_{15}$) naturally found in small amounts in the potato skins and sprouts, and even smaller amounts in the potato itself. When a potato is exposed to sunlight, damaged, or gets too old, it produces additional solanine. An excessive amount of solanine can cause headache, cramps, and diarrhea. Good rules to live by: don't eat potato sprouts or old or damaged potatoes; don't eat green potatoes or yellow snow.

////

FALLACY: Spanish moss is a parasitic moss that kills the trees it lives on.
FACT: Spanish moss is not a moss. It is an epiphytic plant, *Tillandsia usneoides*. It is also not a parasite. Spanish moss gets its moisture and nourishment from the air, not from the tree. It depends upon its host only for support and can, like some people, spend its life on telephone lines.

FALLACY: Mixing your drinks will make you more intoxicated.
FACT: Shifting from one kind of alcoholic drink to another will not make you more intoxicated. The intoxicant in all alcoholic beverages is ethyl alcohol. The source of the alcohol makes no difference. Neither does the addition of sugar, foaming agents, coloring, or other additives. The more concentrated the alcohol is (the higher the proof), the more alcohol you get with each swallow. Psychological factors aside, the more alcohol you drink, the more intoxicated you will become. The idea that mixing your drinks will make you more intoxicated may come from the fact that a person who has already had quite a bit to drink is more likely to shift from one type of drink to another. Or several others.

6

History

FALLACY: The last day of the twentieth century will be 31 December 1999.

FACT: The last day of the twentieth century will be 31 December *2000*. The first year was year 1, not year 0, so the first century ended on 31 December 100. The first millennium ended on 31 December 1000. The twentieth century, and the second millennium, will end at midnight on 31 December 2000. The twenty-first century, and the third millennium, will begin on 1 January 2001. Remember to mark that on your calendar.

//

FALLACY: The stock exchange quotes prices in eighths of a dollar to make the system seem more complicated than it is.

FACT: When the stock exchange was set up in the eighteenth century, the American dollar was interchangeable with the Spanish silver dollar. The Spanish silver-dollar coin was so large that it was often broken into eight pieces, or bits. It was common to refer to eighths of an American dollar also, as in "two bits," meaning a quarter of a dollar. The stock exchange used that system when it started in the eighteenth century, and has never changed it. Even without that, the stock exchange is a bit more complicated than a sane person could understand.

//

FALLACY: The Pharaoh Cheops is buried in the Great Pyramid of Cheops.

117

FACT: We know him today by the Greek version of his name, Cheops, but his name was Khufu. When the ancient Greek historian Herodotus went to Egypt more than two thousand years ago, he looked on the pyramids as monuments of an ancient civilization; they were already more than two thousand years old. Khufu was a pharaoh of Egypt's Fourth Dynasty, lived from 2590 to 2567 B.C., and had the Great Pyramid built on the Giza plateau as his tomb. When the pharaoh's chamber deep inside the pyramid was opened, however, there was no body in it.

//

FALLACY: President Ford's only pardon was of Richard Nixon; President Bush's only pardons were of the Iran-Contra Six.
FACT: That brings to mind one of Richard Nixon's more famous quotes, on 19 May 1977: "When the president does it, that means it is not illegal." Although it's not widely publicized, presidents grant quite a few pardons; the Iran-Contra Six were not Bush's only pardons. Among those pardoned by Ford in addition to Nixon was Jimmy (The Greek) Snyder, who had been convicted of gambling violations. Ronald Reagan granted 393 pardons, including one for New York Yankees owner George Steinbrenner, who was convicted of making illegal contributions to Nixon's reelection campaign.

//

FALLACY: Hiawatha was a fictional character created by Longfellow.
FACT: Henry Wadsworth Longfellow's 1855 poem, *The Song of Hiawatha,* was based on a real person. Chief Hiawatha of the Onondaga people, who was born in the mid-1550s, is credited with organizing the Iroquois Confederacy. Also known as the Five Nations, it comprised the Cayuga, Mohawk, Oneida, Onondaga, and Seneca. *Longfellow*, however, is a suspicious name, and may be either an anatomical reference (meaning, of course, that he was tall), or a fictional character created by Hiawatha.

//

FALLACY: Will Rogers, who said "I never met a man I didn't like," entertained the troops in World War II.
FACT: The United States entered World War II at the end of

1941. Will (William Penn Adair) Rogers died in a plane crash near Point Barrow, Alaska, along with pilot Wiley Post, on 15 August 1935. Wiley Post is famous in his own right as the first person to make a solo flight around the world, in 1933. Will Rogers's most often quoted comment, "I never knew a man I didn't like," is almost always misquoted as "I never met a man I didn't like."

//

FALLACY: The Spanish Inquisition lasted almost a hundred years.
FACT: The Roman Catholic Church's Inquisition, begun about 1230 by Pope Gregory IX, was completely separate from the Spanish Inquisition. It later became part of the Holy Office; the name was changed to Congregation for the Doctrine of the Faith in 1965. The Spanish Inquisition was an official part of the government. It was begun by King Ferdinand and Queen Isabella in 1478, fourteen years before they sponsored Christopher Columbus's first voyage; it was not abolished until 1834. The Spanish Inquisition lasted for 356 years. Senator Joseph McCarthy tried to revive the ancient sport of heresy trials in the 1950s, but all that remains of his effort is the word *McCarthyism.*

//

FALLACY: The Kodak camera was invented by Eastman Kodak.
FACT: The Kodak camera was, indeed, invented by a man named Eastman, but his name was George Eastman. According to the Eastman Kodak Company, George created the name *Kodak* because he liked the way it sounded. As he said in a letter he wrote at the time, "The letter 'K' had been a favorite with me—it seems a strong, incisive sort of letter." From there it was just a matter of adding letters until he had a word that he liked. He liked *Kodak* well enough to take out a trademark on it in 1888. Human history is as strange as the mind of man.

//

FALLACY: Columbus was right, and the geographers of his day were wrong, about the size and shape of Earth.
FACT: There was a lot that the geographers of Columbus's day didn't know: that there were continents in the Western Hemisphere, for example, or that Antarctica existed. They did know that Earth was round,

however; that was discovered by the Pythagoreans of ancient Greece. Where Columbus disagreed with them was on the size of Earth, and on the size of Asia. Earth's size was worked out fairly accurately around 200 B.C. by Eratosthenes, who measured shadows cast by the Sun at different places on the planet. Columbus, however, contended that Earth was about 25 percent smaller than it is, and that Asia extended much farther to the east than it does. It was because of those two errors that he believed Asia's east coast was close enough to Europe to be reached. If the lands of the Western Hemisphere hadn't gotten in his way, and he hadn't turned back, he would never have been heard from again.

//

FALLACY: Sirhan Sirhan, who assassinated Robert Kennedy, was sentenced to life in prison without possibility of parole.

FACT: On 5 June 1968, Sirhan Bishara Sirhan shot Senator Robert F. Kennedy at the Ambassador Hotel in Los Angeles during a celebration of Kennedy's victory that day in the California Democratic presidential primary. Kennedy died the following day. Sirhan was sentenced to death, but when the California Supreme Court outlawed the death penalty in 1972, his sentence was changed to life in prison. He became eligible for parole in 1975; parole has been denied at every hearing since then, including one on 4 August 1992.

//

FALLACY: Aphrodite, Eros, Poseidon, and Zeus were Roman gods.

FACT: Not true, by Jove! The Romans borrowed gods from many different cultures. Most of their better-known gods were stolen directly from the previous civilization in the northern Mediterranean, the Greeks. Only the names were changed, to protect the Romans. Aphrodite, for example, became Venus; Dionysus became Bacchus; Eros became Cupid; Poseidon became Neptune; and Zeus became Jupiter or Jove.

//

FALLACY: Camels evolved in the Middle East.

FACT: Camels evolved in North America during the Eocene epoch, fifty-three million to thirty-eight million years ago, and spread to other continents. Along with mammoths, mastodons, saber-toothed tigers, horses, dire wolves, lions, and many other animals, camels became extinct in North America about eleven thousand years ago, at the end of the Pleistocene epoch—the most recent Ice Age.

//

FALLACY: Napoleon was defeated at the Battle of Waterloo.
FACT: The battle was not fought at Waterloo. The decisive battle that Napoleon lost to Wellington in 1815 was fought in a valley below La Belle-Alliance, seven miles south of Waterloo. Interestingly, in Britain a toilet is called both a "water closet" and a "loo."

//

FALLACY: Apaches defeated Custer at the battle of the Little Bighorn.
FACT: The battlefield is on the Crow reservation near Hardin, Montana. Starting in 1990, the Hardin Chamber of Commerce has sponsored an annual reenactment of the 1876 battle. The troops of Custer's 7th Cavalry are played by military-history buffs from around the country. Residents of the Crow reservation play the parts of the original Sioux and Cheyenne warriors. The Apache people didn't live anywhere near the area. Their territory was in what is now the southwestern United States and northern Mexico. Two of Custer's more interesting statements were "The Army is the Indian's best friend," in 1870, and when he first sighted the Native American encampment in the Valley of the Little Big Horn, "Hurrah, boys, we've got them!"

//

FALLACY: The Acropolis is the most famous building in Athens.
FACT: An acropolis, which translates into English as "high city," is a fortified hilltop. Many ancient Greek cities had them. The Athenian Acropolis was dedicated to the city's goddess, Athena. The most famous building on it is the Parthenon, built between 447 and 432 B.C.

//

FALLACY: Abraham Lincoln was born in Illinois, "The Land of Lincoln."

FACT: Abraham Lincoln was born 12 February 1809, to Thomas Lincoln and Nancy Hanks, in Kentucky, "The Bluegrass State." When Abe was seven they moved to Indiana, "The Hoosier State." It wasn't until 1830 that Abe, Thomas, and his second wife, Mrs. Sarah Bush Johnston, moved to Illinois. License plates notwithstanding, Illinois's nickname is not "The Land of Lincoln"—it's "The Prairie State." Honest Abe would want you to know that.

//

FALLACY: Our modern calendar is much more accurate than the Gregorian calendar which it replaced.

FACT: The Julian calendar, named for Julius Caesar in 46 B.C., made the year a little too long because the people who devised it thought that the year was exactly 365.25 days long. The year is actually closer to 365.24 days, so by A.D. 1582 the accumulated error was about ten days. The Gregorian calendar, named for Pope Gregory XIII, decreed that the day after October 4, 1582 would be October 15. The people who devised it were much closer on the exact length of the year, and made their calendar fit by adding leap-year days according to a complicated formula. Our modern calendar did not replace the Gregorian calendar—it *is* the Gregorian calendar. It still isn't in exact agreement with the movement of our planet, so scientists adjust it with leap seconds. The British Empire, including its American colonies, didn't accept the Gregorian calendar until 1752, at which time they declared that the day after September 2, 1752 would be September 14. That's why, although George Washington was born on February 11, his birthday from 1753 onward has been February 22, just in time for the Washington's Birthday Sales.

//

FALLACY: Europeans brought syphilis to the New World.

FACT: Although Europeans brought smallpox to the New World, they can't be blamed for bringing syphilis. Syphilis turned up in Spain in the 1490s, spread throughout Europe, and was known as greatpox to distinguish it from smallpox. The date it turned up is not coincidental. When the Old World invaders raped, robbed, murdered, and pillaged their way through the civilizations of the New World, they carried back to Europe more than they realized.

FALLACY: Timbuktu, like Shangri-la, was a legendary city that never really existed.

FACT: Shangri-la was a purely fictional paradise in James Hilton's novel *Lost Horizon.* Timbuktu, a city in central Mali, northwest Africa, was founded in the eleventh century. It was a major commercial and cultural center from the fourteenth century until 1593, when it was sacked by invaders from Morocco. It was taken over by France in 1896, and although Mali is now an independent country, French remains the official language. Timbuktu, connected to the Niger River by a canal system, still exists; Shangri-la exists only in political campaign promises.

//

FALLACY: Prohibition ended in the United States in 1933.

FACT: Only in some parts of the United States. The Eighteenth Amendment, enforced by the Volstead Act, ushered in federal Prohibition in 1919, and the Twenty-First Amendment repealed it in 1933. Some states, however, had their own Prohibition laws. The last state to end Prohibition was Mississippi, in 1966. Smaller jurisdictions, such as counties, can have their own "How Dry I Am" laws.

//

FALLACY: Mussolini made the trains run on time in Fascist Italy.

FACT: Probably created by Mussolini's ministry of propaganda, this common misbelief is a good example of how long an advertising slogan can last. The trains did not run on time, as many historians and a host of commuters have noted.

//

FALLACY: The Inca empire was held together by a common written language and a system of fast, wheeled vehicles.

FACT: The Inca empire covered an area about 2,500 miles north to south, from the Pacific Ocean high into the Andes. It included what is now Peru, and parts of Ecuador, Chile, Bolivia, and Argentina. Their extensive network of roads included cut-and-fill engineering, suspension bridges over deep Andean gorges, tunnels, ferries over rivers, and relay stations. Their roads not only climbed mountains, but went through swamps and jungles. Because the empire was headed by an absolute ruler and run by a bureaucracy located in Cuzco, swift communication was vital to maintain control. Messages could be carried 150 miles a day by a series of runners—but not written messages. The Incas never developed a written language, relying instead on a system of knots in cords called *quipu*. Considering the extent of their empire, the countless tons of stone moved to their building sites, and the complex engineering of their road system, it is surprising that the Incas never invented the wheel. They didn't, however, so there were no wheeled vehicles on those roads. Spanish invaders arrived in 1532, killed the emperor by treachery, and by 1537 had destroyed the Inca empire. European historians mistakenly reported that religion and civilization had been brought to the savages; European religion and civilization had been brought *by* the savages.

//

FALLACY: The powers of the British monarchy are limited by the British Constitution, which is the oldest Constitution still being used by any country.

FACT: Unlike the United States, neither England nor Britain has a Constitution. The system of government is based on unwritten tradition and custom, and on a collection of written documents such as the Magna Carta (or Charta) of 15 June 1215, and the Bill of Rights of 1689. The oldest Constitution still being used is that of a relatively young country: the United States of America.

//

FALLACY: The Salem witch trials led to hundreds of people being burned to death.

FACT: The Salem witch trials did occur. Twenty people were executed, but not one was burned. Nineteen people were hanged, and one was crushed to death with heavy stones. There was definitely evil afoot, but it was on the other foot.

//

FALLACY: Christopher Columbus discovered North America.

FACT: Christoforo Colombo found both Central America and South America but managed to miss North America completely. He never even saw it. And he couldn't "discover" the Western Hemisphere, because it had been discovered between 12,000 and 30,000 years earlier. Although Columbus Day is celebrated as a national holiday in the United States, it is not one of the major holidays on Native American calendars.

//

FALLACY: A "baker's dozen" is thirteen because bakers used to toss in an extra loaf as a matter of customer relations.

FACT: A baker's dozen is thirteen because bakers didn't want to run afoul of the law. There was a time when bakers skimped on the size of their loaves to increase profits. Laws were enacted making it a crime for bakers to sell underweight bread. This caused a problem. It was difficult to make sure of the exact weight of every loaf. If they put too much dough in every loaf, they'd lose money; if they didn't, they might be breaking the law. So, to make sure that every dozen loaves was up to the legal limit, they tossed in a thirteenth loaf.

//

FALLACY: The Charge of the Light Brigade led to a great military victory.

FACT: The Charge of the Light Brigade did not lead to a great military victory for the Russians, who were being charged, and it led to a great military disaster for the British, who were doing the charging. That famous cavalry charge occurred, on 25 October 1854, because of misunderstood orders; it was a classic result of the military dictum: "Don't think, just follow orders." The British light cavalry brigade charged along the floor of a valley toward cannon at the other end, even though the Russians held the high ground on both sides and the cannon they were heading for were also on high ground. The British military would probably have been happier if this disaster were quickly forgotten, but the British poet Tennyson immortalized it in *The Charge of the Light Brigade*:

> *Half a league, half a league,*
> *Half a league onward,*
> *All in the Valley of Death*
> *Rode the six hundred.*
> *"Forward the Light Brigade!"*
> *Was there a man dismay'd?*
> *Not tho' the soldier knew*
> *Some one had blunder'd:*

Their's not to make reply,
Their's not to reason why,
Their's but to do and die:
Into the Valley of Death
Rode the six hundred.

Using his poetic license, Tennyson fudged the numbers a bit. There were actually 673 men in that charge; 134 were wounded or captured, 113 were killed.

//

FALLACY: The world's first subway was the IRT in New York City.
FACT: The world's first subway was the four-mile London Metropolitan Railway, which opened on January 10, 1863. The Interborough Rapid Transit, which ran between 145th Street in upper Manhattan and the Brooklyn Bridge, opened on October 27, 1904. New York's subway system may look like the world's oldest, but it's not.

//

FALLACY: Saint Patrick was Irish.
FACT: He was born in the fifth century, not in Ireland but in Roman Britain. The name he was born with is not known. When he became a priest he was given the Latin name Patricius. He became associated with Ireland because he headed the campaign to convert the Irish from their religion to Christianity. And no, his mother's name was not Faith Ann Begorra.

//

FALLACY: Generals lead their troops into battle.
FACT: Haven't for a long time. Generals stay way behind the lines except for occasional visits for public-relations purposes. The theory is that generals are too important to risk where the fighting is going on. Generals came up with that theory.

FALLACY: Billy the Kid was born in the West; his real name was William Bonney.

FACT: When Billy the Kid was born in Manhattan, New York, in 1859, he was named Henry McCarty. It was about 1875 that he began calling himself Billy Bonney. He was twenty-one years old when he was killed by Pat Garret in 1881.

//

FALLACY: When he was a boy, George Washington threw a silver dollar across the Potomac.

FACT: There are a couple of small problems with that. George Washington was born to Augustine Washington and Mary Ball at Wakefield, Virginia, on Pope's Creek. Most of his boyhood was spent on a farm near Fredericksburg, on the Rappahannock River, nowhere near the Potomac. The other small problem is that when George was a lad he lived in the British colonies. There was no U.S. dollar to throw, because there was no United States. Because of inflation, doing the equivalent today would be far more difficult; it's not easy to throw a $100 bill.

//

FALLACY: D.B. Cooper hijacked an airliner in the Pacific Northwest, bailed out with $200,000 ransom money, and was never found.

FACT: Someone did, but not D.B. Cooper. The FBI suspected him, and investigated him, but he was in jail at the time of the hijacking. The name on the passenger list, probably false, was Dan Cooper.

//

FALLACY: The United States has never invaded Russia.

FACT: After the Russian Revolution overthrew the Czar in 1917, there was a civil war between the Czarist Whites and the Bolshevik Reds. In 1918 the United States landed troops at both Archangel on the White Sea and Vladivostok on the Pacific. American troops fought against the Reds, but even with their help the Whites lost. U.S. troops didn't leave Russia until 1920. Russia, though, has never invaded the United States.

//

FALLACY: The Arc de Triomphe in Paris was built to celebrate France's triumphs in World War I.

FACT: The Arc de Triomphe de l'Etoile, 163 feet high and 147 feet wide, was begun in 1806 to celebrate Napoleon's triumphs. Not coincidentally, Napoleon was emperor in 1806.

//

FALLACY: The first presidential election covered on television was the 1948 contest between Thomas E. Dewey and Harry S. Truman.
FACT: Television has been around longer than you might think. The first presidential election covered on television was the 1932 contest between Herbert C. Hoover and Franklin D. Roosevelt. Proving the persistence of hope over experience, some of the same campaign promises were believed in the last election.

//

FALLACY: Henry Ford's Model A came a long time before his Model T.
FACT: Just the opposite. The Model T came a long time before the Model A. Between 1908 and 1927, Henry Ford made more than 15 million Model Ts. The cause of its demise was its successor, the Model A, introduced in 1927.

//

FALLACY: The Hundred Years War lasted 100 years.
FACT: The Hundred Years War was fought between England and France. England wanted to control France, but France was not fond of the idea. There were breaks now and again, but the war started in 1337 and ended in 1453. The Hundred Years War lasted 116 years.

//

FALLACY: "Hooch," meaning alcohol, is from the name of a famous bootlegger in the Prohibition era.
FACT: Hooch is from Hoochinoo, the name of an Alaskan Tinglit tribe. During the Alaskan Gold Rush, which began in 1896, the Hoochinoo were famous among thirsty miners for making rotgut booze. Although the miners doubtless saw many strange things after drinking Hooch, the

Hoochinoo lived on mainland Alaska, not on the Aleutian Island chain, and cannot therefore be blamed for optical Aleutians.

// //

FALLACY: Cleopatra was Egyptian.
FACT: Cleopatra was not Egyptian. She belonged to the Ptolemy dynasty, Macedonians who ruled Egypt for 250 years after Alexander the Great conquered it in 332 B.C. She was the daughter of Ptolemy XI, wife of her brother Ptolemy XII and later of her brother Ptolemy XIII, and mother of Ptolemy XIV, whose father was Julius Caesar. Cleopatra died of suicide, not of ptomaine or ptosis.

// //

FALLACY: If women hadn't gotten the vote, Prohibition wouldn't have been voted in.
FACT: Prohibition did not become the law of the land as the result of a popular vote. The Eighteenth Amendment to the Constitution was ratified on 16 January 1919, following the required approval by at least three-fourths of the states. The government of none of those states was controlled by women. Another small problem with that belief is that it was the Nineteenth Amendment, not ratified until 20 August 1920, that gave American women the right to vote. In the words of H.L. Mencken, "A prohibitionist is the sort of man one wouldn't care to drink with—even if he drank."

// //

FALLACY: Sir Walter Raleigh introduced tobacco to Europe.
FACT: He was much too late to make such an introduction. Europe and tobacco were already well acquainted. Tobacco was brought to Europe from Cuba by crew members who sailed with Columbus in the fifteenth century. Raleigh wasn't born until the mid-sixteenth century. Blame your cough on Columbus.

// //

FALLACY: The name ferris wheel comes from *ferrous,* the word for iron, and was used to distinguish that type of amusement wheel from earlier wheels made of wood.

FACT: The name has nothing to do with the structural material, and everything to do with the design. The original Ferris wheel, with a 250-foot diameter and weighing 1,285 tons, was built in Chicago for the 1893 World's Columbian Exposition (World's Fair). It was designed by engineer and inventor George Washington Gale Ferris, who died three years later, but from nothing related to his Ferris wheel.

//

FALLACY: The first colonial victory in the Revolutionary War was on Bunker Hill.
FACT: The Battle of Bunker Hill, the first major battle of the Revolutionary War, was not fought on Bunker Hill. It was fought on Breed's Hill in Charlestown, near Bunker Hill. And it wasn't a colonial victory: the Americans lost the battle, and the hill. So many British troops were killed, though, that it was no real victory for them, either. For both sides, The Battle of Bunker Hill was a bummer.

//

FALLACY: Byzantium is in Greece.
FACT: Byzantium was founded by the ancient Greeks, but not in Greece. It was in Thrace, southeastern Balkan Peninsula, on the shore of the Bosphorus Strait between the Black Sea and the Sea of Marmara. In A.D. 330 its name was changed to Constantinople. Today it is called Istanbul; it is the largest city in Turkey.

//

FALLACY: *Gestapo* is a German word.
FACT: Gestapo is not a word but an acronym from: *Ge*heime *Sta*ats*po*lizei, which translates into English as Secret State Police. The Gestapo organization was created by the Nazis, and died with them.

//

FALLACY: Everyone in the Alamo was killed.
FACT: Mexico allowed Americans to settle in the part of Mexico that is now Texas. In 1836 President Santa Anna announced a new Con-

stitution that applied to all of Mexico and that outlawed slavery. Many in the American-Mexican community were aroused by patriotic feelings for the United States; many were aroused by what they saw as a threat to their property rights—their right to own slaves. When the American-Mexicans tried to seize Texas and make it part of the United States, Mexico considered it treason and sent an army to defend its territory. The famous siege of the Alamo by General Santa Anna lasted from February 24 to March 6, 1836. Although all the combatants in the Alamo were killed, a woman, her child, and a slave were not.

//

FALLACY: There were four Crusades.
FACT: The first of the Crusades by European Christians began in 1095; they recaptured Jerusalem from the Muslims in 1099. The Muslims not only won the Second Crusade, but in 1187 they recaptured Jerusalem. The Third Crusade, again for Jerusalem, was a tie, with the Muslims keeping Jerusalem. In the Fourth Crusade the Christians got Constantinople. The next Crusade was an unnumbered disaster called the Children's Crusade, in which thousands of children were sold into slavery or died of hunger and disease. The Fifth Crusade was for control of Egypt, which the Muslims retained. The Sixth Crusade and the three that tailed off from there were more or less ties, with the Muslims winning on points in 1291 when they recaptured Akko (now called Acre), the last Christian stronghold in Muslim territory. Officially there were nine numbered Crusades plus the Children's Crusade, but during that long and bloody period it's difficult to say what was a "Crusade" and what was merely a war.

//

FALLACY: Nobody knows the real names of Calamity Jane, Molly Pitcher, Nellie Bly, or The Swedish Nightingale.
FACT: Some people do, but not many. Most people know them only by those famous sobriquets. The real names: Calamity Jane was Martha Burke; Molly Pitcher was Mary Ludwig Hays McCauley; Nellie Bly was Elizabeth Cochrane; and The Swedish Nightingale was Jenny Lind, a name famous in its own right.

//

FALLACY: Otis invented the elevator.
FACT: Various types of elevators had been in use for centuries

before Elisha Graves Otis was born. What Otis invented in 1852 was the "safety" elevator, which used a mechanism called a ratchet: a hinged catch that engaged the sloping teeth of a wheel, allowing movement in only one direction. The practical effect was that if the supporting cable broke, the elevator would not fall. It was only after Otis's invention that elevators became popular, and high-rise buildings therefore became practical.

//

FALLACY: There were no survivors of the battle at Little Big Horn, where War Chief Sitting Bull defeated Custer.

FACT: There were many survivors of the battle at Little Big Horn. None of them belonged to Lieutenant Colonel George Armstrong Custer's invading military force, but hundreds of the Cheyenne and Sioux defenders survived. Sitting Bull was not a War Chief; he was a Sioux Medicine Man who stayed behind the lines. The War Chief who led the Native Americans in the battle at Little Big Horn was Crazy Horse.

//

FALLACY: Charles Lindbergh was the first person to make a nonstop flight across the Atlantic Ocean.

FACT: Charles Lindbergh was the sixty-seventh person to make a nonstop flight across the Atlantic. His only claim to fame is that he was the first person to make a *solo* nonstop flight across the Atlantic.

//

FALLACY: Hitler invented the swastika as a symbol for the Nazis.

FACT: The swastika has been around since prehistoric times. The word *swastika* comes from the Sanskrit *svastikah*. Ancient Greeks used the symbol, as did Native Americans.

//

FALLACY: The letters in the distress signal S.O.S. stand for Save Our Ship.

FACT: There are no periods after the letters *SOS*, since they do not stand for anything. *SOS* was agreed upon as an international distress signal because in Morse Code those letters are easy to remember, easy to send, and easy to recognize. The letter *S* is three dots, the letter *O* is three dashes. Morse Code, of course, should not be confused with the Norse Code of the Vikings.

//

FALLACY: Casey Jones is a mythical American folk hero.

FACT: Because of "The Ballad of Casey Jones," he would probably be the most famous of all railroad engineers even if he never existed. He did exist, though. His nickname was Casey, he was born in 1864 with the name John Luther Jones, and he was a locomotive engineer. On April 30, 1900 he was driving the *Cannon Ball Express* from Memphis, Tennessee, to Canton, Mississippi, when he saw a train ahead on the same track at Vaughn, Mississippi. Rather than jumping to safety he stayed with his locomotive, trying to stop it and save the passengers. The passengers were saved, but Casey died in the crash.

//

FALLACY: There are no Incas left in Peru, and the Incan language has been lost.

FACT: About 45 percent of the population of Peru are Incan Native Americans; another 37 percent are people of mixed European and Native American ancestry, known as mestizos. Peru has two official languages; one is Spanish, and the other is Quechua, the Incan language.

//

FALLACY: Unlike the British navy, the U.S. navy never used flogging as a punishment.

FACT: The U.S. navy used flogging as a punishment from its very beginning. Flogging was not stopped until 1850. Among the states, Maryland law allowed it as a penalty until 1953, and Delaware law until 1972.

//

FALLACY: Robert Fulton invented the steamboat.

FACT: In 1542, Spanish navigator Blasco da Garay gave Charles V the design for a steamboat. In 1783, Jouffroy d'Abbans of France sailed a steamboat on the Saône River. In 1787, John Fitch of America sailed a steamboat on the Delaware River, and by 1790 he was advertising regularly scheduled steamboat runs between Philadelphia and Trenton. In 1807, Robert Fulton sailed a steamboat on the Hudson River.

//

FALLACY: Atlas holds the world on his shoulders.
FACT: Looks that way in some statues and pictures, but not true. It's the sky that Atlas holds up, not Earth. The Atlas Mountains in northwestern Africa were named after him, because they seemed to be supporting the sky.

//

FALLACY: Houdini died when he couldn't escape from a box underwater.
FACT: Harry Houdini, born Erich Weiss, died at the age of fifty-two on Halloween, 1926, of appendicitis.

//

FALLACY: The United States was the first country in the Western Hemisphere to outlaw slavery.
FACT: Unfortunately, that's not true. Argentina outlawed slavery in 1813, Colombia in 1821, and Mexico in 1829. The United States didn't outlaw slavery until 1866, with the Thirteenth Amendment. The Emancipation Proclamation of 1863 did not free all slaves in the United States, but only those in territories in rebellion: the Confederacy. And even the Thirteenth Amendment didn't completely outlaw it: "Neither slavery nor involuntary servitude, except as a punishment for crime whereof the party shall have been duly convicted, shall exist within the United States or any place subject to their jurisdiction."

//

FALLACY: Nero fiddled while Rome burned.
FACT: Nero neither had a fiddle, also called a violin, nor did he know how to play one. Couldn't have known how to play one because he

couldn't have had one. That famous burning of Rome was in A.D. 64. The fiddle wasn't invented until the 1500s.

//

FALLACY: The internment of Japanese-Americans during World War II was a matter of national security, not a matter of racism.
FACT: The Executive Order was signed on 19 February 1942. At that time we were at war with Italy, Japan, and Germany. The order did not apply to persons of Italian or German ancestry—it applied only to persons of Japanese ancestry. In all, 110,000 Japanese-Americans were interned for three years. Of those, 75,000 were citizens of the United States.

//

FALLACY: Traffic signals have red, yellow, and green lights because those colors are the easiest to see.
FACT: Traffic signals began with only two colors, red and green. Some had two arms, with the word *Stop* on one and the word *Go* on the other, which swung out to make sure that everybody knew what the light colors meant. Traffic signals use the colors red and green to mean stop and go because that's what the railroads were using when traffic signals were invented. The third light was added later; yellow was chosen because it is easy to distinguish from both red and green.

//

FALLACY: The British navy stopped giving British sailors a rum ration in the nineteenth century.
FACT: The British navy started giving sailors a rum ration in place of the previous beer ration in 1687, after discovering Jamaican rum. In the words of Robert Louis Stevenson's 1883 novel *Treasure Island*: "Fifteen men on the dead man's chest, Yo-ho-ho, and a bottle of rum!" The tradition was officially abolished on 31 July 1970.

//

FALLACY: Mercedes-Benz invented the automobile.
FACT: In 1805, Isaac de Rivaz built a gasoline-powered vehicle, but it wasn't practical. In 1860, Etienne Lenoir built the first practical

internal-combustion vehicle. In 1885, Karl Benz drove his gasoline-powered three-wheeler around a track at his factory. Gottlieb Daimler, who had been working independently, made a test run of his own vehicle a few months later. It wasn't until 1926 that their companies merged, forming Mercedes-Benz. A vehicle didn't have to be powered by gasoline to be an auto-mobile, however. In 1769 Nicholas Joseph Cugnot built an impractical steam vehicle, and in 1801 Richard Trevithick built the first successful steam vehicle. Some credit should go to Denis Papin, the inventor of the pressure cooker, who first proposed a steam-powered vehicle in 1690.

//

FALLACY: IWW stands for International Workers of the World.
FACT: IWW stands for *Industrial* Workers of the World, a union formed in 1905. The nickname for its members is "Wobblies."

//

FALLACY: Prehistoric humans hunted dinosaurs.
FACT: Modern humans are *Homo sapiens sapiens,* and appeared about 35,000 years ago as Cro-Magnon man. *Homo sapiens neandertalensis,* Neandertal man, appeared about 100,000 years ago. The species *Homo sapiens* first appeared about 250,000 years ago. The oldest fossils yet found of the genus *Homo* date to between 2 million and 3 million years ago. That's not nearly old enough. Dinosaurs, after dominating the world for more than 150 million years, became extinct 65 million years ago.

//

FALLACY: The first American military casualties of World War II were at Pearl Harbor.
FACT: Considering World War II, and not when the United States joined it, the first American military casualties were in the North Atlantic. On 31 October 1941, a German submarine torpedoed a U.S. destroyer there, killing 100 U.S. servicemen. Technically, the attack on Pearl Harbor also happened before the United States joined the war.

FALLACY: The oldest inhabited city on Earth is Rome.

FACT: According to tradition, Rome was founded by twin brothers Romulus and Remus, sons of the god Mars, in 753 B.C. No one knows when Damascus, Syria, was founded, but it was inhabited before 2000 B.C. The oldest continuously inhabited city on Earth discovered so far is Damascus.

//

FALLACY: In Doolittle's raid early in World War II, a single plane dashed in, dropped bombs on Tokyo, and dashed back out.

FACT: That famous raid, commanded by Lieutenant Colonel James Doolittle, took place on April 18, 1942. Sixteen B-25s took off from the USS *Hornet*. In addition to Tokyo, they bombed Kobe and Yokohama. Of the eighty raiders, only seven died in the surprise attack.

//

FALLACY: Executions for witchcraft ended in the American colonies long before they ended in England.

FACT: Between the fourteenth and eighteenth centuries, thousands of "witches" were tortured and killed in Europe by religious people who said that they were fighting evil spirits. On September 5, 1682, three women were executed for witchcraft in England. That was the end in England. A decade later, on September 22, 1692, eight women were executed for witchcraft at Salem, Massachusetts. That was the end in the American colonies.

//

FALLACY: In the *Hindenburg* disaster, everyone aboard was killed when the hydrogen in the dirigible burst into flame and the airship crashed to the ground.

FACT: More than 60 percent of the passengers and crew aboard at the time of the disaster survived—fifty-six out of ninety-two.

FALLACY: Jefferson Davis and Robert E. Lee were citizens of the United States when they died.

FACT: Abraham Lincoln declared a general amnesty, but Davis and Lee were excluded because of the offices they held in the Confederacy. Although never brought to trial, Davis was held prisoner from the end of the Civil War until May 1867, then released. He died in 1889 without having regained his American citizenship. Lee, unlike Davis, tried to regain his citizenship, but when he died in 1879 he was still a man without a country. More than a century after they died, Congress restored Lee's citizenship in 1975 and Davis's in 1978.

//

FALLACY: Stonehenge was built by the druids.

FACT: No one knows exactly who did build Stonehenge, but it definitely wasn't the druids. Stonehenge was built between 2000 and 1500 B.C., more than a thousand years before the druids arrived in that area.

//

FALLACY: The first shots of the Civil War were fired at Fort Sumter.

FACT: The first shots of the Civil War were fired three months before the April 12, 1861 attack on Fort Sumter. On January 9, a Union ship named *Star of the West* was fired on while it was bringing supplies to Fort Sumter, and forced to turn back.

7

Humans

FALLACY: Only women can be college Homecoming Queens.

FACT: Students are an intelligent and curious group. At colleges and universities where rules for Homecoming Queen candidacy were written many decades ago, it didn't occur to the writers that anyone but a woman would even try. So there were no rules about gender, species, or even whether or not the candidate was alive. At Rice University in Texas, founded in 1891, winning candidates for Homecoming Queen have included a male student, a dog, and a refrigerator.

//

FALLACY: Humans are the only animals who dream.

FACT: Anyone who has lived with a dog knows that they dream, too. The only mammals that *don't* have the rapid-eye-movement (REM) stage of sleep characteristic of dreaming are the egg-laying monotremes.

//

FALLACY: If a tossed coin comes up heads, the odds are that on the next toss it will come up tails.

FACT: The odds of a coin coming up heads on any toss are 50–50. If it has just come up heads, the odds of it coming up heads on the next toss are still 50–50. If it has come up heads twenty times in a row, the odds of it coming up heads on the next toss are still 50–50. If it has come up heads several times in a row, though, the odds are extremely high that nobody's going to call heads.

139

FALLACY: The busiest travel day, and the busiest telephone day, is Christmas.

FACT: The record for the greatest number of telephone calls on a single day is held by Mother's Day. Since people let their fingers do the walking so that their feet won't have to, Mother's Day is not the busiest travel day. That record is held by the day before Thanksgiving. Why not the day after Thanksgiving? Because that's a Friday, and people aren't in a rush to get back. Why not the day before Christmas? Because travel during the year-end holiday season is spread out over many days.

//

FALLACY: Casey Stengel's real name was Casey Stengel.

FACT: Before the New York Yankees' famous manager became known as "Casey," he was known as "K.C."—a nickname from his hometown, Kansas City. His parents named him Charles Dillon Stengel. Using his hometown's initials rather than his own was a good move. "Casey" sounds a lot better than "Seedy."

//

FALLACY: Humans in good health can hear and see everything around them.

FACT: Humans in even the best of health can hear and see only a tiny percentage of what's around them. What humans can hear is limited to what their listening apparatus can deal with. They can't hear sounds above or below certain frequencies. Dogs, bats, and many other animals can hear frequencies that are inaudible to humans. What humans can see is also limited to what their physical apparatus can deal with. When you look at the night sky you are seeing only a small fraction of what's there. If you used an infrared telescope, you would see an entirely different pattern of stars and other energy sources. And yet another pattern if you used an ultraviolet telescope.

//

FALLACY: Aside from the obvious, there's no great difference between men and women.

FACT: On the contrary, there's a vas deferens between men and women.

//

FALLACY: In poker, the odds of getting a pair are 1 to 1; the odds of getting a royal straight flush arc about 100,000 to 1.

FACT: In a game with no wild cards, there are 2,598,960 possible poker hands. The odds of getting absolutely nothing are 1 to 1—even odds. The odds of getting a pair are 1.37 to 1. Two pairs: 20 to 1. Three of a kind: 46 to 1. Straight: 254 to 1. Flush: 508 to 1. Full house: 693 to 1. Four of a kind: 4,164 to 1. Nonroyal straight flush: 72,192 to 1. Royal straight flush: 649,739 to 1. Read 'em and weep.

//

FALLACY: B.V.D. stands for what they were originally called: Brief Vented Drawers.

FACT: B.V.D. doesn't stand for Brief Vented Drawers, or for the next most common guess, Boys' Vented Drawers. Deliberately kept secret, probably for the advertising value of having people wonder about it, the B.V.D. trademark stands for the names of the three men who founded the company: Bradley, Voorhies, and Day. In spite of the aging of the Baby Boom generation, there is no truth to the rumor that they're planning a line of orthopedic underwear.

//

FALLACY: Although there were arrests, no one was ever convicted of the murder of Malcolm X.

FACT: Three men were convicted of murdering Malcolm X as he spoke at a New York City rally at the Audobon Ballroom on February 21, 1965: Muhammed Abdul Aziz, known at the time as Norman 3X Butler; Kalil Islam, known then as Thomas 15X Johnson; and Mujahid Abdul Halim, earlier known as Thomas Hagen and Talmadge Hayer. As of the beginning of 1993, Hagan/Hayer had been denied parole from his minimum-twenty-year sentence seven times. Aziz and Islam had already been paroled.

FALLACY: You shouldn't go swimming for at least an hour after eating, or you'll get stomach cramps.
FACT: There is absolutely no truth to this old saw. Its origins are unknown, but it has been disproven repeatedly. Ask the swimming coach at the nearest college; ask the Red Cross; ask the YMCA; ask Tarzan.

//

FALLACY: Prostitution is legal throughout Nevada.
FACT: Prostitution is not legal in Las Vegas, nor is it legal in Reno. And not, as commonly supposed, because of the gambling there. Nevada law says that prostitution is legal by county option only in counties that have a population of less than 200,000.

//

FALLACY: National Football League teams get most of their money from the high ticket prices.
FACT: National Football League teams get a lot of money from those high ticket prices, but that's not their major source of income. In July 1992 the NFL revealed that its twenty-eight teams took in $402 million the previous year in ticket sales. Their income from radio and television, though, was $850 million—more than twice as much as from ticket sales. Adding in the loose change, the NFL's total revenue for the year was $1.4 billion.

//

FALLACY: It's amazing that things are always in the last place you look for them.
FACT: Would be more amazing if they weren't. Once you find them, you don't look anywhere else.

//

FALLACY: Printing pictures of money on cloth is not counterfeiting, because no one is going to mistake it for money.
FACT: That's logical, and makes perfect sense, so that's not what the counterfeiting laws say. An underwear company printed pictures of

$500 bills on cotton shorts. No one could possibly mistake them for money. One of the reasons the pictures were of $500 bills is that the largest bill now in general circulation is the $100 bill. Secret Service agents seized the underpants.

/ /

FALLACY: If you shuffle a deck of cards three times, they're completely mixed.
FACT: You wouldn't believe the research that went into this one. Turns out that there is now a mathematical proof for exactly how many shuffles it takes to completely mix a deck. If you're a serious shuffler don't play cards with impatient people, because it takes seven shuffles.

/ /

FALLACY: The dinosaurs didn't last very long.
FACT: Dinosaurs were the dominant form of life on Earth from the late Triassic, 215 million years ago, until the end of the Cretaceous, 65 million years ago. They lasted for more than 150 million years. Our genus, *Homo,* has been around two to three million years. Our species, *Homo sapiens,* has been around about 250,000 years. Our subspecies, *Homo sapiens sapiens,* has been around about 35,000 years. If you think the dinosaurs didn't last very long, what do you have to say about the Homo saps?

/ /

FALLACY: There are nearly 1,000 bank robberies in the Los Angeles area every year.
FACT: Much too modest a claim. There were 1,854 bank robberies in the Los Angeles area in 1983, a record that held until 1991. With the recession in full swing and everyone working harder to make ends meet, the number of bank robberies that year went up to 2,355. In just the first seven months of 1992, there were 1,516. These are money banks; not a single sperm bank was robbed.

/ /

FALLACY: The number of triplets, quadruplets, and quintuplets born each year increases because the population increases, but the percentages remain about the same.

FACT: That was true for a long, long time, and then came the fertility drugs. According to a government study, from 1972 to 1989 there was a 156 percent increase in triplet births to U.S. white women; a 356 percent increase in quadruplet births; and a 182 percent increase in quintuplet-and-greater births. Black women have much less access to fertility drugs, so the percentage increases were much smaller: 18 percent for triplets; 126 percent for quadruplets.

//

FALLACY: An official baseball weighs about half a pound.
FACT: An official baseball weighs less than a third of a pound: between 5 ounces and 5.25 ounces. That's a dry baseball; a spitball weighs more.

//

FALLACY: Laws against going topless apply only to women.
FACT: In 1935, forty-two men who went topless on the beach at Atlantic City were arrested for violating the law. In 1985, a Public Defender in Palm Beach, Florida, who had been arrested for jogging without a shirt, lost his case in federal court against a city law that made it illegal for anybody over the age of fourteen to go topless except at the beach (in 1987 he finally won in the U.S. Court of Appeals). In 1986—half a century after those men were arrested for violating a state law against going topless in New Jersey—seven women were arrested for violating a state law against going topless in New York. Related topic: most people are not in favor of topless waitresses; it's bad enough when they get a *thumb* in your food.

//

FALLACY: Because mail-order catalogs are made of low-grade paper, they don't use up many trees.
FACT: Those mailbox-to-trashcan catalogs that trickle down all year, and rise to a flood before the winter holidays, use an amazing amount of paper of all grades. In an average year, 14,000,000 trees give their lives so that advertisers can show us just how many useless things we desperately need but can't afford.

FALLACY: Egyptian mummies are the oldest human bodies.

FACT: The oldest known complete mummy is that of a man buried in a royal tomb in Saqqâra, Egypt, about 2400 B.C. The oldest known partial mummy is that of a woman buried near Giza, Egypt, about 2600 B.C. Even that woman's mummy, however, is not the oldest human body. In September 1991, the freeze-dried body of a late Stone Age man was found in the Alps. The body was so well preserved that tattoos could still be seen; artifacts found with the body included clothing fragments, a knapsack, a bow and a quiver that still held arrows, and a copper ax. Carbon dating of the straw he used as insulation in his boots indicates that he died about 3300 B.C. This is the oldest known human body—about 5,300 years old.

// /

FALLACY: Hoyle didn't invent poker, but he did write the official rules for it.

FACT: Most poker players accept the rules "according to Hoyle," but Edmond Hoyle didn't write them. Although he wrote works on backgammon, chess, and whist (the ancestor of bridge), he never wrote one on poker. Couldn't have. He died in 1769, about a century before poker was invented.

// /

FALLACY: Siamese twins don't live long, and can't have children.

FACT: Siamese twins are just as able to have children as anyone else, limited only by where they're joined. The famous pair whose birth led to the term *Siamese twins* were Chang and Eng, born on 11 May 1811 in Siam (Thailand). In the Thai language, their names mean Left and Right, respectively. Although they were joined at the chest, Chang fathered ten children and Eng fathered twelve. They died within a few hours of each other on 17 January 1874, at the age of sixty-two.

// /

FALLACY: Our voice sounds the same to us as it does to everyone else.

FACT: What other people hear is sound waves traveling through air. We hear those, but that's not all. We also hear vibrations that are affected by the bones, fluids, and air pockets in our head. Instead of the complex symphony of sounds that we hear when we speak, other people hear only a band.

↗↗

FALLACY: There have been only a few executions since the 1976 Supreme Court ruling allowing states to resume the death penalty.
FACT: Between that 1976 U.S. Supreme Court decision and the beginning of 1993, there were a total of 189 executions in the United States: 188 men and 1 woman. Thirty-eight states had death-penalty laws at the end of that period, but only twenty-one states had carried out executions. Of those, six states accounted for 145 of the 189 executions: Texas, 54; Florida, 29; Louisiana, 20; Virginia, 17; Georgia, 15; and Alabama, 10.

↗↗

FALLACY: It never rains on the Rose Bowl game.
FACT: It's not true that it never rains in Southern California, but it is rare that it rains on that parade. That's what makes 1934 (Columbia 7, Stanford 0) and 1955 (Ohio State 20, Southern California 7) stand out. As of 1993, those were the last two years that it rained on the Rose Bowl game. They should have had rain again in the 1970s to keep things regular, but California was having a bout of drought.

↗↗

FALLACY: Even during a recession, American charities take in nearly a billion dollars a year.
FACT: In 1991, a recession year, American charities took in $124.8 billion in cash donations alone, according to the American Association of Fund-Raising Counsel. Eighty-three percent of that came from individuals, the rest from bequests, corporations, and foundations.

↗↗

FALLACY: In spite of junk mail, the great majority of all mail is still personal letters.

FACT: How many personal letters have you written in the past year? According to the U.S. General Accounting Office, 95.5 percent of all domestic mail carried by the U.S. Postal Service is something other than personal letters. Doesn't leave much, does it?

↗↗

FALLACY: The official distance between a baseball pitcher and home plate is sixty feet.

FACT: The story goes that in 1893, baseball officials decided that the then-current fifty feet between pitcher and home base was too short. They roughed-out a diagram showing the field as it should be. The diagram was labeled by hand. There's many a slip between the hand and the eye. The new dimension was written as 60'0"—sixty feet, zero inches. It was read, and put onto the official plans, as 60'6". Whether that's history or apocrypha, it's a fact that since 1893 the official distance between the pitching rubber and home plate has been sixty feet, six inches.

↗↗

FALLACY: Cutting or shaving hair makes it grow faster.

FACT: There's not a whisker of truth in this myth, so widely believed by adolescents. The onset and rate of growth are determined by genes. The growth itself occurs at the root of the hair, which is unaffected by cutting off the hair's end, or by even the closest of shaves.

↗↗

FALLACY: The Olympic Games have been held every four years, except during wars, since the time of Ancient Greece.

FACT: The first recorded Greek Olympic Games were held in 776 B.C., near Olympia. The Games degenerated after Greece was conquered by Rome, and Roman Emperor Theodosius banned them in A.D. 394. The modern Olympic Games were first held in Athens in 1896; Winter Olympic Games were added in 1924.

↗↗

FALLACY: Some people sweat like pigs.

FACT: In a pig's eye. Any human who sweated like a pig

wouldn't last very long. The reason why pigs spend so much time wallowing in water and wet mud is to lower their body temperature. Except for a few sweat glands on the snout, pigs don't sweat. Pigs, like humans, would overheat and die if they didn't have some way to dissipate excess heat.

/ /

FALLACY: Baseball wasn't played at night until after World War II.
FACT: The first major night baseball game was played on June 2, 1883, between a professional team and a college team. The first big-league night game was on May 24, 1935, between the Cincinnati Reds and the Philadelphia Phillies. Phil Wrigley of Wrigley Field, owner of the Chicago Cubs, commented: "Just a fad, a passing fancy." After 6,852 day games, the first baseball game under the lights at Wrigley Field since it became home to the Cubs in 1916 was played on August 8, 1988. The other team was, historically enough, the Philadelphia Phillies.

/ /

FALLACY: Tissues that come in a box are called facial tissues because that's the part of the body they're used on.
FACT: If tissues that come in a box are called facial tissues because that's the part of the body they're used on, then tissues that come in a roll are badly misnamed. Although originally designed as cold-cream removers, facial tissues are overwhelmingly used for nose blowing. According to the where-it's-used theory, they should be called nasal tissues.

/ /

FALLACY: No one can swim all the way from one continent to another.
FACT: Depends on where you make the attempt. Daniel Carpio, for example, swam from Europe to Africa on July 22, 1948. He did that by swimming across the Strait of Gibraltar from Spain to Morocco: about eight miles. Turning that sideways, Mihir Sen swam from one ocean to another between two continents, when in 1966 he swam the length of the Panama Canal.

FALLACY: The morning sickness that all pregnant women get occurs in the morning.

FACT: Only some pregnant women get the nausea and vomiting called morning sickness. Unfortunately, it can strike at any time of the day, and sometimes lasts all day. Fortunately, it usually occurs only during the first trimester of pregnancy.

//

FALLACY: Forest Lawn Cemetery is in Los Angeles.

FACT: Forest Lawn Memorial Park started in Glendale, not Los Angeles, as a fifty-acre cemetery in 1917. By the beginning of World War II it was a three-hundred-acre theme-park cemetery. Today it includes not only the Glendale location with its Renaissance Art theme, but Forest Lawn–Cypress (Orange County), Forest Lawn–Covina Hills, and Forest Lawn–Hollywood Hills with an American History theme.

//

FALLACY: The tennis term *love* is just a politeness to soften the blow of getting a zero.

FACT: The original of that tennis term is the French word *l'oeuf.* That's what the French called the zero on the scoreboard—an egg, because of its shape. An American term based on the same visual concept is "goose egg" for zero. When the stock market crashed in 1929, introducing the Great Depression, the front-page headline of *Variety*'s 30 October edition read: "WALL STREET LAYS AN EGG." It was a real stinker.

//

FALLACY: The cerebral cortex is the core of the brain.

FACT: The word *cortex* comes from the Latin word for bark, and in zoology refers to the outer layer of an organ: the adrenal cortex, for example, or the cerebral cortex, or the renal (kidney) cortex. When you hear someone refer to the brain as "gray matter," they're referring to the cerebral cortex: the gray, two-millimeter-thick outer layer of the cerebrum. According to Aristotle, "The seat of the soul and the control of voluntary movement—in fact, of nervous functions in general—are to be sought in the heart. The brain is an organ of minor importance."

FALLACY: For the convenience of their customers, Las Vegas casinos have clocks in every room except the bathroom.

FACT: Gambling rooms in Las Vegas casinos—and gambling rooms in Lake Tahoe, Reno, Atlantic City, and elsewhere—almost never have clocks. The purpose is to create an artificial environment where time is suspended. For the same reason, gambling rooms almost never have windows. Many's the gambler who has gone out the door and been amazed at how low his wallet is and how high the Sun is.

//

FALLACY: Because of technological advances in baseball equipment, the record for longest home run changes every few years.

FACT: Technology doesn't have that much to do with baseball. Anything that might ruin the game is kept out of it. The current record for longest home run in a regular-season major league game is 573 feet. It was set by Dave Nicholson of the Chicago White Sox on 6 May 1964 at Comisky Park.

//

FALLACY: When women get older, their hair turns bluish gray.

FACT: Most people's hair turns yellowish gray rather than gray when they get older. Women, more often than men, use a blue rinse to counteract the yellow color. If someone uses a bit too much blue to cancel out the yellow, the overall effect is bluish gray.

//

FALLACY: As humans evolved, they lost all vestige of a tail.

FACT: The human tailbone is well named. At the bottom of our spine and officially called the coccyx, it is what remains of our tail. Some of us are born with a five-vertebrae-long coccyx, some with four vertebrae, but each of us still has a tailbone.

//

FALLACY: ''Instant replays'' in the National Football League caused very few decisions to be reversed.

FACT: Well, let's see. In 1986, a total of thirty-eight decisions were reversed after the instant replay was checked. In 1987, that increased to fifty-seven. It decreased in 1988 to fifty-three, but rose to sixty-five in 1989, seventy-three in 1990, and ninety in 1991. That may explain why instant replays were dropped in 1992.

/ /

FALLACY: Pygmies are an African tribe.
FACT: There is no such tribe, and never has been. "Pygmy" came from a Greek myth. It is now a general term used for any human group whose males average less than five feet tall. The favorite sport of such groups is not basketball.

/ /

FALLACY: Among the states, California has the highest divorce rate.
FACT: Among the states, California's divorce rate is not even among the top ten. According to the U.S. National Center for Health Statistics (NCHS), Nevada has the highest divorce rate. Because of its liberal divorce laws, people come to Nevada from other states. To keep things balanced, though, Nevada also has liberal marriage laws, and people come to Nevada for that as well as for other forms of gambling.

/ /

FALLACY: Because of wind resistance, skiers can't reach much more than 60 miles per hour.
FACT: Wind resistance is definitely a factor, and so is the size of the skier (width and weight); friction between snow and skis varies greatly depending on the type of ski and the condition of the snow surface. All that taken into consideration, at the 1992 Olympics at Les Arcs, France, skier Michaël Prüfer attained a speed of 142.165 miles per hour.

/ /

FALLACY: *Olé!* is a Spanish bullfight cheer derived from *Hollar!*
FACT: Only if you're cheering for the bull. *Hollar!* means "Trample Down!" The exclamation *Olé!*, not reserved for bullfights,

came from the time when Spain was an Islamic country. It derives from *Allah!*

////

FALLACY: The odds against dealing a hand containing all thirteen cards of one suit are a million to one.

FACT: If you're offered those odds to try it, don't take them. The actual odds are 160 billion to one. That's even worse than the odds you get when you buy a lottery ticket.

////

FALLACY: No jockey has ridden more than 1,000 winning horses.

FACT: Eddie Arcaro rode a total of 4,779 winning horses. On 10 March 1993, Eddie Delahoussaye won in the fifth race at Santa Anita, becoming the fourteenth jockey in North American thoroughbred racing history to ride 5,000 winning horses. Billy Lee (Willie) Shoemaker holds many horse-racing records, including riding the greatest number of winners. His first career win was in 1949; he went on to ride a total of 8,833 winning horses by the time he retired in 1990. Blazing Saddles Shoemaker?

////

FALLACY: If someone's eyes show up red in a photograph, it means they have red-eye.

FACT: If someone's eyes show up red in a photograph, it means that the angle of the light was just right to reflect from the retina at the back of the eye. The retina is red because of blood vessels. It also means that the room was relatively dark, causing the person's pupils to be open wide so that a significant amount of light could reach the retina and bounce back out to the camera. Red-eye is cheap whiskey, or a late-night flight, either of which could cause the whites of your eyes to look bloodshot-red.

////

FALLACY: No one knows when the name Olympic Games was first used.

FACT: Although there were Greek ceremonies at Olympus before the earliest historical reports, we do have official records of the first time the name Olympic Games was used. That was the term used for the artistic and religious events held there in 776 B.C. The only athletic event mentioned was a two hundred-yard footrace.

//

FALLACY: Goose bumps are just the skin shriveling when it gets cold.
FACT: When birds get cold they fluff out their feathers, trapping a layer of warm air next to their skin. When hairy animals get cold, they do the same with their hair. Tightening muscles at the end of hair shafts causes the hair to raise up—the mammal version of feather fluffing. It also puckers the skin into what we call goose bumps. Humans used to be a lot hairier than they are today, and the body's mechanism for using that hair to keep warm still functions, especially when one is naked as a jaybird.

//

FALLACY: The longest boomerang round-trip, about 200 feet, was recorded in Australia.
FACT: The boomerang record may have come from Australia, but it didn't return there. Although longer boomerang round-trips may have been accomplished, the longest recorded was over 440 feet, in the United States.

//

FALLACY: Because of their abuse by some athletes, steroids are now prescription drugs.
FACT: A law signed in November 1990 classified anabolic steroids as controlled substances. Until that law went into effect they had been prescription drugs, under the jurisdiction of the Food and Drug Administration. As controlled substances, they are now under the jurisdiction of the Drug Enforcement Administration.

//

FALLACY: Humans have stopped evolving.
FACT: Definitely not. The appendix is now a vestigial organ, and

many people are born without wisdom teeth. Where there's life, there's evolution.

//

FALLACY: A poker hand with a queen of spades is called a Deadman's Hand.
FACT: There is no queen of spades in a Deadman's Hand. That's the name given to the cards held by James Butler (Wild Bill) Hickok when he was shot and killed in Deadwood, South Dakota, in August 1876. The hand he held: an ace of spades, an ace of clubs, a jack of diamonds, an eight of spades, and an eight of clubs. Another name for the hand is Aces and Eights.

//

FALLACY: When people say "mush" to sled dogs, they're using an Eskimo word.
FACT: When people say "mush" to sled dogs, they're using a nonsense word. It probably originated with French explorers who used *Marchons!* (We go!). English speakers mashed it to "mush."

//

FALLACY: Champagne corks have been known to fly as far as fifty feet.
FACT: Most champagne corks are fired accidentally, but occasionally an innocent bottle of champagne has been sacrificed to see how far a cork will go. The longest known flight involving no gimmicks was launched by Heinrich Medicus in New York in 1988. The cork flew 177 feet 9 inches: just cause to celebrate with the bottle's contents.

//

FALLACY: Baseballs are covered with horsehide.
FACT: Baseballs were covered with horsehide until 1973; since then they've been covered with cowhide. Although baseball is known as a U.S. sport, virtually all baseballs used in this country are sewn in Caribbean countries because of the much lower wages.

FALLACY: The Baby Ruth candy bar was named for Babe Ruth.
FACT: Although Babe Ruth didn't get that girth by avoiding candy bars, the Baby Ruth candy bar was named for President Cleveland's daughter, "Baby" Ruth.

/ /

FALLACY: Florence Chadwick was the first woman to swim the English Channel.
FACT: Florence Chadwick was the first woman to swim the Catalina Channel, between Catalina Island and the California coast, in 1952. She broke the existing record time, held by a man. The first woman to swim the English Channel, from France to England, was Gertrude Ederle, on 6 August 1926. Her time was nearly two hours shorter than that of the record holder, Enrique Tiraboschi.

/ /

FALLACY: Although some major league players make more than $1 million a season, the average is way below that.
FACT: According to Associated Press figures, at the close of the 1990 baseball season the average salary for all major league baseball players was $597,537. When the 1991 season opened, the average was $891,188; when the 1992 season opened, it was $1,084,408. Although the figures continue to climb, Ryne Sandberg's 1993–1996 contract with the Chicago Cubs was noticed in passing because his annual average passed another million milestone: $7,100,000 per year. And then there's Barry Bonds: his $43,750,000 six-year contract, with "incentives" that could raise the total above $54,750,000, calls for $8 million for the 1996 season. Basketball players are paid even more than baseball players. Patrick Ewing signed a two-season contract extension (1995–1996 and 1996–1997) with the New York Knicks for an average of $9.4 million per year. Magic Johnson signed a one-season contract extension (1994–1995) with the Los Angeles Lakers for $14.6 million. Not including basketballs.

/ /

FALLACY: When people dream, they move as if they were acting out their dream; their arms move if they're swimming, their legs move if they're running.

FACT: We typically have four dream periods during a normal night's sleep. When we dream, our breathing becomes irregular and our heart rate increases. Motor neurons are inhibited, however, so we are virtually paralyzed. The brain probably does this as a survival mechanism, to keep us from thrashing around and damaging our bodies. The muscles of the eyes are a major exception. The eyes seem to follow the action of what we're dreaming, which may explain why so few of us dream about long tennis matches.

// /

FALLACY: Insurance companies want you to lock your car because it takes a thief a lot longer to get into a locked car.
FACT: Depends on what you consider a lot. In New York City, the police estimate that it takes approximately thirty seconds longer.

// /

FALLACY: Climbing to the top of the Empire State Building would take more than twenty-four hours.
FACT: Possibly, if you were climbing the outside and had to contend with a giant ape. Using the stairs inside, though, it would take about a tenth that long. Geoff Case of Australia won the 1993 annual run up the stairs of the Empire State Building in a record ten minutes and thirty-eight seconds. The Empire State Building, not including its TV tower, is 1,250 feet (102 stories) tall.

// /

FALLACY: The worldwide "population bomb" fizzled out years ago.
FACT: In 1800, the worldwide human population was 954 million. In 1900 it was 1.6 billion. In 1990 it was 5.3 billion. In just ninety years, the human population more than tripled. According to a study released by the U.S. Census Bureau in 1992, the world's population had doubled to 5.4 billion since 1955, and will double again by 2036. Birth rates go down when birth control is used, but where birth control is not available populations continue to explode because lighting the fuse is so much fun.

// /

FALLACY: Humans evolved from apes like the ones alive today, but scientists haven't yet found the "missing link" between us.

FACT: There is no "missing link." Humans did not evolve from modern apes, or from monkeys. All three are primates; long ago they had a common ancestor. The first primates evolved from tree-dwelling mammals about sixty-five million years ago. The primate tree branched many times after that. One branch led to modern apes, and a completely separate branch led to humans. It was between five million and nine million years ago when the family that would lead to humans diverged from our common ancestor.

//

FALLACY: Members of the Baseball Hall of Fame are elected by coaches of the major league teams.
FACT: Taking 1993 as a typical year, not a single major league coach voted for Reggie Jackson, who was elected to the Baseball Hall of Fame after being named on 93.6 percent of the ballots. The ballots are cast not by coaches, but by members of the Baseball Writers Association of America.

//

FALLACY: The largest organ of the human body is the liver.
FACT: An average human liver weighs about three pounds. Raymond Burr, Nell Carter, and Orson Welles included, an average human skin comprises fourteen to eighteen square feet and weighs about six pounds. The largest organ of the human body is the skin.

//

FALLACY: All Camp Fire Girls are girls.
FACT: All Camp Fire Girls used to be girls, before the organization changed its name to Camp Fire Boys and Girls. Forty-five percent of those engaged in Camp Fire Boys and Girls programs as of 1992 were boys.

//

FALLACY: Not even the best golfer can hit a ball more than three times the length of a football field.

FACT: On 12 July 1986, Jack Hamm hit a ball 406 yards—more than four times the length of a football field—to win the official Professional Golf Association record. The most famous Jack of all was "Jack be nimble, Jack be quick; Jack jumped over the candlestick." It has been unreliably reported that in an attempt to break into the *Guinness Book of World Records,* a streaker named Jack jumped over *two* candlesticks. With apologies to Edna St. Vincent Millay, he burned his end at both candles.

//

FALLACY: The percentage of children in the U.S. population has increased significantly since the end of the 1950s.

FACT: The number of children in the United States has remained fairly constant, rising only slightly from 63,727,000 in 1960 to 64,137,000 in 1990. Since the overall population has grown from 179 million in 1960 to 249 million in 1990, however, the percentage of children has *decreased* significantly.

//

FALLACY: Franklin Delano Roosevelt began the tradition of the president throwing out the first baseball of the season.

FACT: Probably would have if it hadn't already been a tradition. It was started by our largest president (over 350 pounds), William Howard Taft, on Opening Day, 14 April 1910. The person who caught the ball wasn't as well known as Taft, but he was a lot more important to the game: Senators' pitcher Walter Johnson.

//

FALLACY: In spite of the tall tales, no one has ever jumped out of an airplane at several thousand feet without a parachute, and survived.

FACT: Nicholas Alkemade, a sergeant in the British air force, jumped out of a burning plane at eighteen thousand feet without a parachute, and survived. He landed in deep snow after losing a lot of his velocity by crashing through pine trees. He was not seriously injured, but he was seriously surprised: the reason he jumped was to end it quickly, rather than slowly in a burning plane.

FALLACY: Adults have more bones than children do.
FACT: Children have almost 50 percent more bones than adults
do. An adult human has 206 bones; a child has 300. As the child gets
older, short bones grow together into longer ones.

//

FALLACY: With some major exceptions such as Los Angeles, the
majority of commuters in most cities travel by mass transit.
FACT: Other exceptions are Boston, Chicago, Houston, Miami,
Philadelphia, Seattle, and Washington. In fact, New York City is the only
metropolis in the country where the majority of commuters use mass transit. In every other city, more use their private automobiles than all forms
of mass transit combined. According to data from the 1990 U.S. Census,
72.3 percent of all commuters travel alone in their cars.

//

FALLACY: There haven't been any pirates for at least a hundred
years.
FACT: There are still pirates, in many of the same places. Sometimes the booty is cargo; often it is cash and valuables. Pirates are most
active today in the Gulf of Thailand, the Straits of Malacca between the
South China Sea and the Indian Ocean, the Mediterranean, the Caribbean,
off the west coast of Africa, and near the Philippines. Pirates seized a
petroleum tanker in Manila Bay in January 1988. South of Singapore,
about 100 major ships and tankers are attacked each year, according to
local shipping officials. In April 1989, pirates robbed, raped, and killed
Vietnamese refugees in a boat off the coast of Thailand; of about 130
refugees, one survived. In February 1990, police and pirates fought a
three-hour gun battle in the Bay of Bengal. In February 1992, pirates
boarded a tanker off the coast of Rio de Janeiro, Brazil, killed two crew
members and wounded two others, then stole cash and electronic equipment. Pirates are people on a ship who plunder other ships or coasts
without the approval of some government. If they have government approval, they're not pirates.

//

FALLACY: The golf term *Fore!* means "Four coming through!" and
derives from the usual number of golfers in a group: a foursome.

FACT: "Fore!" comes from the time when soldiers fired one rank at a time. When the second and subsequent ranks were ready to fire, an officer would shout "Beware before!" to warn the ranks in front to get down. That original meaning has not become obsolete on the golf course, as was demonstrated by President Gerald Ford.

8

International

FALLACY: The world's largest pyramid is in Egypt.
FACT: The world's largest pyramid is in Mexico. The Quetzalcóatl pyramid, 63 miles southeast of Mexico City, is 177 feet tall with a base covering about 45 acres, and a volume of approximately 120 million cubic feet. Egypt's largest, the Cheops (Khufu), was originally 481 feet tall but has a base covering only about 13 acres, and a volume of approximately 90 million cubic feet. Egypt does have the world's oldest, though. The Djoser step pyramid at Saqqâra was built about 2650 B.C.—more than 4,600 years ago.

//

FALLACY: New York City has more taxis than any other city.
FACT: If so, they're water-soluble: it's impossible to find one when it's raining. Truth is, New York City doesn't hold the record. Mexico City does, with more than sixty thousand taxis.

//

FALLACY: About 100 nations are members of the United Nations.
FACT: As recently as 1988, the United Nations had 159 members. Georgia was the last of the former Soviet republics to request membership in the United Nations. When it was admitted on 31 July 1992, it became the 179th member nation. As of the beginning of 1993, following the admission of both the Czech Republic and Slovakia in place of the former Czechoslovakia, 180 nations were members of the United Nations.

FALLACY: If you flew due south from Detroit, you'd be over the United States, then the Gulf of Mexico, then western South America, then the Pacific Ocean.

FACT: If you flew due south from Detroit (not Detroit Metro Airport), you'd be over the United States, then Canada, then the United States, then the Gulf of Mexico, then Cuba, then the Caribbean Sea, then the border area between Costa Rica and Panama, then the Pacific Ocean. As far as the Pacific goes, you'd get your feet wet faster by heading west.

//

FALLACY: The initials *MG* stand for Motor Garage; the initials *BMW* stand for Bavarian Motor Works.

FACT: The initials *MG* are the famous British automotive letters, as in MGA and MGB; *MG* originally stood for Morris Garage. In 1992 the MG line was resurrected by British automaker Rover in the form of the MG RV8. Although BMW is a German company, the *B* does not stand for Bavarian; the initials represent the words *Bayerische Motoren Werke*. The world's largest automaker, though, is neither BMW nor MG, but GM. OK?

//

FALLACY: The foreign students in our universities cost U.S. taxpayers millions of dollars every year.

FACT: There are approximately 500,000 students in U.S. colleges and universities from other countries; they are not supported by U.S. taxpayers. Schools compete for these students because they pay full tuition. According to the Department of Commerce, students from other countries bring more than $5 billion a year into the U.S. economy.

//

FALLACY: Casablanca is the capital of Morocco.

FACT: Casablanca is Morocco's largest city. Thanks to the classic movie of that name, Casablanca's Casbah is the most famous in the world. *Casbah* is a north African word meaning either a fortress, or the native section of a city. In spite of these claims to fame, Casablanca is not the capital of Morocco. Neither is the country's next most famous city, Tangier. Morocco's capital is Rabat.

////

FALLACY: Turkeys are called that because they originated in Turkey.
FACT: Unlike eagles, turkeys are native only to North America. That's why Benjamin Franklin tried to get the turkey accepted as the symbol of the new North American country. The turkey was called that because some Europeans confused it with the guinea fowl, which they thought had come to the Old World from Turkey. It's a compound confusion, because the guinea fowl actually came from Africa.

////

FALLACY: Although Wake Island belongs to the United States, residents of Wake Island are not U.S. citizens.
FACT: The United States took formal possession of Wake Island in 1899. About 2,300 miles west of Hawaii and 1,290 miles east of Guam, it is of particular importance because it lies on the direct route between Hawaii and Hong Kong. It's safe to say that the residents of Wake Island are U.S. citizens: there are no native residents. The island has been administered by the Air Force since 1972, and is basically a U.S. Air Force base.

////

FALLACY: The Leaning Tower of Pisa has been leaning at the same angle for more than a hundred years.
FACT: The Leaning Tower of Pisa, which the people of Pisa call *La Torre Pendente,* has been leaning for *way* more than a hundred years, but not at the same angle. Construction began in 1174 and was completed in 1350. Because of an inadequate foundation, the famous marble bell tower began tilting even before it was finished. According to measurements begun in 1918, the rate of tilt averaged one millimeter per year; during the second half of the twentieth century that rate nearly doubled. The 180-foot tower now leans toward the south at an angle of 5.5°.

////

FALLACY: Wales, in western Britain, was originally called Whales.
FACT: The original prehistoric settlers of the area were Celts; the

Celtic name is *Cymru*. Anglo-Saxon invaders called the people *Waelise* (foreign); from that we got Wales. The title "Prince of Whales" is purely pelagic.

//

FALLACY: About 90 percent of U.S. patents go to U.S. applicants.
FACT: Between 1969 and 1990, General Electric Company came in first with 18,541 patents, followed by IBM Corporation. In the single year 1990, however, only three of the top ten were U.S. corporations. The top four were all Japanese. In order, Hitachi, Toshiba, Canon, and Mitsubishi. Of the patents issued in 1990, 52.4 percent went to U.S. corporations or government agencies, and 21.6 percent went to Japanese applicants. In fiscal 1991, the U.S. Patent and Trademark Office issued 101,860 patents; 21,464 went to Japanese applicants; in number of patents awarded, four of the top five corporations were Japanese. For seventeen consecutive years including 1991, Japan received more U.S. patents than any other foreign country.

//

FALLACY: Saudi Arabia is one of the few countries that does not import oil.
FACT: Saudi Arabia imports more than $1 billion worth of oil every year. Not petroleum, but cooking oil.

//

FALLACY: Carioca is a tropical plant related to the tapioca plant.
FACT: There is no tapioca plant. Tapioca is a starch derived from the root of the cassava or manioc plant (*Manihot esculenta*). There is no carioca plant, either. A Carioca is a resident of Rio de Janeiro, Brazil, or a dance popularized there. In the interest of brevity, the residents are not called Rio de Janeiroans.

//

FALLACY: Buckingham Palace is the world's largest palace.
FACT: Definitely not "four rooms and a path," Buckingham Palace has been the official residence of British monarchs since 1837. It was

built by the Duke of Buckingham in 1703, and purchased in 1761 by King George III of American Revolution fame. Even though it has about 600 rooms, it's not the world's largest palace. That title goes to the Palace of Versailles on the other side of the Channel, fourteen miles southwest of Paris. The Palace of Versailles was completed in 1682 for King Louis XIV. The front of the palace has 375 windows, but it's probably only coincidental that window washers were among those who supported the French Revolution of 1789 and forced Louis XVI to move back to Paris.

//

FALLACY: African slaves were brought to what is now the United States almost a hundred years before the Civil War.
FACT: Africans were brought as slaves to what is now the United States more than 240 years before the Civil War. A Dutch ship brought the first slaves to the English colony of Virginia in 1619. The first European to deal in New World slavery, however, did it the other way; Christopher Columbus sent Native Americans back to Europe as slaves.

//

FALLACY: Sydney is the capital of Australia.
FACT: Sydney, in the state of New South Wales, is the largest city in Australia and the best known outside of Australia. It is not the capital of Australia, however, nor is the next largest city, Melbourne, in Victoria. The capital is Canberra, in the aptly named Australian Capital Territory.

//

FALLACY: Upper Egypt is north of Lower Egypt.
FACT: That's the way almost everything else on the planet is named, because north-south is the major determinant. In ancient Egypt, though, the major determinant was the direction of flow of the single most important thing in Egyptians' lives: the Nile. The Nile rises in the south and flows north to the Mediterranean Sea, so Upper Egypt is south of Lower Egypt. Keeps the Nile from defying gravity, and flowing from lower to upper.

FALLACY: Mexico is the official name of that country.

FACT: No more than America is the official name of the United States of America. The official name of our southern neighbor is the United Mexican States.

/ /

FALLACY: Belgian Congo, British Honduras, Burma, Ceylon, East Pakistan, Northern Rhodesia, Southern Rhodesia, Tanganyika, and Zanzibar are members of the United Nations.

FACT: You won't find any of them listed among the membership. They are now, respectively, Zaire, Belize, Myanmar, Sri Lanka, Bangladesh, Zambia, and Zimbabwe; Tanganyika and Zanzibar merged to become Tanzania.

/ /

FALLACY: Because cows are sacred in India, there are no fast-food hamburger restaurants.

FACT: Beef is taboo to the 80 percent of India's people who are Hindus. Just to complicate the issue for the bacon-cheeseburger crowd, pork is taboo to the 10 percent of India's people who are Muslims. This hasn't stopped the fast-food hamburger chains, though. Wimpy's biggest seller is a chickenburger, and it has 100 percent lamb "hamburgers." Restaurants can sell beef in India if they have a special government license, but those licenses are restricted to only a few luxury tourist hotels.

/ /

FALLACY: The world's oldest parliament is in Britain.

FACT: A parliament is a representative assembly having the supreme legislative power of a nation. Britain's parliament evolved from the Curia Regis, a group composed of members of the nobility and the church, which was merely advisory to the monarch. It wasn't until the thirteenth century that knights and burgesses were added, and it wasn't until the seventeenth century that Britain's parliament received power over taxation and expenditures. Congress became the supreme legislative body of the United States in 1789. Parliament became the supreme legislative body of Britain as a result of the Glorious Revolution in 1688. Althing became the supreme legislative body of Iceland in 930, making it the world's oldest parliament. Will Rogers, always ready to lighten anything that sounded too serious, said: "This country has come to feel the same when Congress is in session as when the baby gets hold of a hammer."

//

FALLACY: Wombats are African bats.
FACT: Wombats are not bats, and these members of the family Vombatidae are natives of Australia, not Africa. Although they look like small bears they're actually marsupials; their diet consists mainly of grass, leaves, and roots.

//

FALLACY: Spanish is the official language of the Latin American countries.
FACT: The official language of Brazil, which is not only the largest of the Latin American countries but is larger than the forty-eight contiguous United States, is not Spanish. The citizens of Brazil—who make up more than half the population of South America—speak Portuguese.

//

FALLACY: Holland is the Dutch homeland.
FACT: There is no nation named Holland. The name of the Dutch homeland is Koninkrijk der Nederlanden, or Kingdom of the Netherlands. There is an area in the Netherlands named Holland, but thinking of the Netherlands as Holland would be like thinking of the United States as New York. Only New Yorkers do that.

//

FALLACY: There is an elephant graveyard somewhere in central Africa where elephants go to die.
FACT: There is no such elephant graveyard in Africa, or anywhere else. Elephants, like all other living things, die wherever they die.

FALLACY: Bagpipes originated in Scotland.

FACT: First off, the name: even though there are five pipes, the name of the instrument is bagpipe. It originated in the Middle East several centuries B.C., spread throughout Europe, and didn't reach Scotland until the fifteenth century. It is unkind to suggest that it be sent back.

//

FALLACY: Ship captains can perform marriages once they are in international waters.

FACT: Ship captains can no more perform marriages than they can perform divorces. To perform a legal marriage, a person must be authorized by the government of the area. There is no national government with jurisdiction over the high seas, and no international body has authorized ship captains to perform marriages.

//

FALLACY: The United States closed Subic Bay in the Philippines, but it still has other bases there.

FACT: U.S. military forces seized the Philippines from Spain in 1898, during the Spanish-American War. Clark Air Base, home of the 13th Air Force, was officially closed on November 27, 1991 after being virtually destroyed by eruptions of nearby Mount Pinatubo. Subic Bay Naval Base was the largest U.S. naval base in Asia, until it was officially closed on November 24, 1992. As of the closing of Subic Bay, the Philippines were free of foreign troops for the first time since the sixteenth century.

//

FALLACY: A quahog is a miniature Chinese hog.

FACT: A quahog is a thick-shelled, North American, Atlantic-coast clam (*Venus mercenaria*). The name comes from the Native American Narragansett word *poquauhock*. Interestingly, all quahogs start out as males. When young and tender enough to be eaten raw, they're called littleneck clams. When half-grown they're called cherrystone clams. When fully grown they become females and stay that way the rest of their lives, which often end not with a bang but with a chowder.

FALLACY: World War II was the longest war in this century, followed by the war between Iran and Iraq.

FACT: World War II lasted from 1939 to 1945: six years. The Iran-Iraq War lasted from 1980 to 1988: eight years. The Vietnam War lasted from 1954 to 1975: twenty-one years.

//

FALLACY: Bananas were brought to Europe from South America.

FACT: Many people slip up on this one. Bananas originated in Asia. The first Europeans to eat them were ancient Greeks and Romans. Bananas were brought to South America by Europeans.

//

FALLACY: The Khyber Pass is in India.

FACT: The Khyber Pass is a 3,500-foot-high, 33-mile-long pass on an ancient route between India and the West. It is not in India, however. It's part of the route between the capitals of Islamabad, Pakistan, and Kabul, Afghanistan, on the border between those two countries. The Khyber Pass was used by both Tamerlane, a Mongolian from the east, and Alexander the Great, a Macedonian from the west.

//

FALLACY: Britain is a monarchy, not a democracy.

FACT: Britain is very definitely a democracy. Although it maintains the trappings of a monarchy, the government is run by a democratically elected parliament. Parliament could abolish the monarchy, but the monarchy could not abolish Parliament. Main reasons for keeping the monarchy are tradition and economics. Those at the top of the class system enjoy it, and there's no doubt that the royal pomp and circumstance are among Britain's greatest tourist attractions.

//

FALLACY: The United States acquired its Caribbean territories from Spain.

FACT: Puerto Rico was acquired from Spain. The U.S. Virgin Islands were purchased for strategic reasons during World War I, but not from Spain. At the time of their acquisition in 1917, they were known as the Danish West Indies.

//

FALLACY: The Great Wall of China is hundreds of miles long.
FACT: The Great Wall of China was begun by Ch'in Shih Hwang-ti, in the third century B.C. The name of the country is derived from the Ch'in (Qin) dynasty. The Great Wall averages 12 feet in width and 25 feet in height, and extends for 1,500 miles, from the Yellow Sea to the Gobi Desert. If all the curves, bends, and offshoots were included, its total length would be about 2,500 miles.

//

FALLACY: Karl Marx was Russian.
FACT: Karl Marx was born in the Rhineland in 1818, left Germany twenty-five years later, spent a few years in Paris, then lived the rest of his life in London. He never even visited Russia. Marx died in 1883, more than three decades before the Russian Revolution of 1917. And no, his grave is not in Moscow; it's in London.

//

FALLACY: The shilling, bob, and quid are units of British currency.
FACT: The shilling, equal to twelve pence or one-twentieth of a pound, was a British monetary unit until 15 February 1971, when Britain shifted to a decimal currency system. There are now 100 pence to a pound. "Bob" was a popular term for a shilling, similar to "buck" for a dollar. "Quid" is a popular term for a pound.

//

FALLACY: The only countries where cars drive on the left side of the road are Britain and a few other English-speaking countries.
FACT: That would come as a great surprise to the people of Finland, India, Indonesia, Japan, Suriname, and Thailand, which are among the more than fifty countries where people drive on the left side of the road.

FALLACY: The Kremlin is a building in Moscow.

FACT: The Kremlin in Moscow is a ninety-acre walled area. The word *kremlin* is a version of the word *citadel*. In medieval times there were outer walls around many major cities, and inner walls as a last line of defense protecting an area at the center. This inner area was known as a citadel or kremlin. The Russian Kremlin was built in the fifteenth century.

//

FALLACY: The largest gathering of heads of government was at the signing of the United Nations' Charter in New York City.

FACT: The United Nations charter was signed by fifty nations on 26 June 1945 at the end of the United Nations Conference on International Organization, held in San Francisco from 25 April to 26 June; the charter came into effect on 24 October 1945. A larger gathering was the September 1990 World Summit for Children, held at United Nations headquarters and attended by seventy-one world leaders. The largest gathering of heads of government in the history of the world was at the United Nations Conference on Environment and Development (also called the Earth Summit), held in Rio de Janeiro, Brazil, in June 1992. A total of 117 heads of government and heads of state attended.

//

FALLACY: The Opium War was fought by Britain to keep China from exporting opium.

FACT: The Opium War started in 1839 after China outlawed the importing, not exporting, of opium. When British opium was destroyed at Canton, Britain began the Opium War. It was not really about opium, though. The British wanted to end Chinese trade restrictions, and used the Canton incident as an excuse. Britain won an easy military victory. The 1842 Treaty of Nanking gave Hong Kong to Britain, and forced China to open five ports to British trade.

//

FALLACY: Puerto Rico is a country.

FACT: Puerto Rico's full name is Estado Libre Asociado de Puerto Rico. It is not an independent country, but a self-governing part of the United States, with roughly the same control over its internal affairs as one of the states. Although Puerto Ricans are not allowed to vote in national elections, they do vote in national primary elections. They have no senators or representatives in Congress, but they are citizens of the United States. As with all other citizens, Puerto Ricans are subject to military service, but in keeping with the principle of "no taxation without representation," they are not subject to federal taxes.

//

FALLACY: London Bridge is in London.
FACT: London Bridge was built in London between 1824 and 1831. It was sold by the Court of Common Council of the Corporation of London to the McCulloch Oil Company of Los Angeles in 1968 for $2.47 million, disassembled, shipped across the Atlantic, then transported across most of North America. Reassembled at Lake Havasu City, Arizona, it was officially opened on October 10, 1971. London Bridge may not be in London, but it was solidly reconstructed and is in no danger of falling down.

//

FALLACY: More than a million U.S. military personnel were sent to the Middle East for the Persian Gulf War, and a large percentage of them were women.
FACT: A total of 540,000 U.S. military personnel were sent to the Middle East for the Persian Gulf War. Of those, 32,000, or less than 6 percent, were women.

//

FALLACY: Big Ben is the clock in the British Parliament's tower.
FACT: Big Ben is not the name of the clock, or of the tower at the Houses of Parliament in London. It's the name of the *bell* of the clock.

//

FALLACY: Citizens of the Philippines are Philippinos.
FACT: The Spanish, who once ruled the Philippines and named it after their King Phillip, spell the name Filipinos. Natives of the Phil-

ippines spell it Pilipinos, for the simple reason that there is no *F* in their language, Tagalog. Since Americans would pronounce Pilipinos incorrectly, they use the Spanish spelling.

//

FALLACY: The dollar, although accepted elsewhere, is the national currency of only one country: the United States.
FACT: The word *dollar* comes from Low German *Daler,* which comes from German *Taler,* short for *Joachimstaler,* which comes from the name of a European town where taler coins were first minted, Joachimstal. Although we're fond of calling our dollar *the* dollar, there are twenty-six jurisdictions that call their currency a dollar: Australia, Bahamas, Barbados, Belize, Brunei, Canada, Cayman Islands, Dominica, Fiji, Grenada, Guyana, Hong Kong, Jamaica, Kiribati, Liberia, Nauru, New Zealand, Saint Lucia, Saint Vincent and the Grenadines, Singapore, Solomon Islands, Taiwan, Trinidad and Tobago, Tuvalu, United States, and Zimbabwe.

//

FALLACY: Ostriches are native to Australia.
FACT: Ostrichlike birds called ratites, including cassowaries and emus, are native to Australia; ostriches are not. Once common throughout Africa and southwest Asia, ostriches are now found only in eastern Africa. Ostriches are definitely not Australians, as proven by the fact that they are not fond of Foster's lager.

//

FALLACY: Scotland Yard is the headquarters of England's national police.
FACT: Scotland Yard, named after a street in London although it is no longer on that street, is not the headquarters of any national organization. It houses the Criminal Investigation Department of a city police force, the London Metropolitan Police. Britain's "national police" organization is MI-5, a branch of the military.

FALLACY: Most of the "Seven Wonders of the World" still exist.
FACT: The Seven Wonders of the World: the Pyramids of Egypt, the Hanging Gardens of Babylon, the Statue of Zeus at Olympia, the Temple of Artemis at Ephesus, the Mausoleum at Halicarnassus, the Colossus of Rhodes, and the Pharos (Lighthouse) at Alexandria. Only the Pyramids of Egypt still exist.

//

FALLACY: France, Germany, and Italy are Western countries.
FACT: Italy, Germany, and most of France are east of the Zero Meridian, which runs through Greenwich, England, and are therefore Eastern countries. That's real. In the unreal world of politics, they are Western countries. New Zealand, one of the "Western" countries, is actually about as far east as you can go. And speaking of the Far East, where does that put the Far West, the Near East, the Near West, the Mideast, and the Midwest?

//

FALLACY: The world's largest airport is O'Hare Field in Chicago.
FACT: The world's largest airport is not O'Hare Field, or Kennedy International, or Dallas–Fort Worth. By far the largest is King Khalid International Airport at Riyadh, Saudi Arabia. Spread out beneath the 243-foot-high world's largest control tower, Khalid International covers 86 square miles. O'Hare may not be the largest airport, but it is the world's busiest, with a twenty-four-hour average of one takeoff or landing every forty seconds; some of them are on time, and a few even have the right baggage.

//

FALLACY: Interpol hasn't existed since World War II.
FACT: Interpol, short for International Criminal Police Organization, was founded in Vienna in 1923, at a conference of police chiefs. Its headquarters were seized in the Nazi takeover of Austria in 1938. Interpol resumed operations in Paris in 1946. Each member country has its own National Central Bureau through which its police communicate with Interpol or with the police of other member nations. On November 27, 1989, Interpol opened a new headquarters in Paris. At a closed meeting

in Ottawa in September 1990, at least four new members were accepted: Czechoslovakia, the Marshall Islands, Poland, and the Soviet Union. The Soviet Union's membership was later transferred to Russia; Czechoslovakia broke into two countries, the Czech Republic and Slovakia.

//

FALLACY: Florence, Venice, and Rome are the Italian names of those cities.
FACT: People who live in those cities, as well as the people who live elsewhere in Italia, call them Firenze, Venezia, and Roma.

//

FALLACY: Guinea pigs are small pigs from Guinea.
FACT: Guinea pigs are not from Equatorial Guinea, Guinea-Bissau, or the Republic of Guinea, all of which are nations in western Africa. Guinea pigs are native to South America. They are plump, small-legged, nearly tailless, domesticated rodents. They do not resemble pigs, and are in no way related to them.

//

FALLACY: The world's tallest obelisk is in Egypt.
FACT: The world's most famous obelisks were built in ancient Egypt, at Aswan and Heliopolis. The world's tallest obelisk, though, was built in the United States, at Washington. It's the 555.43-foot Washington Monument, on the nonshopping Mall between the Capitol and the Lincoln Memorial.

//

FALLACY: Saint Patrick drove the snakes out of Ireland.
FACT: That *would* have been a miracle, because snakes never made it to Ireland from the continent. The same is true for many of the world's other islands, including Hawaii.

//

FALLACY: The Chinese people speak Mandarin Chinese.
FACT: The people of China speak many languages, and many

different dialects of Chinese. *Putonghua,* known in the West as Mandarin, is the most common dialect, and one variety or another is known in about four-fifths of the country; the "approved" variety is that spoken in the Beijing area. Mandarin is the official dialect, and the national government has tried several times in the past to get all of the people to use it. The current attempt has less sweeping goals: government officials at all levels, from province down to township, are supposed to use Mandarin. One of the most familiar dialects to Americans is Cantonese, spoken in Guangdong province, its capital, Guangzhou (formerly Canton), and neighboring Hong Kong.

//

FALLACY: The Mexican border with the United States is only about a fourth as long as the Canadian-U.S. border.
FACT: The Mexican border is about two thousand miles long; the Canadian border about four thousand miles.

//

FALLACY: Most Muslims are Arabs.
FACT: Although many people think "Arab" when they hear the word *Muslim,* most of the world's Muslims are *not* Arabs. India, for example, has a Muslim population of about 95 million. Indonesia, a Pacific Ocean archipelago, has a total population of more than 190 million; 90 percent of the people are Muslims, giving Indonesia the largest Muslim population of any nation on Earth. The world's Muslim population is approximately 1 billion; about 80 percent of them are *not* Arabs.

//

FALLACY: Gypsies originated in Hungary.
FACT: The idea that Gypsies originated in Hungary was popularized by Hollywood films, but it's pure fiction. Gypsies were long believed by Europeans to have originated in Egypt, hence the name Gypsy. They were, indeed, in Egypt by the fifteenth century, but probably originated in India. Research indicates that they began their migration from India about A.D. 1000. Their language, Romany, is not related to European or Egyptian languages, but to Sanskrit, an ancient language of India. By

the sixteenth century they were traveling all over Europe. Along with communists, homosexuals, and Jews, Gypsies were targets of the Nazis, who killed more than 500,000 European Gypsies.

//

FALLACY: The spitting cobra of India can spit its stream of venom as far as six feet.

FACT: Spitting or ringhals cobras, which live only in Africa, fire two streams of venom, just as they have two fangs. Venom can be washed off the skin without harm, but the cobra aims for the eyes. If venom gets in the eyes and is not removed immediately it can cause blindness, but a simple pair of glasses will protect the eyes. As for distance, ringhals cobras can spit venom as far as twelve feet. The world's longest poisonous snake is also a cobra, the king cobra (*Ophiophagus hannah*), which can grow to eighteen feet in length. For obvious reasons, these are not the snakes of choice for snake charmers. Their favorites are the Egyptian and Indian cobras, *Naja haja* and *Naja naja* respectively. Cobras, as is true of other snakes, have no ears and do not hear music. What they react to is the nearness of the swaying snake charmer, who stays just beyond the distance at which the snake will strike. The music is not to charm the cobra; the music is to tame the tourist.

//

FALLACY: In Egyptian mythology, the sphinx killed people who couldn't answer its riddle.

FACT: The sphinx was a mythical monster in many parts of the ancient world, including Greece and Egypt. Greek mythology gave us the sphinx with a woman's head and a lion's body, which killed anyone who couldn't answer its riddle. The riddle was: "What goes on four legs in the morning, on two at noon, and on three at night?" Oedipus gave the correct answer: "Man. In infancy he crawls; in his prime he walks; and in old age, he leans on a staff." In Egyptian mythology, the sphinx represented the pharaoh, and had a man's head and a lion's body. The one we think of most often today is The Great Sphinx, near the pyramids on the Giza plateau. It was built about 4,500 years ago, and the face is probably that of the pharaoh Khafre.

//

FALLACY: The wall that divided the city of Berlin was only a few miles long.

FACT: The Berlin Wall, built on the night of August 12–13, 1961, was 26.5 miles long. It came down on November 9, 1989, with a lot more joy than it went up.

/ /

FALLACY: Cinco de Mayo is Mexico's Independence Day.

FACT: That is commonly believed because the 5th of May is celebrated so widely in Mexican-American communities. Historically, Cinco de Mayo memorializes a battle at Puebla on May 5, 1862 between outnumbered Mexican troops and a powerful French army, which the Mexicans won. What is often forgotten is that although they won the battle, they lost that war. Cinco de Mayo is not a major holiday in Mexico. Mexico's Independence Day is Dieciseis de Septiembre, which commemorates the beginning of the War of Independence against Spain on September 16, 1810. It is celebrated in Mexico with all the gusto of the 4th of July in the United States.

/ /

FALLACY: Parking meters were invented in Europe after World War II.

FACT: Parking meters were invented by Carl Magee of the United States. They were first installed in Oklahoma City on July 19, 1935. European drivers have never forgiven us.

/ /

FALLACY: MI-5 is Britain's equivalent of the CIA.

FACT: MI-5 is Britain's equivalent of the FBI. The equivalent of the CIA is MI-6. Their official names are Military Intelligence, Department 5 and Department 6. MI-6 is also known as the Secret Intelligence Service. Ian Fleming's novels about James Bond were based on MI-6.

/ /

FALLACY: Panama hats, woven from palm fronds, are made in Panama.

FACT: Panama hats were originally made in Ecuador, from *to-*

quilla fiber. There was no direct trade route from Ecuador, so the hats were sent first to U.S.-controlled Panama, then into the world trade pattern. That's why they are mistakenly called "Panama" hats. French fries aren't from France, either.

/ /

FALLACY: Leningrad used to be in the Soviet Union; now it's in Russia.
FACT: Leningrad isn't anywhere anymore. In 1914, the city's name was changed from Saint Petersburg to Petrograd. In 1924, the city's name was changed from Petrograd to Leningrad. In 1991, the city's name was changed from Leningrad to Saint Petersburg.

/ /

FALLACY: Skunks live on all the continents except Antarctica.
FACT: Skunks don't live on the African continent. Skunks don't live on the Australian continent. Skunks don't live on the Eurasian continent. That doesn't leave many.

/ /

FALLACY: The only vehicles with right-hand-drive made in the United States are for export.
FACT: Worldwide, one of the biggest customers for right-hand-drive vehicles made in the United States is the U.S. Postal Service. For most drivers, it's best to be near the middle of the road so as to get a better view of the whole road. That's why motorists in countries with standard right-hand-drive, drive on the left of the road. For people delivering mail to boxes on the side of the road, though, it's best to be near the side of the road.

/ /

FALLACY: The Canary Islands were named for the canaries that live there.
FACT: The Canary Islands, off the northwest coast of Africa, did not get their name from that bird. Quite the opposite. The small finches

we call canaries are abundant there, and were named for the islands. Our word *canary* comes from the Latin *Insulae Canariae*, which means "Dog Islands." Although no doubt impressed by the wild songbirds, the Romans were much more impressed by the large number of wild dogs living on the islands. Among the best known of the many islands, which have roughly 3,000 square miles of land surface and comprise two Spanish provinces, are Grand Canary, Palma, and Tenerife.

//

FALLACY: On a ship, "eight bells" means 8:00 A.M.

FACT: A ship's bell is rung eight times to announce any of these: 12:00 A.M. or P.M., 4:00 A.M. or P.M., 8:00 A.M. or P.M. After the eight bells at midnight, the daily cycle goes to one bell at 12:30 A.M., adds one bell for each half hour until it reaches eight bells at 4:00 A.M., then goes back to one bell at 4:30 A.M.

//

FALLACY: The language spoken in the Irish parliament is Irish.

FACT: The name of Ireland's pre-English language is Gaelic. Although some of the Irish people speak Gaelic, which is a Goidelic branch of the Celtic languages, all of the Irish people speak English. The language spoken in Ireland's parliament, called the Dail, is English.

//

FALLACY: Russia is the only diamond-mining country that does not sell its diamonds through South Africa's De Beers company.

FACT: De Beers Centenary AG, based in Switzerland, handles all of De Beers's diamond-buying outside of South Africa. In 1990 it signed an agreement with the Soviet government diamond-selling organization Glavalmazzoloto, which has since been replaced by the Russian Rossalmazzoloto. For at least three decades before the signed agreement, the Soviet Union had been selling diamonds through De Beers. De Beers sells diamonds through its Central Selling Organization in London. All of the world's other major diamond-mining countries also sell their rough stones to De Beers: Angola, Australia, Botswana, Namibia, South Africa, and Zaire.

FALLACY: Because it is a communist country, China has no stock market.

FACT: One of the most despised symbols of the capitalist system, the stock market was thrown out of China in 1949 following the revolution. As part of the Chinese leadership's shift back toward capitalism, the Shanghai and Shenzhen stock exchanges were opened in 1992.

//

FALLACY: South Africa is the most populous nation in Africa.

FACT: For a number of reasons, we hear more about South Africa than we do about other African nations, but that's not because of its population of 40 million. Egypt, which is also an African country, has a population of 55 million. The most populous nation in Africa, though, is Nigeria, with 120 million.

//

FALLACY: OPEC is made up of Middle Eastern oil-producing countries.

FACT: OPEC members include a South American country, Venezuela, which was a founding member; three African countries, Algeria, Gabon, and Nigeria; and the Pacific Ocean nation of Indonesia. Ecuador was also a long-time member, joining in 1973. On 27 November 1992, Ecuador became the first oil-producing country to leave OPEC, saying that it could not afford the annual $4 million in dues and other costs.

9

Medicine

FALLACY: Doctors learn Latin in medical school.
FACT: Students learn a few Latin phrases and abbreviations in medical school, but not the language itself. Latin is no more a requirement for a medical degree than is legible handwriting.

//

FALLACY: The only ways to remove a tattoo are burning, freezing, or plastic surgery.
FACT: Those are the traditional methods, always painful and often scarring. The Food and Drug Administration approved a new laser technique in 1992 that works on blue and black tattoo dyes. Using very short bursts, it doesn't create enough heat to damage skin. This will be of particular interest to people with a name tattooed on some part of their body, who are currently interested in someone with a different name.

//

FALLACY: Because of worldwide health programs, very few people die of malaria any more.
FACT: In spite of worldwide health programs, notably a major effort by the United Nations, more than 100 million people are infected with malaria by mosquitoes each year. The death rate from malaria has dropped, but even now about 1.5 million people die from it each year.

FALLACY: Although not a serious medical problem, heartburn is caused by a condition that irritates the bottom of the heart.

FACT: From the bottom of my heart: heartburn has nothing to do with the heart. Medically, it's gastroesophageal reflux, which defines both its cause and its location: a regurgitation of acid from stomach into esophagus.

//

FALLACY: Humans see the universe as it is.

FACT: Light, usually reflected, reaches receptors in the eye where it triggers nerve cells. Those cells send chemically moderated electrical impulses along nerve pathways: the light itself does not travel along those pathways. When they reach the brain, the electrical impulses are translated into symbols that are understood as light and color and form. Humans are incapable of directly experiencing the universe. Not only light, but every incoming stimulus, must be translated into a form that the brain can comprehend. By definition, any stimulus that cannot be translated cannot be comprehended.

//

FALLACY: Mother and father are equally responsible for the sex of their child.

FACT: The mother donates an X chromosome. The father donates either an X or a Y. Two Xs result in a female; an X and a Y in a male. Since only the father can donate a Y, the father is 100 percent responsible for the sex of their child.

//

FALLACY: The best thing to do for frostbite is to rub snow on it.

FACT: About the worst thing you could do for frostbite is to rub snow on it. Any type of rubbing, even by a person's hands, can cause serious skin damage. Add the abrasive power of snow crystals and you compound the damage. The second problem with using snow is that you want to gently warm the frostbitten skin, and snow is by definition below the freezing point of water. Best bets are to blow warm air on the frostbitten area or, if possible, to get it next to warm skin. Armpits are a good place to put your hands, but you could do yourself an injury trying to put your feet there.

FALLACY: You can't get too many vitamins.

FACT: You can get too much of anything. Excessive amounts of most water-soluble vitamins are excreted, but fat-soluble vitamins such as A and D can build to toxic levels. Eating polar-bear liver, an extremely concentrated source of vitamin A, can be fatal.

↗↗

FALLACY: Most people worldwide who have the AIDS virus got it from homosexual sex or drug needles.

FACT: Worldwide, about 15 percent of people infected with HIV, the AIDS virus, got it from homosexual sex. About 7 percent were infected through intravenous-drug needles. Another 5 percent got it from tainted blood products. More than 70 percent of people infected with the AIDS virus got it from heterosexual sex.

↗↗

FALLACY: Nothing available in a drugstore can kill the AIDS virus.

FACT: Most spermicides and some condoms available in drugstores contain nonoxynol-9. In laboratory tests, this chemical has killed not only sperm but HIV (human immunodeficiency virus), which causes AIDS. It is also effective against the organisms that cause gonorrhea, herpes, syphilis, trichomoniasis, and possibly chlamydia. Nonoxynol-9 will not eliminate HIV once the virus has entered the blood, but using condoms and vaginal spermicides containing nonoxynol-9 will greatly reduce the chances of infection.

↗↗

FALLACY: Within the field of medicine, Ear, Eye, Nose, and Throat are four separate specialties.

FACT: Eye doctors have a specialty all their own: Ophthalmology, which covers diseases and surgery of the eye. Ear, Nose, and Throat doctors all belong to the same specialty. The words *Ear, Nose,* and *Throat* are obviously too small and simple to justify large and complicated bills, so the specialty is officially called Otorhinolaryngology. Trying to spell that word as you read it will send you to an ophthalmologist; trying to pronounce that word will send you to an otorhinolaryngologist.

FALLACY: An extreme mental shock can turn someone's hair white overnight.

FACT: It's an extreme mental shock that anyone still believes this. The color of a strand of hair starts at its root and gradually grows outward. Unless the shock caused the person to grow an entire new head of hair overnight, the color couldn't change.

/ /

FALLACY: Blue peter is a venereal disease.

FACT: *Blue peter* is a naval term, referring to a blue flag with a white square in its center. When a ship hoists the blue peter it is signaling that it is ready to sail. In the International Code of Symbols, a blue flag with a white square is the symbol for the letter *P*.

/ /

FALLACY: Perfect vision is 20/20.

FACT: Normal vision is 20/20. What the numbers mean is that a person can see at twenty feet what it is normal to see at twenty feet (letters on an eye chart, for example). If a person can see only at twenty feet what it is normal to see at fifty feet, that person has 20/50 vision. If a person has sharper than normal eyesight, however, and can see at twenty feet what it is normal to see only at ten feet, that person has 20/10 vision. See?

/ /

FALLACY: Feed a cold, starve a fever.

FACT: That bit of folk wisdom has been around for a long time. Doesn't make it true, though. To fight off any infection, your body needs nutrition. There's no definitive rule on this one, but the best rule of thumb seems to be: Drink a lot of liquids (alcohol, coffee, and tea don't count), and eat what appeals to you. Your body often knows what it needs, and what it doesn't need. As with a pregnancy, a cold or a fever may call for some unusual gustatorial combinations. Anyone for pickles and chicken soup?

FALLACY: Penicillin is bread mold.

FACT: Penicillin is a general term for a whole group of broad-spectrum antibiotic drugs that are effective against gram-positive bacteria. Penicillin can be produced synthetically in a laboratory, or from bluish green molds (fungi) of the genus *Penicillium*, which grow mainly on over-ripe fruit and ripening cheese. Although penicillin can be produced from *Penicillium* molds, the molds are not penicillin. You can get rid of that green loaf of bread in your kitchen.

//

FALLACY: Heating water to the boiling point, and keeping it there for a few minutes, will kill any bacteria.

FACT: Water boils at 100° Centigrade. Heating water to the boiling point, and keeping it there for a few minutes, will kill *most* bacteria. There are bacteria, however, that not only survive at temperatures up to 110° C, but actually grow. Bacteria discovered in deep-sea sediments at hot-water vents in the Guaymas Basin in the Gulf of California actually grow best in water between 103° C and 106° C. Unless you're getting your drinking water from a deep-sea hot-water vent, though, boiling it for a few minutes will do the job.

//

FALLACY: The condom was invented by Dr. Condom.

FACT: Dr. Charles Condom of England may have contributed his name to it, but the condom was in use under other names long, long before he was born in 1630.

//

FALLACY: Schizophrenics have split personalities.

FACT: Schizophrenia refers to a large group of serious mental illnesses (psychoses), characterized by withdrawal from reality and often involving delusions or hallucinations. Current research indicates that schizophrenia may have a genetic basis, and is related to dopamine levels in the brain. Schizophrenia does not refer specifically to split or multiple personalities, which is a category of its own: multiple personality disorder. The huge majority of people suffering from schizophrenia do not have split personalities.

FALLACY: If you eat enough food, you won't get constipated.

FACT: Depends entirely on what kind of food. You could eat a huge amount of low-fiber food and become very constipated. Fiber and fluid are what count. Insoluble fiber found in such things as wheat bran absorbs water, providing bulk and stimulating the process of elimination. As for the speed at which food moves through the gastrointestinal tract, fast food is just the opposite.

/ /

FALLACY: When medical thermometers aren't being used, they register room temperature.

FACT: Two problems with that. First, a higher temperature can cause the mercury to rise, but a lower temperature can't cause it to drop. The tube that holds the mercury has a constriction just above the bulb at the bottom; that constriction keeps the mercury from dropping until the thermometer is shaken down. Second, it would have to be a very hot room to make the temperature rise; the scale on a typical medical thermometer runs from a low of 96° Fahrenheit to a high of 106°F.

/ /

FALLACY: Cancer is the leading cause of death in the United States.

FACT: The leading cause of death in the United States is heart disease, accounting for about a third of all deaths. Cancer is second, followed by stroke. The death rate from heart disease has been declining steadily, but the death rate from cancer has been rising.

/ /

FALLACY: Circumcision is a routine medical procedure in most of the Western world.

FACT: Circumcision is based on religious tradition, not on medical necessity. It became fashionable in this country around the turn of the century, then became so routine that most parents didn't even think about it. For those parents who did think about it, the argument was that they wouldn't want their boy to look different from the majority. About 55 percent of the male newborns in the United States are still circumcised, but the percentage has been dropping for two decades. It is a painful operation, usually performed without anesthetic. The United States is the only Western country where the procedure is commonly performed for other than religious reasons. In Australia, Canada, and most of Europe, the rate is about 30 percent. Circumcision is sometimes called the unkindest cut of all.

FALLACY: The best thing to drink when your mouth is burning from hot peppers is plain old water.
FACT: The best thing to drink when your mouth is burning from hot peppers is plain old milk. The substance doing the burning is capsaicin, which binds to receptors in your mouth. The main protein in milk, casein, clears the receptors and stops the burning. Water will momentarily cool your mouth, but it won't remove the capsaicin, so the burning comes right back. If you don't have milk quickly to hand, chomp on some cheese—it also contains casein.

FALLACY: Polio was eradicated in the United States in the 1960s.
FACT: Polio, previously called infantile paralysis, is caused by the *Poliomyelitis* virus, and viruses are notoriously difficult to eradicate. The first major polio epidemic hit the United States in 1916, killing 6,000 children and paralyzing 27,000 more. The nationwide epidemics were finally brought to a halt by the development of two vaccines: Salk's in 1955, and Sabin's, which replaced it in 1961. These vaccines can prevent polio, but there is so far no drug that can cure it. The effect of the vaccines was dramatic. According to the federal Centers for Disease Control and Prevention (CDC), there were 33,300 reported cases in 1950; 3,190 in 1960; 33 in 1970; 9 in 1980; 7 in 1985; and none in 1990. But that's only one small part of the story. The Pan American Health Organization began a program in 1985 to eliminate polio from the Americas. On August 23, 1991, one case of polio was reported in Peru. As of August 23, 1992, there had not been a single new case anywhere in the Western Hemisphere. It is too early, though, to say that polio has been eradicated in the Americas. On the other half of the planet, polio still strikes 120,000 people each year. The United Nations World Health Organization has a goal of eliminating polio worldwide by the year 2000.

FALLACY: Fish is brain food.
FACT: Most people who still believe that attribute it to B-complex vitamins in fish, but originally it was attributed to phosphorus. Although fish have some of each, there are many foods that have much more. The brain is a very complicated organ and requires a wide range of minerals and vitamins to function; there is no specific "brain food." Fish, by the way, are not noted for their intelligence.

//

FALLACY: You can get warts from handling toads.
FACT: Although toads do not like to be handled, and probably wish you could get warts from handling them, you can't. Warts are caused by viruses.

//

FALLACY: Female circumcision is used in some cultures for sanitary and medical reasons.
FACT: There is no such thing as female circumcision. The term is sometimes mistakenly applied to genital mutilation, including removal of the clitoris, the inner or outer labia, or all of those. There is no sanitary or medical justification for this genital mutilation, which is used in some parts of the world to prevent women from enjoying sex.

//

FALLACY: You shouldn't drink milk when you have a cold, because milk causes the body to produce mucus.
FACT: Drinking milk has no effect on the production of mucus. A scientific experiment at the University of Adelaide, Australia, measured the mucus production of volunteers who had colds. Two-thirds of the volunteers believed that milk had such an effect. Measurements before, during, and after drinking milk showed no increased mucus production.

//

FALLACY: A loss of circulation causes a hand or a foot or whatever to "fall asleep."

FACT: The "falling asleep" effect is caused by pressure on nerves, not on blood vessels. Sensation returning to the temporarily restricted nerves causes the tingling sensation. Loss of blood circulation has far different, and far more serious, symptoms.

//

FALLACY: The military and some boys' schools slip saltpeter into food because it causes temporary impotence.

FACT: The name itself probably helped to create this myth. Saltpeter does not cause impotence, or affect sexual drive or performance in any other way. Saltpeter is sodium nitrate or potassium nitrate. The word comes from the Latin *sal petra*, which means nothing more sinister than "salt of the rock."

//

FALLACY: Salmonella bacteria, which cause food poisoning, got their name from spoiled salmon.

FACT: Salmonella bacteria got their name from Daniel E. Salmon, an American veterinarian. People most often get salmonella from eggs, milk, or poultry, not from salmon. That noble fish is often blamed, but innocent.

//

FALLACY: The most frequent cosmetic surgery for women in the United States is a face-lift.

FACT: The most frequent cosmetic or plastic surgery for women in the United States is liposuction, popularly known as "fat sucking." More than 100,000 liposuction operations were performed on women in 1991. The second most frequent process is collagen injections, usually to plump out wrinkles; the effect lasts only a few months. The collagen is extracted from cattle hide and, according to some critics, is injected back into the same.

//

FALLACY: Muscle spasms that wake you up are a sign that something's wrong with you.

FACT: Muscle spasms that wake you up are a sign that you're normal. Actually, there are two different types of muscle spasms associated with sleep. The one that strikes just as you're drifting off is called a hypnic jerk, and often occurs in the legs. No one is certain why they occur, but it might be as simple as a major muscle system suddenly tightening and then relaxing, so as to release residual tension. The other type, called a myoclonic jerk, happens routinely while you're sound asleep. Although some people who wake you might justly be called jerks, myoclonic jerks usually go unnoticed, and rarely wake you.

//

FALLACY: All vegetable oils are more healthful than animal fats because vegetable oils are unsaturated.

FACT: "Oil" and "fat" are interchangeable here. Generally, an unsaturated fat is liquid at room temperature; a saturated fat is solid. Hydrogenating an oil makes it more solid and more saturated. Liquid corn oil, for example, is less saturated than hydrogenated corn-oil margarine in a tub, and that is less saturated than a solid stick of corn-oil margarine. Many vegetable fats are unsaturated, but a few are very highly saturated. Among the worst are the tropical oils—coconut oil, palm oil, and palm kernel oil—which are as highly saturated as some animal fats. Humans, who consider themselves the wisest of animals, take liquid corn oil and hydrogenate it to make it solid, then take that saturated fat and put it on hot food to make it liquid.

//

FALLACY: Some people are double-jointed.

FACT: In its proper location, each of us has one joint. Just one. There is no such thing as a double-jointed person. People who can perform those amazing feats of movement simply have ligaments that are longer than average.

//

FALLACY: The heart is on the left side of the chest.

FACT: The center of the heart in most people is in the center of the chest. The human heart is not completely symmetrical, and a small portion at the bottom curves slightly to the left. That's all, though. A straight line through the breastbone would go through the middle of the heart.

//

FALLACY: Los Angeles was the first major city to distribute condoms to its high school students.
FACT: The debate took more than two years, but when the Los Angeles Unified School District finally began the practice in 1992, it was not the first. Other major cities that already distributed condoms to their high school students included New York, Philadelphia, and San Francisco.

//

FALLACY: Cold-remedy ads refer to "post-nasal drip," but never to "pre-nasal drip" because there is no such thing.
FACT: Sure there is. It's called a runny nose.

//

FALLACY: Petroleum jelly is not a petroleum product.
FACT: Petroleum jelly is a common name for petrolatum, which is gelatinous and ranges in color from clear to amber. Petrolatum is obtained from petroleum; both names are derived from the same Latin root. The best known trademarked brand of white petrolatum is Vaseline.

//

FALLACY: Milk is good for heartburn and ulcers.
FACT: Milk is not good for either heartburn or ulcers. Although it gives momentary relief because it dilutes the stomach contents and because it contains the antacid calcium, it also contains protein. To digest protein, more acid is pumped into the stomach. More acid is the last thing you want. Better to take calcium without milk's other ingredients.

//

FALLACY: The funny bone is another name for the elbow bone.
FACT: The funny bone is not a bone. What you're hitting when you get that electricitylike jolt is the ulnar nerve, which crosses the elbow.

FALLACY: Being cold and wet can cause you to catch a cold.
FACT: The only thing that can cause you to catch a cold is a virus; specifically, a type of picornavirus called a rhinovirus. One reason why people catch colds more often in the winter is that they're packed together indoors, so the virus is more easily transmitted. You can get as cold as you want and as wet as you want, but if the virus isn't present, you cannot catch a cold. A rhinovirus is considerably smaller than a rhinoceros; the only connection between them is the root *rhino*, which means "nose."

//

FALLACY: People who are bitten by a black widow spider die unless they can get to a doctor.
FACT: People definitely have died from the bite of a black widow spider; the young, the old, and the ill are particularly susceptible. The vast majority of people bitten, though, do not die, even if they receive no treatment.

//

FALLACY: Rubbing butter or oil on a burn will help it.
FACT: The best thing you can put on a burn is cool water. Hold it under a running tap for about five minutes, or as long as it takes for the burning sensation to go away. That will minimize the damage, and speed healing. And no, you don't put oil or butter on it after the cool water.

//

FALLACY: All blood is red.
FACT: It's true that there's no such thing as a "blue blood" human. That was just a notion of some people who mistakenly thought that they were better than other people. To be true blue-bloods they'd have to be lobsters, which do have blue blood. Insects don't have either red blood or blue blood; many of them have yellow or white blood.

FALLACY: Malaria is named for the doctor who discovered its cause.
FACT: Malaria is named that because the people who named it were very mistaken about its cause. The word comes from the Italian *mala aira*, "bad air." Before it was discovered that the disease was transmitted by female *Anopheles* mosquitoes, many people believed that it was caused by breathing bad air.

///

FALLACY: Whiskey is a snakebite remedy.
FACT: Antivenin is a snakebite remedy. Removing the venom is a snakebite remedy. Whiskey is not only not a snakebite remedy, it will make the situation worse. The last thing you want is to cause the venom to spread more rapidly. Alcohol causes blood vessels to dilate, and speeds the venom through the system.

///

FALLACY: Only antibiotics from a doctor can cure a cold, and they usually won't give them to you because they don't want you to build up an immunity to the antibiotics.
FACT: What do doctors take to treat a cold? About $50. No doctor knows of any antibiotic that will cure a cold. Colds are caused by viruses. Antibiotics work against bacteria, but not against viruses. Doctors will give you antibiotics for pneumonia, however, because that is caused by bacteria. If you have both a cold and pneumonia, antibiotics will work against the pneumonia bacteria, but not against the cold viruses. That's a good arrangement: it's better to suffer from a cold than to die from pneumonia.

///

FALLACY: Food is digested in the stomach.
FACT: Very little digestion takes place in the stomach. The stomach is a place where food is broken down, mainly by hydrochloric acid, into a digestible mass. That mass then moves on to the small intestine, and several hours later to the large intestine. It is in the small intestine, consisting of the duodenum, jejunum, and ileum, that most of the digestion occurs.

FALLACY: A good sneeze can reach speeds up to 50 miles per hour.

FACT: Although some unofficial ones would doubtless blow this record away, sneezes have been scientifically clocked at up to 104 miles per hour.

//

FALLACY: Once a woman has delivered a baby by Caesarean section, any subsequent deliveries must also be by Caesarean section.

FACT: That belief arose fairly recently, and is rapidly declining. In 1970 only 5.5 percent of births in this country were by Caesarean section. It was 24.7 percent in 1988, when the American College of Obstetricians and Gynecologists issued a statement saying that women who had had a Caesarean section should deliver subsequent children by normal, vaginal birth. According to the federal Centers for Disease Control and Prevention (CDC), 23.5 percent of all births in 1991 were by Caesarean section, and 349,000 of those 966,000 operations were unnecessary. C-sections are more convenient, seldom being scheduled on holidays, weekends, or at odd hours. Since they involve major surgery, they are also more dangerous, and much more costly.

//

FALLACY: Typhoid fever is caused by typhus.

FACT: The two are often confused because of the similarity of names and of some symptoms. They are two separate infectious diseases, however, caused by two different agents. Typhoid fever is caused by *Salmonella typhosa,* and is usually contracted from someone who has it, or from food or water that they've handled. Typhoid Mary, for example, was a food-service worker. Typhus is caused by rickettsia, and is carried by lice. Unlike typhoid fever, typhus is usually fatal if not treated.

//

FALLACY: Herbal tea is better for you than regular tea.

FACT: Officially, the only tea plant is the shrub *Camellia sinensis,* of eastern Asia. Unofficially, practically anything steeped in water makes a tea. As many a gardener knows, one of the best things for a growing plant is manure tea. Herbal teas usually have no caffeine, and many of them have beneficial ingredients. Some traditional ingredients, however, are definitely not better for you than those in regular tea. Large amounts of germander or of comfrey, for example, can cause liver damage. Lobelia can be an emetic, causing vomiting. Melilot, tonka beans, and woodruff contain anticoagulants, which thin the blood and can cause bleeding.

//

FALLACY: Drinking milk or oil before drinking alcohol will coat the stomach and keep you from getting drunk.
FACT: Neither milk nor oil will "coat the stomach" to prevent absorption of ethyl alcohol, most of which is absorbed from the intestines in any event. Eating something will slow emptying of the stomach, and drinking something nonalcoholic will dilute the ethanol, but nothing will keep you from getting drunk if you drink too much alcohol.

//

FALLACY: A headache is the brain feeling pain.
FACT: The brain cannot feel pain, because it has no pain receptors. The pain you feel in your head is caused by receptors in structures outside the brain, most commonly blood vessels or the covering of the brain (dura mater). As long suspected by cynics, comedians, and other astute observers, the human brain is numb.

//

FALLACY: Sterilization is the least-used form of birth control.
FACT: Although sterilization is not widely used by unmarried women in the United States, nearly one in four married American women has undergone the procedure. Because marriage rates are higher in Third World countries, female sterilization accounts for 26 percent of all human contraception, making it the most-used form of birth control. Male sterilization accounts for 19 percent of all contraception, and oral contraceptives for 15 percent.

FALLACY: Green apples will give you a stomachache.

FACT: Although green apples taste tart, there is nothing in them that will give you a stomachache. That tall tale may first have been told by a farmer trying to protect his apple crop between the end of school and the beginning of harvest. The only thing worse than finding a worm in the apple you've just bitten into is finding half a worm.

//

FALLACY: Tuberculosis is virtually extinct in the United States.

FACT: Tuberculosis was once the leading cause of death among Americans, but declined rapidly after the 1944 discovery of streptomycin. By the 1970s it seemed headed for extinction in this country, although it was still rampant elsewhere on the planet. Then, after three decades of decline, the number of new cases in the United States rose 2 percent in 1986. In 1990, 25,701 new cases of tuberculosis were reported, a 15 percent increase over 1985. In 1991, 26,283 new cases were reported. Every state reported cases of tuberculosis in 1991; drug-resistant strains of *Mycobacterium tuberculosis* were reported in more than thirty-five states, including Florida, Michigan, Mississippi, Missouri, and New York. Worldwide, there are about 8 million new cases of tuberculosis each year, and about 3 million people die of it.

//

FALLACY: Only surgery will get rid of liver spots.

FACT: First off, liver spots have nothing to do with the liver. They're caused by lifelong exposure to sunlight, which prompts cells below the skin to produce excess pigment. They are completely harmless; they are also difficult to remove. Most creams do not work, and for cosmetic reasons thousands of people each year have them removed surgically. Recent research suggests that there's another way for those who feel the need to remove them. A prescription skin cream containing Tretinoin, commercially known as Retin-A, will not only fade the spots but will inhibit the pigment production that causes them.

//

FALLACY: AIDS is like a modern Black Death.

FACT: The Black Death was a highly contagious disease, bubonic plague, transmitted by rat fleas. Since both the cause (a bacterium) and the means of transmission were unknown, it was virtually impossible to defend against catching it. Both the cause (the human immunodeficiency virus, HIV) and the means of transmission of AIDS are known. The only way to catch AIDS is by getting body fluids from an infected person into your body fluids.

//

FALLACY: Women have always outlived men.
FACT: For most of human history, men outlived women. It wasn't until this century, when the death rate from childbirth dropped precipitously, that women began to outlive men.

//

FALLACY: Smallpox vaccinations are required in some states before a child can be enrolled in school, and are necessary before traveling to some parts of the world.
FACT: Smallpox vaccinations are no longer required anywhere, for anyone. The last smallpox death (from an escaped lab sample) occurred in England in 1978; the last smallpox case was found and cured in Somalia in 1979. The U.N. World Health Organization declared smallpox extinct in nature as of 1980. Smallpox virus is now known to exist only at the Research Institute for Virus Preparations in Moscow, and the Centers for Disease Control and Prevention (CDC) in Atlanta. Scientists are working to sequence smallpox's DNA and store it on computer. Once that is done, the last smallpox virus on Earth may be destroyed.

//

FALLACY: Reading in dim light, too-bright light, or in unusual positions will harm your eyes.
FACT: The worst thing that reading in dim light may cause is a bit of eye strain, which is neither dangerous nor permanent. The same is true of reading in very bright light, or in unusual positions. And if reading under the covers with a flashlight were harmful, a large percentage of us would have been blind before we got out of our teens.

10

Science

FALLACY: The black box on an airplane is black.
FACT: The black box or flight data recorder on an airplane is orange, which makes it easier to find in case of an accident. It's called a black box because it's sealed and no one on the airplane can open it. A black box has no relation to a black hole, which is strictly for luggage.

/ /

FALLACY: There's no scientific answer to the question, Which came first, the chicken or the egg?
FACT: There's a definite scientific answer. The egg came first. Dinosaurs were laying eggs millions of years before the first chicken evolved. We're talking a *big* omelet here.

/ /

FALLACY: No American vehicle—other than an airplane—really gets such bad mileage that it's measured in gallons per mile.
FACT: The M-1 tank uses about two gallons per mile. Some models, weighing in at more than 120,000 pounds, use about five gallons per mile. The space shuttle transporter, which moves the shuttle from the vehicle assembly building to the launch pad, uses more than 500 gallons per mile. Doesn't your car's mileage sound a lot better now?

FALLACY: 12:15 P.M. is later than 10:15 P.M.

FACT: Anyone who can add 1 and 1 knows that 12 is two numbers past 10, but that doesn't always work in the magic world of time. 12:15 P.M. is *earlier* than 10:15 P.M. The 12:15 that comes two hours later than 10:15 P.M. is 12:15 A.M. Tempus fidgets.

//

FALLACY: Antimatter is strictly a matter of science fiction.

FACT: Antimatter not only exists, it is used in laboratory experiments. The antimatter equivalent of an electron, for example, is called an antielectron or a positron. When an electron and a positron collide they annihilate each other, releasing a huge amount of energy, which in turn generates elementary particles. The existence of the positron was first predicted by Paul Dirac and Erwin Schrödinger long before the first particle was actually detected in 1932; Dirac and Schrödinger shared the 1933 Nobel Prize in physics. Although particle accelerators have created antimatter counterparts to nearly all of the normal particles, combining them into antimatter *atoms* is another matter entirely. The simplest possible atom is hydrogen, which has one proton and one electron; work is already underway on creating an atom of antihydrogen.

//

FALLACY: A barrel is 30 gallons.

FACT: Depends on what kind of barrel you're talking about. In the U.S. Customary System a barrel of wine is 31.5 gallons, a barrel of beer is 36 gallons, and a barrel of oil is 42 gallons. You've got me over a barrel, though, when it comes to the capacity of a barrel of monkeys.

//

FALLACY: The Manhattan Project was carried out in Manhattan.

FACT: That would have been very messy, indeed. The Manhattan Project was the United States' original project to build nuclear weapons. Begun in 1942, it had facilities in several states, including Illinois, New Mexico, Tennessee, and Washington. On 2 December 1942, in a squash court under Stagg Field at the University of Chicago, a team led by Enrico Fermi created the first controlled, self-sustained nuclear chain reaction. The bombs were designed and constructed by a team of scientists headed by J. Robert Oppenheimer at Los Alamos, New Mexico. The world's first atomic bomb was exploded near Alamagordo, New Mexico, on 16 July 1945. Manhattan's streets may be dangerous, but they're not *that* dangerous.

/ /

FALLACY: Nonchlorine laundry brighteners bleach just as well as chlorine.

FACT: Although there are peroxides in some nonchlorine brighteners, the main brightening effect does not come from bleaching. Chlorine bleaches out the yellowish color that darkens both whites and colors. Nonchlorine brighteners add blue coloring to the clothes, to cancel out the yellow.

/ /

FALLACY: Computer chips are made from silicone.

FACT: Computer chips are made from silicon. Silicon is an element, Si, common in the silica of Earth's crust. Silicone is a polymer based on R_2SiO, where R is an organic group, Si is silicon, and O is oxygen. Silicone is what plastic surgeons used to make mountains out of molehills. Easy way to remember the difference: silicon makes computer chips; silicone makes silly cones.

/ /

FALLACY: Mastodon is the scientific name for what's popularly called a mammoth.

FACT: Mastodon refers to any of several Oligocene animals found in Africa that belonged to the extinct genus *Mammut*. They were considerably different from mammoths and from modern elephants. Mammoth refers to any of several Pleistocene animals found in Eurasia and North America that belonged to the extinct genus *Mammuthus*. Although mammoths were elephants, and the largest of the prehistoric elephants, they were not direct ancestors of today's elephants.

/ /

FALLACY: There are hundreds of different types of force in nature.

FACT: As scientific method has uncovered more and more of nature's secrets, what appeared to be hundreds of different types of force have turned out to be variations of just a few fundamental forces. Electricity and magnetism, for example, were found to be different manifestations of what is now called electromagnetism. The four forces of nature recognized today are: strong and weak, which act within an atom's nucleus; electromagnetic; and gravitational. The current goal is to unite the first three of those in a Grand Unified Theory. Ideally, the gravitational force would then be added, but that's beyond today's theoretical horizon.

//

FALLACY: Alfred Nobel, who established the Nobel Prizes, invented nitroglycerin.

FACT: It's commonly believed that Swedish chemist Alfred Bernhard Nobel invented nitroglycerin, $CH_2(NO_3)CH(NO_3)CH_2(NO_3)$, but he didn't. It was invented by Ascanio Sobrero. Nitroglycerin is highly unstable and sensitive to both heat and shock, and while it makes a very satisfying explosion, it tends to go off at unexpected and therefore inconvenient times. To make his fame and fortune, Nobel devised a way to make the touchy explosive safe to use. He poured it into absorbent and inert materials such as sawdust, inventing an explosive that was safe to handle and to transport: dynamite.

//

FALLACY: When you buy a container of something in a store, it weighs less after it's empty than it did when it was full.

FACT: If you buy a balloon filled with helium, it will weigh more after it's empty. Helium weighs less than even fondly remembered clean air.

//

FALLACY: The transistor, and the transistor radio, were invented in Japan.

FACT: A transistor contains a semiconductor and at least three electrical contacts, and is used in a circuit. The name comes from trans(fer) (res)istor. The transistor revolution definitely spread outward from Japan, but that's not where the transistor was born. The transistor was invented in the United States, at Bell Laboratories division of American Telephone and Telegraph, in 1947. The first transistor radio, named TR-1, was made by the Regency division of IDEA for Texas Instruments in 1954. The first Japanese transistor was made by Tokyo Telecommunications in 1954. The first Japanese transistor radio, named Sony, was made by Tokyo Telecommunications in 1955. It was so popular worldwide that in 1957 Tokyo Telecommunications changed its name to Sony.

FALLACY: *Quark* is a nonsense word made up to name subatomic particles.
FACT: The word *quark* comes from James Joyce's *Finnegans Wake*: "Three quarks for Muster Mark!" In physics, a quark is an elementary particle that carries a fractional electrical charge. Among the six types of quarks, also imaginatively named, are the strange quark and the charmed quark.

FALLACY: Most American homes have a hot-water heater.
FACT: Very few, if any, American homes have a hot-water heater. They do have water heaters, though. Why heat water that is already hot?

FALLACY: Food laced with ground glass is a good way to kill a person.
FACT: Ground glass would probably taste gritty, but it would be harmless. Like other forms of indigestible matter that we eat, it would simply be eliminated. Ground glass has no sharp edges. Glass shards would do harm, but nobody is going to eat food laced with them.

FALLACY: Einstein won many Nobel Prizes, including those for his theories of gravity, general relativity, special relativity, and quantum mechanics.
FACT: Albert Einstein, whose many theories revolutionized phys-

ics and our view of the universe, won no Nobel Prizes for his work on gravity, general relativity, special relativity, or quantum mechanics. He won a grand total of one Nobel Prize: for his work on the photoelectric effect.

//

FALLACY: Stealth aircraft are hidden from radar by their shape and the use of nonmetallic materials, not by their paint job.

FACT: The shape of stealth aircraft, specifically avoiding any sharp angles, lowers their radar reflectivity. The use of nonmetallic materials also helps. Their paint job, however, does play a very significant role in hiding them from radar. The coating is made of three layers: two ferrite layers, with a dielectric layer sandwiched between them. Radar waves pass through the outer layer, then reflect between the two ferrite layers; the dielectric layer slows them just enough for the incoming waves and the outgoing waves to meet peak-to-trough, canceling each other.

//

FALLACY: Diamonds, rubies, and sapphires are valuable because of what they're made of.

FACT: Diamonds are made of carbon, the same thing that coal is made of. Rubies and sapphires are both made of aluminum oxide, the same thing that a common abrasive often used on sandpaper is made of.

//

FALLACY: Bell's telephone was accepted as a scientific breakthrough.

FACT: Alexander Graham Bell's telephone was hardly accepted at all. He patented it in 1876, and then offered to sell it to the Western Union Telegraph Company for $100,000. Western Union's president, William Orton said, "What use could this company make of an electrical toy?" Also in 1876, U.S. president Rutherford B. Hayes took part in a telephone call between Washington and Philadelphia. His comment after the call: "That's an amazing invention, but who would ever want to use one of them?" It was during this time that the phrase "Bell's Folly" became popular.

FALLACY: Aluminum doesn't rust.

FACT: Scratch a piece of aluminum. That shiny scratch will soon be gone, covered by aluminum oxide (rust). When iron combines with oxygen and forms rust (iron oxide), the process continues until the entire piece of iron is oxidized to rust. The handy thing about aluminum rust is that it seals the surface, keeping oxygen away from the aluminum inside. Aluminum is useful not because it doesn't rust, but because it rusts so well.

//

FALLACY: After the Chernobyl nuclear power plant disaster in Russia, the whole plant was decontaminated and buried in concrete.

FACT: The Chernobyl nuclear power plant, then in the Soviet Union and now in Ukraine, had four nuclear reactors. On 26 April 1986, Unit 4 reactor exploded, heavily contaminating the Soviet republics of Ukraine and Byelorussia, and sending radioactive clouds as high as fifty thousand feet to spread contamination around the world. To stop the contamination, Unit 4 reactor was encased in a 300,000-ton concrete sarcophagus (*Ukritiye*) with the highly radioactive material still inside. The concrete has since cracked, however, so the radioactive material inside is not completely sealed: if water leaks through the sarcophagus, it will contaminate the groundwater; if the sarcophagus collapses, a dust cloud will contaminate the air. In October 1991, Unit 2 reactor was shut down when its roof was damaged by fire. During the winter of 1993/1994, Ukraine was getting more than 25 percent of its electricity from nuclear power plants, including Chernobyl's Unit 1 and Unit 3 reactors.

//

FALLACY: A pound of gold weighs the same as a pound of feathers or a pound of anything else.

FACT: There are two different systems involved here. Feathers and people and most other things are weighed with the avoirdupois system, which has a pound equal to sixteen 437.5-grain ounces or 7,000 grains. Gold is weighed with the troy system, which has a pound equal to twelve 480-grain ounces or 5,760 grains. A pound of gold weighs less than a pound of feathers or a pound of person.

FALLACY: The Richter earthquake scale goes all the way up to 10.

FACT: Although there have been no recorded earthquakes of Richter 10 or above, the Richter (M_L) scale is open-ended because it takes into account that nature can do whatever it wants. There is no upper limit to the Richter scale.

⚡⚡

FALLACY: Electronic equipment emits electromagnetic radiation; animals don't.

FACT: The electromagnetic spectrum includes, in decreasing frequency: cosmic rays, gamma rays, X rays, ultraviolet, visible light, infrared, microwaves, and radio waves. With the exception of black holes, everything in the known universe emits some form of electromagnetic radiation. Generally, animals emit in the infrared (heat); specifically, the outer surface of a human emits infrared at about 68° Fahrenheit.

⚡⚡

FALLACY: Dew is caused by moisture coming up from the ground.

FACT: The dew point is the temperature at which a vapor begins to condense. When the temperature of the air drops below its dew point, water condenses out as dew. The same process occurs when room air is cooled by contact with a window—that's dew, too.

⚡⚡

FALLACY: Arabs use Arabic numerals.

FACT: Arabs are among the few who do *not* use what we call Arabic numerals. There are symbols in the Arabic language for numbers, but with few exceptions they look nothing like the ones you're used to. "Arabic" numerals were developed in India. They passed through Arabia on their way to Europe, and Europeans mistakenly thought that those symbols had been invented by Arabs.

⚡⚡

FALLACY: Duck tape is one of the most common types of tape among home-repair supplies.

FACT: Only if the folks who live there are planning to repair ducks. Although that heavy, silver-backed tape is often referred to as duck tape, it's actually duct tape. It was originally developed for sealing joints in air ducts.

//

FALLACY: The world's first atomic explosion was on 6 August 1945, at Hiroshima.

FACT: The world's first atomic explosion was at 5:30 A.M. local time on 16 July 1945, at Trinity Site on the White Sands Proving Grounds near Alamagordo, New Mexico. The first atomic weapon used against human beings was a uranium bomb dropped on Hiroshima on 6 August 1945. The second was a plutonium bomb dropped on Nagasaki on 9 August 1945.

//

FALLACY: Typewriter and keyboard keys are arranged the way they are because that's the easiest configuration for the fingers.

FACT: They're arranged in what is known as the QWERTY pattern (first six letters on the top row of letters) because of the mechanics of the original typewriters. With manual typewriters, the letters are at the end of arms that fly forward to strike the paper. The original keys were arranged alphabetically. When a good typist got going on a typewriter whose keyboard was arranged alphabetically, the arms bumped into each other and got stuck. The QWERTY keyboard was designed to take advantage of the fact that some letters, and some letter combinations, are used more often than others. By rearranging the keys into the QWERTY pattern, which we still use today, the arms of frequently used letter combinations were moved farther apart, keeping them from hitting each other. It is by no means the easiest configuration for the fingers, and makes no difference to modern typewriters, word processors, or computers, because they have no letter arms. The main reason we still have the QWERTY system is inertia: we've had it for a long time, and current typists know it.

//

FALLACY: The ozone in smog and the ozone in the ozone layer are completely different types.

FACT: The ozone in smog is a potent, unstable, poisonous, bleaching, oxidizing agent; the ozone in the ozone layer is exactly the same molecule. It causes damage when it's at ground level, but it prevents damage when it's in the stratosphere between ten and thirty miles above ground level, protecting us from wavelengths of the Sun's ultraviolet radiation that would otherwise penetrate Earth's atmosphere. As for its family tree, ozone is not only related to oxygen—there's nothing in it *except* oxygen. The symbol for atomic oxygen (one oxygen atom) is the letter *O*. The symbol for diatomic oxygen, which makes up 21 percent of Earth's atmosphere and is the type we're after when we breathe, is O_2. The symbol for ozone, made up of three oxygen atoms, is O_3.

//

FALLACY: A billion is 1,000,000,000.
FACT: Depends on where you are. The word comes from French, meaning "a million million." In the British system, billion means 1,000,000,000,000 (10^{12})—a million million. In the United States, billion means 1,000,000,000 (10^9)—a thousand million. If you're offered a billion of something you want, take delivery in Britain.

//

FALLACY: An airplane drops suddenly when it hits an air pocket.
FACT: There is no such thing as an "air pocket." Among the many different air currents, there are updrafts and downdrafts. The sudden drop in altitude is the result of flying into a downdraft. Wind shear, on the other hand, occurs when an aircraft, changing altitude only slightly, encounters winds with radically different speed and direction.

//

FALLACY: The white tape that plumbers wrap around the end of pipes before putting them together is called plumber's tape.
FACT: The white tape that plumbers wrap around the end of pipes before putting them together is called pipe-thread tape. It's made of Teflon, and helps to form a watertight seal. Plumber's tape is made of metal, and has a line of holes down the middle. It's used to hold pipes against a wall or floor or whatever. The holes are for nails. It's called plumber's tape because except for its thickness it looks like tape, it comes in a roll, and it was developed for plumbers.

FALLACY: There's a difference of about 32° between Fahrenheit and Centigrade (Celsius) temperatures.

FACT: The conversion is easy, but not that easy. Subtract 32° from the Fahrenheit temperature, multiply by five, divide by nine, and that's the temperature in Centigrade. Going the other way, do just the reverse: multiply the Centigrade temperature by nine, divide by five, and add 32°. There's one temperature that comes out the same in both systems: −40° Fahrenheit = −40° Centigrade.

//

FALLACY: The lead in a lead pencil is lead.

FACT: If that were true, people who repeatedly wet the end of their pencil with their tongue would get lead poisoning. The "lead" in a pencil is actually a mixture of graphite and clay. The clay is a binder and hardener; the graphite makes the mark. Graphite is a soft form of carbon.

//

FALLACY: Rockets were invented in Germany during World War II.

FACT: A great deal of rocket research went on in Germany during World War II, but that's not where rockets were invented. At least nine centuries earlier the Chinese were using gunpowder-fueled rockets in combat; Europeans started using them about two centuries later. In 1750, a rocket launched from London attained an altitude of 0.71 miles. The first rocket to reach an altitude of more than a mile was launched by Reinhold Tiling in 1931 from Germany. The first to reach more than 100 miles was a German A.4, launched from Poland in 1944. The first to reach more than 1,000 miles (actually reached almost 3,000 miles) was a four-stage American rocket launched from Eniwetok Atoll in the Marshall Islands, in 1957.

//

FALLACY: Nails come in such sizes as eightpenny, tenpenny, and sixteenpenny because "penny" is an old unit of length.

FACT: It's true that the larger the number the larger the nail, but that's because of its weight, not its length. The main factor was the price of the metal involved; the heavier the nail, the more metal. When the system was devised, the number was the price for 100 of that size, and meant eight pennies for 100 of this size, sixteen pennies for 100 of that size.

✓✓

FALLACY: The atom was originally proposed as the smallest unit of matter in the eighteenth century.

FACT: The atom was originally proposed as the smallest unit of matter by the Greek philosopher Democritus, in the fourth or fifth century B.C. That theory held until the 1890s, when Joseph John Thompson discovered the first subatomic particle, the electron, which orbits the nucleus. The nucleus was later discovered to contain protons and neutrons. As we approach the twenty-first century, current theory holds that all matter in the universe is composed of twelve elementary particles: six quarks and six leptons.

✓✓

FALLACY: A rainbow contains all colors, including white and black.

FACT: There is no white or black in a rainbow. A handy mnemonic for remembering the order of colors in a rainbow is that mythical man, Roy G. Biv. The colors, in order, are: red, orange, yellow, green, blue, indigo, violet. That's what you get when you break white light into the spectrum of colors. White light is all colors; although ultraviolet is sometimes called ''black light,'' there is actually no such thing as black light.

✓✓

FALLACY: Except in Superman stories, Krypton doesn't exist.

FACT: Krypton is one of the six noble gases. The other five are helium, neon, argon, xenon, and radon. They're called ''noble'' because they're inert and refuse to interact.

✓✓

FALLACY: Fish get their oxygen by breaking down water molecules, which are made of hydrogen and oxygen.

FACT: Water molecules are, indeed, made of two hydrogen atoms and one oxygen atom. A molecular bond is very difficult to break, however, and breaking one requires a large energy investment. Fish don't do that, because they have a much easier source of oxygen. Their gills simply absorb gaseous oxygen that has been dissolved in, but is not part of, the water. Dissolved oxygen in the ocean comes from the water's interchange with the atmosphere, from underwater plants, from undersea eruptions, and from waves that mix air and water.

//

FALLACY: Teflon was invented after World War II.

FACT: Teflon (polytetrafluoroethylene) was invented quite accidentally by Roy J. Plunkett on 6 April 1938. What he was trying to come up with was a new, nontoxic coolant gas to be used in refrigerators and air conditioners. A routine experiment went wrong, and he ended up with a waxy, opaque, extremely stable material more slippery than any natural substance: Teflon. The military clamped a lid of secrecy on the new product, and the public wasn't allowed to know about it until 1946, after World War II had ended. Slippery, those military censors.

//

FALLACY: Hot water will freeze faster than cold water.

FACT: This old saw has been passed down for generations, in spite of common sense. The problem with it is that hot water must become cold water before it can freeze.

//

FALLACY: Albert Einstein had no formal training in physics.

FACT: Einstein entered the Swiss Federal Polytechnic School in 1896, studied to become a teacher of mathematics and physics, and was graduated in 1900. While studying for his Ph.D. at the University of Zurich, he worked as a clerk in the Swiss Patent Office. He received his Ph.D. in 1905, the same year that he published four revolutionary papers in the field of physics, including his special theory of relativity. His general theory of relativity was published in 1916.

FALLACY: A two-by-four piece of lumber measures two inches by four inches.

FACT: A two-by-four originally measured two inches by four inches, but now measures 1.5 inches by 3.5 inches. The difference is because lumber used to come rough-cut, and now comes smooth. In planing the wood down to make it smooth on all sides, that much is lost. A two-by-twelve is 1.5 inches by 11.25 inches, and a four-by-four is 3.5 inches by 3.5 inches.

//

FALLACY: You can't see a rainbow after sunset.

FACT: It's not only possible to see a rainbow after sunset, it's easy. And it doesn't have to be associated with a rainstorm. A rainbow is simply light broken into the visible spectrum by moisture in the air. On foggy nights in San Francisco, you can see rainbows near bright lights. Given enough moisture in the air, you can also see them on bright-moon nights.

//

FALLACY: Manholes are round because that's the easiest shape to climb through.

FACT: Given the shape of the human body, an oval or rectangular hole would be easier to climb through. Manholes are round so manhole covers cannot fall in. With a rectangle or an oval or a square, for example, the cover could be turned so that it fell through, and Halloween would be hell for the maintenance department.

//

FALLACY: Rainbows always have red as the outside arc, and violet as the inside arc.

FACT: Most of the rainbows you see have that arrangement: red as the largest arc; then, in order, orange, yellow, green, blue, indigo, and violet arcs. Those are called primary rainbows. There is always a secondary rainbow, too, although usually too faint to be seen. The colors in the secondary rainbow are exactly reversed. A rain "bow" is actually a segment of a circle. We usually see only a bow because Earth gets in the way of the rest of it.

FALLACY: The Boeing 747 Jumbo Jet has the longest wingspan of any plane built in the United States.

FACT: The Boeing 747 Jumbo Jet, which can carry 500 passengers, does have an amazing wingspan. Orville Wright's first flight lasted for 120 feet; the 747's wingspan is almost double that, at 232 feet. That's not the largest wingspan of an American-built airplane, though. Howard Hughes's H.4 Hercules flying boat, nicknamed the Spruce Goose, has a wingspan of 319 feet. It was flown only once, on November 2, 1947, by Howard Hughes himself. Long at Long Beach, California, it left by barge in October 1992 for McMinnville, Oregon, about thirty miles south of Portland, to become the main attraction of the Evergreen AirVenture Museum; when it arrived in February 1993, most of McMinnville turned out for the parade.

/ /

FALLACY: The terms for computer memory and storage are complicated.

FACT: Actually, they're very simple once you learn a few four-letter words from the metric system:

kilobyte	=	1,024 bytes
megabyte	=	1,024 kilobytes
gigabyte	=	1,024 megabytes
terabyte	=	1,024 gigabytes
petabyte	=	1,024 terabytes
exabyte	=	1,024 petabytes

Why 1,024 rather than 1,000? Because computers work with the two-part binary system, and 2^{10} (1,024) is the power of 2 closest to 1,000.

/ /

FALLACY: Most UFOs, if they exist, are flying saucers.

FACT: UFOs definitely exist, but that's exactly what they are: Unidentified Flying Objects. If one were identified as a flying saucer, it would no longer be a UFO.

/ /

FALLACY: The Centigrade (Celsius) thermometer is more scientific and more accurate than the Fahrenheit thermometer.

FACT: Actually, there is no difference in the thermometer itself. The only difference is in the scale written on it. The two scales are equally scientific. When it comes to accuracy and ease of reading the scale, though, Fahrenheit comes out ahead. The Centigrade scale, as its name says, has 100 divisions from freezing to boiling: from 0° to 100°. The Fahrenheit scale has 180 divisions between those two points: from 32° to 212°. The Centigrade scale is used in most nations and by virtually all scientists because it is a decimal scale (based on the number 10), and therefore compatible with the metric system.

//

FALLACY: Ships measure speed in knots per hour, not miles per hour.
FACT: Knots per hour is redundant. "Knot" means "nautical mile per hour." A nautical mile is an international unit equal to 1,852 meters, or 6,076.115 feet.

//

FALLACY: Phillips screws were invented to make people buy Phillips screwdrivers.
FACT: Phillips screws and Phillips screwdrivers were invented at the same time. With a regular straight-slot screw, the screwdriver can slip out at either end of the slot—and does, frequently. With the X-shaped indentation in a Phillips screw, there is no slot to slip out of.

//

FALLACY: Lightning never strikes the same place twice.
FACT: Lightning is *more* likely to strike a place it has struck before. Lightning follows the path of least resistance between cloud and ground. Within a radius of about a hundred feet it usually strikes the highest point; a person or a tree farther away than that is too far from the path for height to make much difference. A tree in an open field will be struck, and it will be struck again and again, so long as it is the tallest thing in that field. The Empire State Building is struck by lightning more than twenty times a year, but no harm is done because the metal communications tower on the roof acts as a lightning rod. Both buildings of the World Trade Center (1,362 feet and 1,368 feet) are taller than the Empire State *Building* (1,250 feet), but the communications tower goes

up another 164 feet. Standing high above the flat expanse of Upper New York Bay, the copper-sheeted Statue of Liberty is also frequently struck by lightning, usually on the upraised torch.

//

FALLACY: The major advantage of a fiber-optic cable is that it's much smaller than a copper cable.

FACT: Although a half-inch fiber-optic cable is only one-sixth as thick as a conventional three-inch copper cable, that's not its major advantage. A three-inch copper cable has 1,800 copper wires, and can carry 10,800 conversations. A half-inch fiber-optic cable has 144 glass or plastic fibers, and can carry 1,350,000 conversations. Light pulses traveling through optical fibers can carry a lot more information than electricity traveling through copper wires. An economic advantage is that light travels farther than electricity before requiring an expensive signal-boosting amplifier in the line. An advantage for users of communications devices is that light traveling through fiber optics is not affected by electrical or radio interference. In the event of a lightning strike, a fiber-optic cable will not carry a computer-frying surge.

//

FALLACY: *Median, mean*, and *average* are different words for the same thing.

FACT: Mean and average are the same. Median is something else. To get the average of a group of numbers, add them together and divide by however many numbers there are. The average of 2, 4, 7, 11, and 16, for example, is 40/5, or 8. The median is merely the middle value in a distribution. In the above series, the median is 7. Averaging some things can give interesting results; the average adult human, for example, has one breast and one testicle.

//

FALLACY: Steam is white.

FACT: Steam is colorless. When the steam cools enough for water droplets to condense, you see those condensed droplets, a cloud of which look a lot like another form of condensed water vapor: fog.

FALLACY: Just the tip of the iceberg is above water.

FACT: Would a quarter of the iceberg count as a "tip"? Depending on composition and density, anywhere from 10 percent to 15 percent of an iceberg's mass is above water—but up to 25 percent of an iceberg's height is above water. In 1986, an iceberg named A-24 broke off from the Antarctic ice sheet. It was twice the size of Rhode Island.

//

FALLACY: Petrified wood is wood that has turned to stone.

FACT: There are no conditions under which wood can turn to stone. When wood is buried under soil and water for a long time, given very special circumstances the wood is gradually replaced by minerals. The process is so slow and detailed that even the grain of the wood can be reproduced. There is no wood, however, in "petrified wood."

//

FALLACY: Only a few people understand Einstein's theories.

FACT: Any person of average intelligence can understand Einstein's theories. When Einstein wrote them he used complicated mathematical equations, but there are many popular works available explaining them in everyday language.

//

FALLACY: *Laser, maser, quasar, radar,* and *sonar* are scientific words derived from Latin.

FACT: Not a one is derived from Latin. They're all acronyms.
Laser = Light Amplification by Stimulated Emission of Radiation
Maser = Microwave Amplification by Stimulated Emission of Radiation
Quasar = QUASi-stellAR object
Radar = RAdio Detecting And Ranging
Sonar = SOund NAvigating and Ranging

//

FALLACY: The fax machine was invented in the 1970s.

FACT: The first European patents for an experimental facsimile machine were taken out in the 1840s. The first commercial fax system functioned between Paris and Lyons, France, from 1865 to 1870. In the United States, Western Union was routinely faxing photographs to newspapers over telegraph wires in the 1920s. A decade later, by means of "equipment contained in a small, attractive box," anyone who had a radio or telephone could receive a newspaper by fax, according to the June 1938 issue of *Scientific American.* "The name of this service now available is facsimile. It involves the conversion of illustrations or other copy, such as printed matter, into electrical signals, which can be sent over radio or telephone circuits. At the receiver the signal is automatically converted back into visible form, appearing as a recorded replica of the original copy." These were not just office machines—you could have a newspaper faxed to your home overnight, to read with your breakfast.

//

FALLACY: The verdict in the Scopes "Monkey Trial" made it legal to teach evolution.
FACT: John T. Scopes broke a Tennessee state law forbidding the teaching of evolution. The verdict in his 1925 trial was Guilty. That verdict was later reversed on a technicality, but the law forbidding the teaching of evolution in Tennessee was not repealed until 1967.

//

FALLACY: The faster water boils, the faster it cooks whatever's in it.
FACT: When water reaches the boiling point, its vapor pressure equals atmospheric pressure and bubbles begin to form. No matter how high you turn the heat, and no matter how fast the water boils, the temperature of the water will remain the same. When water passes its lowest possible temperature it turns into ice; when it passes its highest possible temperature it turns into vapor. If water is boiling at all, it is cooking as fast as it can.

//

FALLACY: It's not true that you can get a worse sunburn when the ground is covered with snow than when it's covered with plain old dirt or grass.
FACT: Grass absorbs solar energy and turns it into several things, including more grass. Soil absorbs solar energy and turns it into heat.

Snow, on the other hand, reflects about 90 percent of the ultraviolet light from sunlight. Between the rays from above, and the reflected rays from below, you're getting almost a double dose of ultraviolet, which will most definitely give you a worse sunburn. And keep in mind that more and more ultraviolet is getting through the thinning ozone layer.

//

FALLACY: The world's largest nuclear weapon explosion was the U.S. test at Bikini Atoll.

FACT: The 1 March 1954 open-air test at Bikini Atoll in the Marshall Islands was the largest hydrogen bomb ever exploded by the United States. Code-named "Bravo," it was measured at eighteen to twenty-two megatons. On 30 October 1961, the Soviet Union detonated a hydrogen bomb at Novaya Zemlya that sent a shock wave around the world three times and blew a hole up through the atmosphere. It was officially listed as fifty-seven to fifty-eight megatons, but unofficial estimates range from sixty to ninety megatons.

//

FALLACY: You can't burn a diamond.

FACT: Diamond is the hardest and densest known natural substance. It is surprising, therefore, that except for impurities and defects, diamond is also transparent. You can burn a diamond, but you'd need at least a blowtorch. Diamonds, like coal, are made of carbon and will burn if they get hot enough. Hot enough for a diamond is roughly 1,500° Fahrenheit. If you're going to heat your home with carbon, coal's a lot cheaper.

II

United States

FALLACY: Coney Island was named for the man who owned it.
FACT: Only if he was a rabbit, because that's what the word *coney* means. Although the name originally made sense, it is wrong now on both counts. The rabbits have long since been replaced with humans, and what used to be an island is now part of southern Brooklyn.

//

FALLACY: There's no pattern to when U.S. presidents die in office.
FACT: William Harrison was elected in 1840 and died in office. Abraham Lincoln was elected in 1860 and died in office. James Garfield was elected in 1880 and died in office. William McKinley was elected in 1900 and died in office. Warren Harding was elected in 1920 and died in office. Franklin Roosevelt was elected in 1940 and died in office. John Kennedy was elected in 1960 and died in office. See a pattern there? Ronald Reagan was elected in 1980; although he little noted nor long remembered, he did not die in office.

//

FALLACY: Only a small percentage of the visitors to Yosemite National Park are Californians; they've already seen it.
FACT: More than four million people visit Yosemite National Park in an average year. Four hundred thousand of them come from other parts of the United States. Six hundred thousand of them come from outside the United States. Three million of them, or 75 percent, are Califor-

219

nians. Could be that it's that beautiful; could be that there are a lot of Californians; could be that Californians have short memories.

//

FALLACY: The number of people killed by automobiles in each state is many times the number killed by guns.

FACT: The federal Centers for Disease Control and Prevention (CDC) keeps track of fatality statistics. Through 1989, all states had reported that more people were killed by automobiles than by guns. In 1990, Texas became the first state to report more deaths from guns (3,443) than from automobiles (3,309). It's not true, by the way, that pickup trucks in Texas are required by law to have a gun rack and a six-pack.

//

FALLACY: The Mason-Dixon Line was drawn at the time of the Civil War to divide free states from slave states.

FACT: Mason and Dixon's Line, popularly called the Mason-Dixon Line, was drawn a long time before the Civil War, and had nothing to do with slavery. At 39°43'19.11" north latitude, it was surveyed by English astronomers Charles Mason and Jeremiah Dixon in 1767. Originally defining the east-west border between Maryland and Pennsylvania, it was later extended to define the border between Pennsylvania and Virginia (including what is now West Virginia).

//

FALLACY: In the 1992 presidential election, H. Ross Perot came in no better than third in any state.

FACT: H. Ross Perot did better in the 1992 election than many people realize. Nationwide, Perot received about 19 percent of the popular vote, George Bush received 38 percent, and Bill Clinton received 43 percent. Perot came in second in Utah, getting more votes than Clinton. Perot came in second in Maine, getting more votes than Bush.

//

FALLACY: According to the Constitution, the Supreme Court must have nine members.

FACT: The Supreme Court was established by Article 3 of the Constitution. The number of justices is not set by that article. Determined by statute, the number of justices varied in the early years, often with much controversy about "stacking" the court. It is only since 1869 that the Supreme Court has had nine members and, although unlikely, that number could again be changed by statute.

//

FALLACY: Alaska was the most recent state to join the United States.
FACT: On 14 February 1912, Arizona became the forty-eighth state. On 3 January 1959, Alaska became the forty-ninth state. On 21 August 1959, Hawaii became the fiftieth state. Aloha, Alaska!

//

FALLACY: Every U.S. president must have a vice president.
FACT: Although some vice presidents seem to have proven the point that a vice president isn't necessary, the Constitution says in Article 2, Section 1: "The Executive power shall be vested in a President of the United States of America. He shall hold his office during the term of four years, and together with the Vice President, chosen for the same term, be elected as follows . . . " The fact is, though, that a president can serve an entire term without a vice president. Four presidents have done so: John Tyler, Millard Fillmore, Andrew Johnson, and Chester Arthur. Interestingly, each of these presidents who never had a vice president served only one term, and was the vice president of the previous administration.

//

FALLACY: Southern Florida is flat, with no major hills.
FACT: The highest point in all of Florida soars to only 345 feet. Southern Florida does have one major hill, south of Miami. Although the name is not official, it is popularly called Mount Trashmore. Roughly 150 feet high and half a mile long, it is what used to be called a dump and is now called a "refuse disposal area." Plans are underfoot to increase Mount Trashmore to 250 feet.

//

FALLACY: John F. Kennedy was one of the many presidents buried in Washington, D.C.

FACT: John F. Kennedy was buried in Arlington National Cemetery, across the Potomac River from Washington in Arlington, Virginia. The only other president buried there was William Howard Taft. The only president buried in Washington, D.C., was Woodrow Wilson.

//

FALLACY: The Alaska Pipeline is almost 500 miles long.
FACT: The Alaska oil pipeline, finished in 1977, runs 789 miles from Prudhoe Bay in the north to Valdez in the south.

//

FALLACY: Alexander Hamilton, first U.S. secretary of the treasury, was born in England.
FACT: Secretary of the Treasury Alexander Hamilton, who favored aristocracy, was a foe of Secretary of State Thomas Jefferson, who favored democracy. Hamilton was born in the West Indies.

//

FALLACY: The dome of the Capitol is made of white marble.
FACT: The dome of the Capitol building in Washington, D.C., is white, but it is not made of marble—or of any other stone. The dome is made of metal. It is white because it's covered with white paint, not whitewash as some critics of Congress claim.

//

FALLACY: The first three digits of a Social Security number can be anything from 001 to 999.
FACT: There is a 001. Along with 002 and 003, it is assigned to people in New Hampshire. There's no 999, however. The highest number ever assigned was 728. The highest being assigned today is 599, which is one of several given to people in Puerto Rico.

//

FALLACY: William Jefferson Clinton was that president's original name.

FACT: President William Jefferson Clinton was born on 19 August 1946, the son of William and Virginia Blythe. His original name was William Jefferson Blythe, III. His father was killed in an auto accident before he was born, and his mother later married Roger Clinton. When the president was sixteen years old, he changed his name to William Jefferson Clinton.

//

FALLACY: The Pledge of Allegiance was written by Congress.
FACT: The Pledge of Allegiance was written by Francis Bellamy for the 8 September 1892 issue of the children's magazine he edited, *Youth's Companion.* The words *under God* were added by Congress in 1954.

//

FALLACY: Los Angeles is larger in area than any other U.S. city.
FACT: Los Angeles is geographically large because it grew out rather than up. Considering its size, it's surprising that Los Angeles isn't even among the top five. New York City, all five boroughs included, isn't even among the top ten. Juneau, Alaska, is not a major city, with a population of less than 30,000, but its area of 3,108 square miles makes it geographically larger than any other U.S. city. Anchorage, with 1,732 square miles and a population density of 131 people per square mile, is the nation's geographically largest city with a population over 100,000. Jacksonville, Florida, is second, with 760 square miles and 885 people for each one. Oklahoma City is third, with 604 square miles and 736 people for each. Los Angeles, by contrast, has an area of 465 square miles and a population density of 7,495 per square mile. New York City is smaller and denser: 301 square miles and 24,327 people per square mile, although "people per cubic mile" might be more appropriate for the skyscraper city.

//

FALLACY: Edwin Booth, the world-famous actor, assassinated President Abraham Lincoln in Henry Ford's Theater.
FACT: Although there is a connection to Edwin Booth, it's not that close. Abraham Lincoln was assassinated on 14 April 1865, while watching the play *Our American Cousin.* Only five days earlier, the Civil War had formally ended with Robert E. Lee's surrender at Appomattox Courthouse. The assassin was John Wilkes Booth, a younger brother of Edwin. The theater was owned by John T. Ford.

FALLACY: New Year's Day, the 4th of July, and Thanksgiving Day are national holidays.

FACT: Those are federal holidays, not national holidays, and there's a big difference. When the federal government declares a holiday, it applies only to federal employees and to the citizens of the District of Columbia. Individual states may or may not declare a holiday for the same day as a federal holiday, as was shown by the battle in some states over the newest federal holiday, Martin Luther King, Jr., Day, celebrated on the third Monday in January.

//

FALLACY: There are only a few $1,000,000 bills.

FACT: There are no $1,000,000 bills. The largest-denomination U.S. currency is the $100,000 bill, used only in transactions between the Treasury Department and the Federal Reserve. $10,000 Salmon P. Chase bills still exist, but have not been printed since 1944. $5,000 James Madison bills, $1,000 William McKinley bills, and $500 Grover Cleveland bills have not been printed since 1969. The $100 Benjamin Franklin bill is the largest now being issued.

//

FALLACY: The first seat of government in what is now the United States was located at Saint Augustine, Florida.

FACT: We have no idea where the first seat of government in what is now the United States was located. All we know for sure is that the members of that government were all Native Americans. The oldest seat of government established by European immigrants was at Santa Fe, New Mexico, in 1610. It has been a capital city ever since, and is today both the county seat of Santa Fe County and the capital city of New Mexico. Saint Augustine, Florida, is the oldest city in the United States. It was established in 1565, but not as a seat of government.

//

FALLACY: Adlai Stevenson was never president or vice president of the United States.

FACT: He was, but there's some confusion, because there were two famous Adlai Stevensons: Adlai Ewing Stevenson and Adlai Ewing Stevenson. Adlai Ewing Stevenson, who ran against Dwight David Eisenhower, was never president or vice president of the United States. Adlai Ewing Stevenson, on the other hand, was vice president from 1893 to 1897 during the second administration of (Stephen) Grover Cleveland. Just to clear things up, Adlai Ewing Stevenson was the grandson of Adlai Ewing Stevenson. Or was it the other way around?

//

FALLACY: The War of 1812 began and ended in 1812.

FACT: The War of 1812, between Great Britain and the United States, was declared by Congress on June 18, 1812. American forces invaded Canada almost immediately, and were almost immediately driven back. The war continued into 1813, and British ships cleared American ships from the seas. The war continued into 1814, and in August, British troops burned Washington. The War of 1812 was finally ended by the December 1814 Treaty of Ghent, which wasn't ratified until 1815. That's what most Americans think of as the War of 1812. Most of the rest of the world thinks of Napoleon's invasion of Russia and capture of Moscow in 1812; Napoleon won the battle, but lost the war to the Russian winter. That's the War of 1812 commemorated in Tchaikovsky's 1812 Overture.

//

FALLACY: According to the Constitution, justices of the Supreme Court must have a law degree.

FACT: The authors of the Constitution may have made mistakes, but none that bad. There is no such requirement in Article 3, which established the Supreme Court. There is no law to that effect, either; it's strictly a matter of tradition. By the time President Clinton took office in 1993, the situation had gotten even worse: seven of the nine sitting justices had previously been not only lawyers, but judges.

//

FALLACY: Lake Okefenokee is in Georgia, not in Florida.

FACT: Let me make one thing perfectly clear: Lake Okeechobee, which is a link in the Okeechobee Waterway, is in Florida, north of the

Everglades and east of the Galoosahatchee River. Okefenokee Swamp, no respecter of silly survey lines, is in both southeast Georgia and northern Florida. In Okefenokee Swamp, Georgia's Suwanoochee River flows into Georgia's Suwannee River, which becomes Florida's Suwannee River, is joined by the Withlacoochee River, and flows all the way to the Gulf of Mexico at Hog Island near the town of Suwannee.

/ /

FALLACY: Lincoln wrote the Gettysburg Address on the way to Gettysburg, on the back of an envelope.

FACT: The only part of that that's true is that Lincoln wrote the Gettysburg Address. After he wrote the first draft, it went through many rewrites and revisions. In addition to the final Gettysburg Address, several earlier drafts are still in existence. None is on an envelope. In one of the best-remembered lines of that November 19, 1863 speech, Lincoln couldn't have been more wrong: "The world will little note nor long remember what we say here."

/ /

FALLACY: The names of individual states are not allowed on federal currency.

FACT: The $5 bill has an engraving of Abraham Lincoln on the front, and an engraving of the Lincoln Memorial on the back. Just above and between the columns of the Lincoln Memorial, both in the engraving and in reality, are the names of eleven states. In order, they are: Delaware, Pennsylvania, New Jersey, Georgia, Connecticut, Massachusetts, Maryland, Carolina (not North or South), Hampshire (not New), Virginia, New York. I'm told that on the smaller, top layer of the memorial are the names of another fifteen states. You're going to need good eyes, good light, a good magnifying glass—and good luck to you.

/ /

FALLACY: The "Star Spangled Banner" has been the national anthem since Francis Scott Key wrote the words and music in 1814.

FACT: Francis Scott Key wrote the words in 1814, but he used the music of an English drinking song written in the 1700s by John Stafford Smith. The "Star Spangled Banner" wasn't adopted as the national anthem until 1931.

FALLACY: The Secret Service is part of the Department of Justice.
FACT: There are many parts to the Department of Justice, including the Federal Bureau of Investigation and the U.S. National Central Bureau of Interpol, but the Secret Service is not one of them. The Secret Service, and the Bureau of Alcohol, Tobacco & Firearms, are two of the many parts of the Department of the Treasury. Why is the Secret Service part of the Department of the Treasury when it should so obviously be part of the Department of Justice? Maybe to keep it secret.

//

FALLACY: Harry S. Truman's middle initial stood for an unusual name.
FACT: The letter *S* in "Harry S Truman" is not the initial letter of a name. It was simply *S* and didn't stand for anything else. That's why there's no period after it.

//

FALLACY: Texas is the largest state.
FACT: You'd think so if you listened to some Texans, but it's not even close. Not even when you leave aside territorial waters, which would make Hawaii huge. The land area of Texas is 266,807 square miles. That's impressive when compared to Rhode Island, which has only 1,212 square miles. But it's less than half as big as the largest state. The land area of Alaska is 591,000 square miles.

//

FALLACY: Any U.S. citizen can be elected to the Senate or to the House of Representatives.
FACT: Being a U.S. citizen is necessary, but not sufficient. To be elected to the House a person must have been a U.S. citizen for at least seven years, be at least twenty-five years old, and be a resident of the state his or her district is in. To be elected to the Senate a person must have been a citizen for at least nine years, be at least thirty years old, and be a resident of the state that she or he will represent.

FALLACY: George Washington chopped down his father's cherry tree, then admitted that he'd done it.

FACT: The story came from Mason Locke Weems, who called himself Parson Weems and claimed to have gotten it from an unidentified woman. Born in 1759, Weems was more a commercial writer than a painstaking historian, as demonstrated by his comment that the cherry tree story was "too true to be doubted." He was also a creative writer, and never seemed to have gotten a firm grasp on the difference between fiction and nonfiction. The cherry tree tale did not appear in the first edition of Weems's biography of Washington, *The Life and Memorable Actions of George Washington, General and Commander of the Army of America*; it didn't appear until the 1806 fifth edition, sixty-eight years after the apocryphal event. Little George may have said, "I cannot tell a lie," but that doesn't hold for what people say about him.

//

FALLACY: The U.S. government's Pony Express carried the mail for several decades before it became obsolete when telegraph wires reached the West Coast.

FACT: The Pony Express was not a government organization; it was established by Russell, Majors and Waddell, a freight-shipping company. The Pony Express was in business for only a year and a half, from April 1860 to October 1861. Riders covered an 1,800-mile route from Saint Joseph, Missouri, to San Francisco, within ten days. Gave a whole new meaning to the expression "saddle sore."

//

FALLACY: The Emancipation Proclamation freed the slaves in the United States.

FACT: The Emancipation Proclamation didn't free a single slave; it wasn't intended to. The Emancipation Proclamation issued by President Abraham Lincoln on January 1, 1863 applied only to slaves in the Confederacy, "as a fit and necessary war measure for suppressing said rebellion." Since the proclamation did not free slaves in the North, and the government in Washington had no control over slaves in the South, it freed no one. It did add strength to the antislavery movement, and on December 18, 1865 the Thirteenth Amendment to the Constitution was ratified: "Neither slavery nor involuntary servitude, except as a punishment for crime whereof the party shall have been duly convicted, shall exist within the United States or any place subject to their jurisdiction." Two large sheets of paper were folded to make eight pages; the text of the Emancipation Proclamation is on five of those pages, with the other three blank. For the first time, the complete Emancipation Proclamation was taken out of its airtight vault and put on public display by the National Archives for its 130th anniversary in 1993.

//

FALLACY: Jeannette Rankin was the first female member of the Senate.

FACT: Rebecca Latimer Felton was appointed in 1922 to serve the remaining one day of a Senate term. Although only technically, eighty-seven-year-old Felton was the first female member of the Senate. Elected to the House of Representatives—not the Senate—in her own right in 1916, Jeannette Rankin ran on a platform of peace and women's rights. She was the only member of Congress to vote against the United States entering World War I, and lost her reelection bid. She was elected again in 1941, and was the only member of Congress to vote against the United States entering World War II. It wasn't until 1968 that an African-American woman was finally elected to Congress, Representative Shirley Chisholm. The first African-American woman elected to the U.S. Senate was Carol Mosely-Braun. She and another new senator, Dianne Feinstein, were the first two women ever appointed to the powerful Senate Judiciary Committee, when the 103rd Congress convened in January 1993.

//

FALLACY: Turkey was the centerpiece at the first Thanksgiving feast.
FACT: There actually was no centerpiece-food on the tables. The first Thanksgiving feast included bread, vegetables, fruit, wine, seafood, and three types of meat: duck, goose, and venison. No turkey.

//

FALLACY: The White House is white because it's made of marble.
FACT: The White House is white because it's painted white. The building itself is made of a reddish-brown sandstone, quarried at Aquia Creek, Virginia.

FALLACY: The U.S. Constitution begins, "When in the course of human events . . . "

FACT: Right country, but not the right historical document. That's the opening of the Declaration of Independence. The Constitution of the United States begins, "We, the people of the United States, in order to form a more perfect Union, establish justice, insure domestic tranquility, provide for the common defense, promote the general welfare, and secure the blessings of liberty to ourselves and our posterity do ordain and establish this Constitution for the United States of America." That sentence is the entire Preamble. If it were written by today's politicians, it would probably run to several hundred pages.

//

FALLACY: The first battle between ironclad ships in the Civil War was between the *Monitor* and the *Merrimac.*

FACT: The Union ship was, indeed, the *Monitor.* Another Union ship, named the *Merrimac,* was burned, sunk, and abandoned in 1861. The Confederacy raised the hulk, rebuilt it, and clad it in iron. The new ship was named the *Virginia.* The famous battle in 1862 was between the *Monitor* and the *Virginia.* Since neither ship could sink the other, the battle ended in a draw. Although there was no winner, there was a loser: the centuries-long reign of the wooden warship was over.

//

FALLACY: Grand Central Station is one of the most famous places in New York City.

FACT: There is no railroad station in New York City named Grand Central Station. The world's largest train station is Grand Central Terminal, at 42nd Street and Park Avenue; it covers forty-eight acres on two levels and serves 200,000 commuters a day. The hub of Grand Central Terminal is the Main Room, which has a 250-foot ceiling and 80,000 square feet of floor space.

//

FALLACY: President Richard Nixon was impeached, but was pardoned by his successor, President Gerald Ford.

FACT: There is some confusion about the meaning of "impeachment.'' It means ''indicted,'' not ''convicted.'' When the House of Representatives brings charges against a president, that is impeachment. The trial itself is conducted by the Senate. An impeached president may or may not be convicted. There is no such thing as a pardon for impeachment—or for the penalties of conviction, because there are no penalties other than removal from office and disqualification from holding federal office. The House Judiciary Committee opened impeachment hearings on 9 May 1974, and in July recommended three articles of impeachment, for obstruction of justice, abuse of power, and contempt of Congress. There seemed little doubt that Richard Nixon was going to be impeached. He resigned on 9 August, before the House voted on the three articles, making him the first president ever to resign. The pardon given him by Gerald Ford on 8 September was, therefore, not for impeachment or for its consequences. It was an unconditional pardon for all federal crimes that Nixon ''committed or may have committed.''

//

FALLACY: Benedict Arnold was executed in the United States.
FACT: Benedict Arnold, born in 1741, died of natural causes in England in 1801.

//

FALLACY: Only about 10 percent of Medal of Honor winners are women.
FACT: The first woman to receive the Medal of Honor was Civil War surgeon Mary Walker. President Abraham Lincoln signed an executive order but was murdered before it was carried out. It wasn't until January 24, 1866 that she finally received the medal. Mary Walker was also the last woman to receive the Medal of Honor.

//

FALLACY: Confederate General Robert E. Lee surrendered in the courthouse at Appomattox.
FACT: At the end of the Civil War there was a town in Virginia named Appomattox. That is not the town where the surrender took place. A nearby town named Appomattox Courthouse did have a courthouse. The surrender did not take place in that courthouse. The surrender took

place on April 9, 1865 in a private home in the town of Appomattox
Courthouse. Since 1954, the area has been a national historical park.

✓✓

FALLACY: Harry Truman was the first president born in the twentieth
century.
FACT: President Harry S Truman was born in Missouri in 1884—
the nineteenth century. President Dwight D. Eisenhower, who succeeded
Truman, didn't quite make it, either. He was born in Texas in 1890. The
first president born in the twentieth century was John F. Kennedy. He was
born in Massachusetts in 1917. All the presidents following Kennedy—
even Ronald Reagan—were also born in the twentieth century. William
Jefferson Clinton, by the way, was the first president born after the end
of World War II.

✓✓

FALLACY: The longest ships afloat are the U.S. navy's Nimitz-class
aircraft carriers.
FACT: The six Nimitz-class aircraft carriers each have a flight
deck of 4.5 acres, a displacement of 100,846 tons, and a length of 1,092
feet. The tanker *Jahre Viking* (renamed from *Happy Giant*) is 1,504 feet
long.

✓✓

FALLACY: Immigrants arriving at New York City are processed at
Ellis Island.
FACT: Fifteen-year-old Annie Moore of County Cork, Ireland,
was the first immigrant to pass through Ellis Island on 1 January 1892,
when it became the main point of immigration for the United States. It
remained the major entry point until 1943, and from then until 1955 was
used by the Immigration and Naturalization Service as a detention center.
More than twenty million people entered the United States through Ellis
Island. It has since been renovated, and is now a national monument.

✓✓

FALLACY: Gerald Ford was Nixon's vice president at the time of the
Watergate burglary.

FACT: On June 17, 1972, five men were arrested for breaking into the Watergate office building headquarters of the Democratic National Committee. Richard M. Nixon's vice president at the time was Spiro T. Agnew. Agnew resigned on October 10, 1973, after pleading no contest to charges of not paying taxes on bribes during the time he was governor of Maryland. Gerald R. Ford, Jr., was appointed on October 12 and sworn in on December 6, becoming the first vice president appointed under the Twenty-Fifth Amendment.

//

FALLACY: Los Angeles has the largest population of any state capital.
FACT: Phoenix has the largest population of any state capital, with 983,403 people as of the 1990 U.S. Census. Los Angeles, with 3,485,398 in that census, has several times the population, but California's capital is Sacramento. Just for reference, Illinois's capital is not Chicago but Springfield; Michigan's is not Detroit, but Lansing; New York's is not New York City, but Albany; Pennsylvania's is not Philadelphia, but Harrisburg; Texas's is neither Dallas nor Houston, but Austin.

//

FALLACY: George Washington's inauguration was held in the new capital, Washington, D.C.
FACT: At the time of Washington's first inauguration on April 30, 1789, there was no Washington, D.C. As president, Washington chose the site in 1790. Congress had its first session there in 1800. The first president inaugurated in Washington, D.C., on March 4, 1801, was Thomas Jefferson. As a history buff might note, Washington never lived in Lincoln, but Lincoln lived in Washington.

//

FALLACY: Armistice Day is a federal holiday.
FACT: Armistice Day was a federal holiday established to celebrate the November 11, 1918 armistice ending World War I. It was celebrated in this country from 1919 until the last Armistice Day on November 11, 1953. In 1954, Armistice Day was replaced with Veterans Day, which is celebrated with parades of troops and weapons.

FALLACY: William H. Rehnquist is the chief justice of the Supreme Court.

FACT: There is no "Chief Justice of the Supreme Court." The Supreme Court is comprised of eight associate justices and the chief justice of the United States. All are appointed by the president with the advice and consent of the Senate. William H. Rehnquist was appointed chief justice of the United States by President Ronald Reagan in 1986.

//

FALLACY: About half of the letters of the alphabet are used in the names of the states.

FACT: All but one of the letters of the alphabet are used in the names of the states. If you included the provinces of Canada, the first letter of Quebec would take care of the oversight.

//

FALLACY: There were several attempted presidential assassinations, but only Lincoln and Kennedy were actually killed.

FACT: Four presidents have been assassinated: Abraham Lincoln on 14 April 1865, James A. Garfield on July 2, 1881, William H. McKinley on September 6, 1901, and John F. Kennedy on November 22, 1963. Kennedy died at an earlier age than any other president: forty-six years 6 months.

//

FALLACY: The U.S. Postal Service can depict anyone, living or dead, on a stamp.

FACT: No living person may be depicted on a U.S. postage stamp. Deceased presidents get a slight break in that they may be pictured on a stamp on or after their next birthday. The rest of us have to wait 10 years.

//

FALLACY: The Statue of Liberty is on Bedloe's Island.

FACT: The full name of that 225-ton statue, completed in New York Harbor on October 28, 1886, is the Statue of Liberty Enlightening the World. It was on Bedloe's Island until August 3, 1956, when the name of the island was changed to Liberty Island.

//

FALLACY: Most members of the first few U.S. governments were born in England.
FACT: If true, that would be most true of George Washington's first administration. Washington was born in Virginia. Vice President John Adams was born in Massachusetts. Secretary of State Thomas Jefferson was born in Virginia. And so it goes.

//

FALLACY: The White House was designed by an English architect, and was based on a building in London.
FACT: The White House was designed by an Irish-born American architect, James Hoban, and was based on a building in Dublin. Hoban not only designed the White House, he supervised its construction. After the British so rudely burned it on August 24, 1814, it was Hoban who supervised the restoration.

//

FALLACY: Segregation in the U.S. military ended after World War I.
FACT: Segregation in the U.S. military started during the Civil War. It continued through the "Indian Wars," the Spanish-American War, World War I, and World War II. Segregation was finally ended in the U.S. military on July 26, 1951.

//

FALLACY: The Declaration of Independence was signed on July 4, 1776.
FACT: No one signed "A Declaration by the Representatives of the United States of America, in General Congress assembled" on July 4, 1776. That was the date on which the final draft was approved by the Continental Congress. A copy of the Declaration was signed by members of Congress on and after August 2. All but six signers finally got around to it by August 6. Thomas McKean didn't sign until 1781.

FALLACY: Anyone who has the money can purchase a seat on the New York Stock Exchange.

FACT: First you have to have the money. Then you have to get permission from the NYSE to buy a seat. Then you have to persuade a member to sell you his or her seat, because membership in the New York Stock Exchange is limited to 1,366.

//

FALLACY: John F. Kennedy was the youngest U.S. president.

FACT: John F. Kennedy was 43 years old when he became president. When Theodore Roosevelt took office following the assassination of William McKinley, he was 42 years old, making him the youngest U.S. president. John F. Kennedy was, however, the youngest man ever elected to the presidency. The oldest president ever elected was Ronald Reagan, at 69 years, 349 days.

//

FALLACY: The U.S. government built its first major national highway in the early 1900s.

FACT: The U.S. government began building the first major national highway, called the National Road, in 1815. It ran from Cumberland, Maryland, through the Cumberland Gap, all the way to Saint Louis, Missouri. Completed in 1833, it was a major route for western migration. Many people alive today have driven along the course of the National Highway without realizing it—Highway 40 closely follows that original route.

//

FALLACY: There are four time zones in the United States.

FACT: There are six time zones in the United States: Eastern, Central, Mountain, Pacific, Alaskan, and Hawaiian.

//

FALLACY: All candidates for the U.S. presidency have been male.

FACT: Several candidates for the U.S. presidency have been female.

The first was Victoria C. Woodhull, nominated by the Equal Rights Party in the 1872 election. She was far ahead of the times, advocating such modern topics as birth control, a tax on excess profits, easier divorces, abolition of the death penalty, and world government. She lost the election to Ulysses S. Grant.

/ /

FALLACY: The basic federal crimes are listed in the Constitution.
FACT: Of the thousands and thousands of federal crimes now listed, the Constitution mentions only one: treason.

/ /

FALLACY: Most presidents have come from the largest states.
FACT: The state with the most presidents is Virginia, with eight. Ohio is second, with seven.

/ /

FALLACY: The first U.S. income tax was levied in 1913.
FACT: Legal or not, the government levied its first income tax in 1862 to finance the Civil War. The Supreme Court overturned that tax in 1881. The government levied another income tax in 1894. In 1913, the Sixteenth Amendment was passed, removing any doubt about the legality of a federal income tax.

/ /

FALLACY: The secretary of defense during World War II was Henry Stimson.
FACT: There was no secretary of defense during World War II. Henry Stimson was appointed secretary of war by President Franklin Roosevelt in 1940; Robert Patterson was appointed secretary of war by President Harry Truman in 1945. Kenneth Royall was the last secretary of war, appointed by Truman in 1947. Postwar efforts to reduce the huge military budget probably had something to do with the fact that, on 18 September 1947, the War Department was renamed the Department of

Defense. Truman appointed James Forrestal as the first secretary of defense.

/ /

FALLACY: Betsy Ross designed and sewed the first American flag.
FACT: Folklore, not history. There is no historical record of Betsy Ross having anything to do with the first American flag. The flag was designed by an official U.S. naval flag designer, Francis Hopkinson.

/ /

FALLACY: The highest point in the United States is on the Continental Divide in the Rocky Mountains.
FACT: The highest point in the United States, and in all of North America, is 20,320-foot Mount McKinley (Mount Denali) in Alaska. And no, the highest point in "the lower forty-eight states" isn't in the Rocky Mountains, either. It's California's 14,494-foot Mount Whitney, in the Sierra Nevada.

/ /

FALLACY: The first American skyscraper was in New York City.
FACT: The first American skyscraper was the Home Insurance Building, 1883, in Chicago. One of New York City's earliest was the Flatiron Building, 1902.

/ /

FALLACY: Abraham Lincoln's Gettysburg Address is the source of the phrase, "of the people, by the people, for the people."
FACT: That's what we associate the phrase with, and it's definitely in there, but Lincoln did not originate it. The credit for that goes to Theodore Parker, who coined it and used it many times in his antislavery speeches and writings during the 1850s.

/ /

FALLACY: There are thousands of people in the United States today for each person who was here when the country began.

FACT: The first official census was in 1790. Not counting Native Americans, who were specifically excluded, the population was 3.9 million. The 1790 census cost $300,000 in 1990 dollars, or $13 for each person. The 1990 census counted 248.7 million people. It cost $2.6 billion, or $1,040 for each person. Given those population figures, 63.77 people were counted in 1990 for each person counted in 1790.

//

FALLACY: George Washington was not only the father of our country, but the father of several children.

FACT: Martha Washington had four children from a previous marriage, but none with George, who fathered no known children. He may have been sterile as a complication of malaria.

//

FALLACY: Alcatraz is a maximum-security prison.

FACT: A military prison since 1859, Alcatraz Island in San Francisco Bay became a federal maximum-security prison in 1933. By the 1960s "The Rock" was becoming too expensive to maintain, and in 1963 it was closed. In 1972 it became part of the Golden Gate National Recreation Area, and is now a popular tourist attraction.

//

FALLACY: Chicago is the windiest city in the United States.

FACT: Although Chicago's nickname is "The Windy City," it isn't the windiest city in the United States. According to the U.S. National Oceanic and Atmospheric Administration (NOAA), Chicago isn't even among the top twenty. The top five all have average wind speeds of between twelve and thirteen miles per hour. They are, in order starting with the windiest: Cheyenne, Wyoming; Great Falls, Montana; Boston, Massachusetts; Oklahoma City, Oklahoma; and Wichita, Kansas. If the category were hot air, Washington, D.C. would have no competition.

//

FALLACY: Lincoln's Gettysburg Address begins, "Fourscore and seven years ago, our forefathers brought forth upon this continent a new nation."

FACT: Probably the most famous nine-sentence speech in history, Abraham Lincoln's 19 November 1863 address at Gettysburg begins, "Fourscore and seven years ago our fathers brought forth on this continent a new nation, conceived in liberty and dedicated to the proposition that all men are created equal." No "forefathers," and no "upon." Lincoln could definitely be seen above the crowd when he delivered his address: he still holds the record as the tallest U.S. president at six feet four inches.

//

FALLACY: Most Americans still don't use the 10-based metric system.

FACT: Sure they do. And they have for a lot longer than you might think. The basic unit of money is the dollar. One-tenth of that is a dime. One-tenth of that is a penny. The others are merely "half" coins, for convenience. Half a dollar is a fifty-cent piece, half of that is a quarter; half a dime is a nickel. Wine and liquor bottles are already in metric, and highway signs will be converted by 1996. At last report, American football fields will remain 100 yards long. It's probably time that the United States converted to metric. The only other nation that hasn't is Liberia.

//

FALLACY: J. Edgar Hoover was the head of the FBI for almost a quarter of a century.

FACT: John Edgar Hoover took over as acting director of the FBI on 10 May 1924, and on 10 December 1924 became director. This was during the administration of Calvin Coolidge. He died and was replaced by L. Patrick Gray in 1972—almost half a century later.

//

FALLACY: Alaskans shoot off aerial fireworks on the 4th of July.

FACT: They can if they want to, but it would be a waste. July 4th occurs during the period of the longest days and shortest nights of the year. In southern Alaska there are only a few hours of darkness; in northern Alaska, there is hardly any. Fireworks don't make much of a splash in a bright sky.

FALLACY: U.S. currency can be counterfeited with a high-quality color photocopier.

FACT: Even the best photocopied currency wouldn't pass a close examination, but apparently some slipped through. The Treasury Department has "taken steps." In September 1991, they started introducing a new type of $50 and $100 bills into the money supply. On the new $100 bill, Benjamin Franklin's head is bordered by microprinting too small to be seen without a magnifying glass. The repeated words making up the border are: "The United States of America." That's one way to see if you have one of the new bills. Another is to hold the bill up to a light and look just left of the Federal Reserve seal. The new bills have a "security thread" there. It's a polyester strip about the thickness of a human hair, wider than it is thick. You can see the thread, but a photocopier can't. Even with a magnifying glass, though, you won't be able to read what's repeated along the security thread, alternately facing one direction and then the other: "USA 100."

//

FALLACY: Confederate General Robert E. Lee was a major slave-holder.

FACT: Robert E. Lee not only didn't have a single slave, he was opposed to slavery itself. He was also opposed to the secession of the southern states. Before the Civil War broke out, he was offered the post of field commander of the Union forces by President Abraham Lincoln. He fought on the side of the Confederate states because his native state of Virginia was one of them.

//

FALLACY: Madison Square Garden is on Madison Square.

FACT: Madison Square Garden is nowhere near Madison Square. It runs from West 31st Street to West 33rd Street, between Seventh and Eighth Avenues. The original Madison Square Garden was at Madison Avenue and East 26th Street—on Madison Square.

//

FALLACY: The national debt has been rising fairly steadily since the beginning of the century.

FACT: The total national debt as of 1900 was $1.2 billion. In 1945, including the World War II debt, it was $258.7 billion. In 1950 it had actually been paid *down,* to $256.1 billion. In 1970 it was $370.1 billion, and by 1980 it was up to $907.7 billion. Then it really took off. In 1985 it was $1.8 trillion, and in 1990 it was $3.2 trillion. The debt in 1990 was almost *nine times* the 1970 debt. Interest on the 1970 debt was $19.3 billion; interest in 1990 was $264.8 billion. The national debt is growing by roughly a billion dollars per day—a thousand million dollars every day, including weekends and holidays. From 1980 through 1992, the national debt more than quadrupled, from $908 billion to over $4 trillion.

//

FALLACY: There are more motor vehicles than people in the United States.
FACT: In 1990 there were 190,228,000 registered cars, buses, and trucks; 167,655,000 licensed drivers; and, according to the U.S. Census Bureau, 248,709,873 people.

//

FALLACY: Every president has been elected either to that office, or to the vice presidency.
FACT: All but one. Gerald R. Ford, Jr., was appointed vice president by President Richard M. Nixon, and became president when Nixon resigned. Ford was never elected to either office.

//

FALLACY: Residents of Guam can vote in U.S. elections.
FACT: Guam, the largest and southernmost of the Mariana Islands, is a U.S. territory under the jurisdiction of the Interior Department. Until 1971, the president of the United States appointed the governor of Guam; Guamanians now elect both their governor and their legislators. The island is home to major U.S. military installations, including naval and air bases. Residents of Guam are citizens of the United States, but they are not allowed to vote in U.S. elections.

FALLACY: America no longer uses the U-2 spy plane.

FACT: America no longer uses the SR-71 Blackbird spy plane, which was retired. The U-2 spy plane, first built in the 1950s, is still being used. Seldom mentioned because of the nature of its work, it received a lot of attention when Francis Gary Powers was forced down over the Soviet Union on May Day 1960. The Air Force purchased at least thirty-seven of them during the 1980s, including one delivered by Lockheed Aircraft Corporation in 1989. The U-2 can fly only 430 miles an hour, but with its gliderlike shape and 103-foot wingspan, it has a range of more than 4,000 miles. Its major defensive feature is that it does its spying from an altitude of more than 70,000 feet. A new batwinged spy plane, unofficially named the Aurora, reportedly has a 66-foot wingspan and can fly six times the speed of sound.

//

FALLACY: The color of the Golden Gate Bridge is gold.

FACT: The Golden Gate Bridge is the tallest suspension bridge in the world, with towers reaching 747 feet above the water. All 4,200 feet of it opened in May 1937, but it's not gold. The color of the Golden Gate Bridge is reddish-orange, the color of the rust-preventing paint used to protect it from the salty ocean air. The name of the bridge refers not to its color, but to the entrance into San Francisco Bay which it spans: the Golden Gate.

//

FALLACY: Although the first presidents of the United States were themselves revolutionaries, no president has said that the American people have a right to revolution.

FACT: You don't have to go back to the 1700s to find a president who said exactly that. This is from President Abraham Lincoln's First Inaugural Address, on 4 March 1861: "This country, with its institutions, belongs to the people who inhabit it. Whenever they shall grow weary of the existing Government, they can exercise their constitutional right of amending it, or their revolutionary right to dismember or overthrow it."

//

FALLACY: With modern fire-fighting techniques, even coal-mine fires are now extinguished within a week or so.

FACT: There is a town in Pennsylvania sitting above a coal-mine fire. Most residents of Centralia have left, but some refuse to abandon their homes. The state plans to force them out with its power of eminent domain because there is danger of the ground collapsing. The fire has been burning for thirty years.

//

FALLACY: Woolworth's has always been a five-and-ten-cents store.
FACT: When Frank Winfield Woolworth opened the first one on 22 February 1879, it was called "The Great 5-Cent Store." It wasn't until 1883 that he, "reluctantly," added the first 10-cent item. In 1932 the first 20-cent item was added, and all limits were off.

//

FALLACY: A presidential candidate who gets a majority of the votes wins.
FACT: In the 1876 election, 4,284,757 Americans voted for Samuel J. Tilden, and only 4,033,950 voted for Rutherford B. Hayes. Hayes won. In the 1888 election, 5,540,050 citizens voted for Grover Cleveland, and only 5,444,337 voted for Benjamin Harrison. Harrison won. The reality is that Americans are not allowed to vote for their president. They vote for electors, who later elect the president. The electors almost always vote for the nominee of their party, but they do not have to. Hayes won because he received 185 Electoral College votes compared to Tilden's 184. Harrison won because he received 233 Electoral College votes compared to Cleveland's 168.

//

FALLACY: The number of people who die from accidents in the United States increases each year because the number of people increases each year.
FACT: According to the National Safety Council, the highest number of accidental deaths was in 1969 when the total reached 116,385. By 1990 that had declined to 93,500, and in 1991 it dropped to 88,500. Three-fourths of the decrease between 1990 and 1991 came from a drop in fatal automobile accidents. The 1991 total was the lowest since the

1924 figure of 85,600; the U.S. population in 1991 was more than double the 1924 population.

//

FALLACY: When President Clinton was inaugurated, for the first time in U.S. history there were five living ex-presidents.

FACT: When President William Clinton was inaugurated as the forty-second U.S. president in 1993, there were five living ex-presidents: Richard Nixon, Gerald Ford, Jimmy Carter, Ronald Reagan, and George Bush. When President Abraham Lincoln was inaugurated in 1861, there were also five living ex-presidents: Martin Van Buren, John Tyler, Millard Fillmore, Franklin Pierce, and James Buchanan.

//

FALLACY: The United States imprisons a smaller percentage of its citizens than most other developed nations.

FACT: As of the beginning of 1991, more than 1.1 million Americans were behind bars in local jails and state and federal prisons. That works out to about 455 people for every 100,000 population. South Africa ranked second with 311 prisoners per 100,000. Venezuela was third with 177. There are no 1991 statistics for the Soviet Union, but the previous year it ranked third with 268. For black males, the imprisonment rate was 3,370 per 100,000 in the United States, followed by 681 in South Africa. The figures for imprisonment do not include people who are on probation or parole. In the United States at the beginning of 1991, there were 2.6 million adults on probation and more than 530,000 on parole. Adding those people to the ones behind bars brings the total number of Americans under control of the justice system to more than 4,230,000.

//

FALLACY: None of the flying presidential command posts, popularly known as Doomsday Planes, has ever been damaged during an in-flight encounter.

FACT: One of them was nearly downed during an encounter in December 1987. Not only was a wing damaged, but two of the four engines were knocked out. All this happened when the presidential plane flew into a flock of geese.